Watching *Game of Thrones*

Manchester University Press

Watching *Game of Thrones*

How audiences engage with dark television

Martin Barker, Clarissa Smith and
Feona Attwood

MANCHESTER UNIVERSITY PRESS

Copyright © Martin Barker, Clarissa Smith and Feona Attwood 2021

The rights of Martin Barker, Clarissa Smith and Feona Attwood to be identified as the authors of this work have been asserted by them in accordance with the Copyright, Designs and Patents Act 1988.

Published by Manchester University Press
Oxford Road, Manchester M13 9PL

www.manchesteruniversitypress.co.uk

British Library Cataloguing-in-Publication Data
A catalogue record for this book is available from the British Library

ISBN   978 1 5261 5217 6   hardback
ISBN   978 1 5261 7194 8   paperback

First published 2021
Paperback published 2023

The publisher has no responsibility for the persistence or accuracy of URLs for any external or third-party internet websites referred to in this book, and does not guarantee that any content on such websites is, or will remain, accurate or appropriate.

Typeset
by New Best-set Typesetters Ltd

Contents

List of tables	vi
Acknowledgements	vii
1 The remarkable phenomenon that is *Game of Thrones*	1
2 Generating a 'richly structured combination of data and discourses'	14
3 Distinguishing different kinds of audience	33
4 Favourite characters, favourite survivors	47
5 The significance of favourite character choices	71
6 Winter is coming …	88
7 Conflicts and controversies	117
8 Making predictions for an unpredictable world	143
Postscript: 'If you think this has a happy ending, you haven't been paying attention'	158
Appendix 1: The questionnaire	170
Appendix 2: 'Mentions'	173
Bibliography	176
Index	196

Tables

2.1	Proportions of all respondents covered by three 'ideal-type' searches	28
3.1	Interrelationships of responses to Question 17	36
3.2	Scaled responses among the seven 'ideal-type' audiences	40
4.1	Favourite character and survivor 'mentions'	55
5.1	Gendered choices of favourite characters and survivors	75
5.2	Rank order of character mentions by ideal-type orientation (combining favourite character and favourite survivor answers)	77
5.3	Patterned variations in naming Daenerys Targaryen	84
6.1	Most intriguing lands or peoples	92–93
6.2	Proportions of ideal-type orientations mentioning at least one land/people in answers to Question 13	94
6.3	Codings of 100 randomised responses, the seven ideal-type orientations	98
6.4	Interrelations among choices of answer to the 'roles of fantasy' question	107
6.5	Spread of mentions of 'fantasy' or 'fantasies' by orientation	109
6.6	Distribution of coded mentions of 'fantasy' across the seven orientations	114
7.1	Top ten 'mentions' of most memorable and most uncomfortable elements	120

Acknowledgements

The following people were all members of the *Game of Thrones* research team, including making a financial contribution to its success: Romana Andò (Italy); José Javier Sánchez Aranda (Spain); Feona Attwood (UK); Doris Baltruschat (Canada); Martin Barker (UK); Lucy Bennett (UK); Joseba Bonaut (Spain); Mark Bould (UK); Mélanie Bourdaa (France); Aryong Choi-Hantke (South Korea); Despina Chronaki (Greece); María José Establés (Spain); Maria del mar Grandio (Spain); Jason Grek-Martin (Canada); Jennifer Grek-Martin (Canada); Mar Guerrero (Spain); Briony Hannell (UK); Víctor Hernández-Santaolalla (Spain); Irma Hirsjärvi (Finland); Aino-Kaisa Koistinen (Finland); Jyrki Korpua (Finland); Urpo Kovala (Finland); Katherine Larsen (US); Javier Lozano (Spain); Elia Cornelio Marí (Mexico); Richard McCulloch (UK); Larisa Mikhaylova (Russia); Tom Phillips (UK); Billy Proctor (UK); Sarah Ralph (UK); Regiane Ribeiro (Brazil); Lars Schmeink (Germany); Felix Schröter (Germany); Rikke Schubart (Denmark); Laura Seligman (Brazil); Clarissa Smith (UK); Minhee Son (South Korea); Liza Tsaliki (Greece); Tanja Välisalo (Finland); and Michela Valquiria (Brazil). Our thanks to everyone who took part and made a contribution – and thanks also for trusting us to develop this book of the project's main findings. Our three publicity assistants were Elizabeth Beaton; Briony Hannell; and Sofia Nika – thank you, you did an extraordinarily effective job, for very limited financial reward. Our thanks also to Dave Gregory who, for the umpteenth time, did excellent work imaginatively designing our website and flawlessly constructing our questionnaire and database. And of course – and most importantly – our sincere thanks to the more than 10,000 people who took such time and trouble to respond to yet another academic study. With all your differences, you are very important and interesting people. We hope we have played fair with your responses in every way. Aware of the time and work that completing the questionnaire demanded, whenever we have quoted answers, we have adopted a practice, out of courtesy, of correcting spelling mistakes and grammatical errors where a person's intended meaning was clear to us.

We see this as preferable to drawing attention to errors by inserting '[sic]' after them.

Three people made contributions to the early stages of writing this book: Liza Tsaliki, Maria Ruotsalainen and Sarah Ralph helped us draft sections of Chapters 1 and 4, and we acknowledge their contributions.

Martin Barker, Clarissa Smith, Feona Attwood

1

The remarkable phenomenon that is *Game of Thrones*

Game of Thrones – a cultural phenomenon of our times. Initially the name of the first book in George R. R. Martin's trilogy in (probably) seven parts – a book series that began quite small but went on to break various records for sales. Then, the adopted title of the eight-season HBO TV series – at its outset the most expensive TV series ever filmed, beginning with modest audiences but soon the triumphal topper of lists and winner of awards (including Emmys, for four years running). A rare case where a book-based TV series outruns its source, so that people can ask how far the TV ending presages what the final books will offer.

The story: a vast narrative widely held to be the successor to J. R. R. Tolkien's *Lord of the Rings*, but as it developed it appears to have transformed the status and expectations of 'fantasy'. Grim, murderous, licentious and low on hope; a world of disinterested gods (if they are there at all), collapsing morals, vicious power plays and murderously competing kingships; plus out-of-control dragons and the tendrils of unpredictable, dangerous magic of various kinds. The twin worlds of Westeros and Essos: heading for a long dark winter, with old powers re-emerging, while the human inhabitants cannot stop squabbling and warring among themselves.

Game of Thrones is a rich source of quotable quotes: 'Winter is coming'; 'You know nothing, Jon Snow'; 'I drink and I know stuff'; 'Hold the door!'. It is also a focus for innumerable blogs and websites for wondering, probing, searching for clues and, of course, debating. The setting for cognoscenti shorthand – 'R + L = J?', you betcha! Hot with controversies, angry complaints and strong rebuttals; the refusals to watch any more, but also 'hate watching' and the need to know in spite of dislike. *Game of Thrones* – widely watched, but even more widely heard about and used as a source for metaphors for our time: for the United States today; for the crudities and corruptions of the world's politicians and the super-rich; for global warming and climate chaos; and even for human behaviour more generally.

It is a cultural phenomenon of real import and impact – but what do we know about its viewers, followers and fans? What do we know of their varied interests in the series, of their likes and dislikes? This book tells that story and reports the findings of a major international research project (conducted 2016–17) that sought to capture a whole range of responses from across the world. Based on a set of more than 10,000 completions of a complex online questionnaire, that allows us to discover *patterns and groupings* but also the *rich detail of people's talk*, we believe that it throws important new light on both the *particularities* of George R. R. Martin's/HBO's story-world, and on the wider consequences and implications for 'fantasy' as a cultural repertoire.

Unsurprisingly, *Game of Thrones* (henceforth, mostly *GoT*) has attracted many kinds of commentary and exploration. Literary analysts have looked at Martin's writing styles and literary tropes. Enthusiasts – both academic and amateur – have explored aspects of the story, uncovering its complexities and themes. Medievalists have looked at the relations between Martin's world and the Wars of the Roses or the European Hundred Years War (for some, it has aspects of a 'new feudalism'). Feminists of various stripes have examined the story's presentation of women, sex and sexual violence. Fans have expanded in various ways upon the series, despite Martin's often quoted dislike of fan fiction. In particular, some fan theorists have explored the series as a 'multiverse', a story-world that can be approached at many levels and through many sources. Sociologists meanwhile have been able to take *GoT* as yet another case of leisure or media tourism. Here, in this book, we have tried to summarise the main tendencies of this voluminous literature, particularly with reference to what it may suggest about audience engagement with the series.

Celebratory writing

Game of Thrones is hot public property. Many a marketing outfit has sought to hitch its wagon to *GoT* – and been caught in the act by others attempting to raise their own profiles by reporting on these 'hitchings'. Hootsuite's (2018) 'best 20 branding exercises' is a worthy case in point. Among these stood Red Bull, Spotify, Twitter, Moleskine, Sesame Street and Farrow & Ball – all entities with ambitions to be 'with it'. There are any number of fan books designed to help us spend more time in and around Westeros, each one specialising in a *surprising* aspect – for example, insider books on the series (e.g., Cogman, 2012; Simpson, 2019); quizzing (Jepson, 2017); cooking (Monroe-Cassel and Lehrer, 2012; Lannister, 2016); and just general fun (e.g., Reinhart, 2014). Academia is not, in general, that overt, so celebratory work about *GoT* tends to be more para-academic, looking for unexpected depths in the books and series and thereby justifying their serious attention. Valerie Estelle Frankel's (2014a) edited collection is a good example of this kind of writing. Occasional academics deploy their specialist knowledge to offer specialist insight into the series (see, for instance, Larrington, 2015 and 2019; McNutt, 2018). Beyond these examples, the academic works that come closest to celebration are more likely to be defences against criticisms or misreadings. Dasgupta's (2017) discovery of queer readings of the series in India also serves here.

History, philosophy and politics

That *GoT* was taken seriously is evidenced by the interest shown in its illuminations of history, philosophy and politics. The medieval setting of the series, people's curiosity about its historical accuracy and the interest that it inspired in the past attracted attention (see Locke, 2018). How *GoT* is related to various historical events, practices and periods has been taken up by Rawson (2015), Lushkov (2017) and Pavlac (2017), while others have explored the relations between medieval literature, Martin's novels and *GoT* (Larrington, 2015; Carroll, 2018).

The launch of a course at the University of Glasgow – '*Game of Thrones* and Philosophy: Politics, Power and War' – suggested ways that *GoT* could be used to think about philosophy (Firstpost, 2017), while the collection *Game of Thrones and Philosophy* (Irwin and Jacoby, 2012) considers the series as 'a genuine exploration of human nature in uncertain times' (2012: xi), providing essays on ethics, metaphysics, virtue, consciousness and political philosophy (see also Silverman and Arp, 2017). Other literature has focused on the politics of *GoT*, drawing parallels between its world and ours (Emig, 2016; Kustritz, 2016). There have also been more practical applications of *GoT* in politics – for example, Virino and Ortega (2019) examine how the Spanish political party Podemos used the character Daenerys Targaryen as part of their campaign to attract younger voters.

Game of Thrones as cultural metaphor

The title '*Game of Thrones*' has been used quite extensively as a metaphor. Sometimes this feels like little more than a phrase-grab, as in Mølstad *et al.* (2017) borrowing the term to consider how knowledge forms are legitimated, or Mooney *et al.* (2014) using it to consider neural plasticity. More often, however, uses of the title (and other defining expressions such as 'winter is coming') highlight some of the ways in which the books and TV series have become available as coinage for debating social and political concerns. At its most undisguised (e.g., Halberstam, 2017, writing about Donald Trump), Martin's story is a virtual allegory on current dangers. At other times, it is as though the series has been perceived as a symptom of a broader zeitgeist, capturing various contemporary anxieties, such as international relations (Dolitze, 2015); security concerns (Kar *et al.*, 2015); and climate change (Milkoreit, 2019). Some writing will even ask directly about the series' capacity to operate as a metaphor (see, for instance, van Laer, 2017; Walsh, 2017). Cumulatively, these are the signs of a culture – especially, but not only, American culture – debating its current state through a work of fiction.

Representation

However, it is perhaps the politics of representation – and issues regarding how the series represents groups of people and relations of power – that has attracted the most attention. The centrality of the dwarf Tyrion Lannister to the series and the popularity of actor Peter Dinklage have been hailed as evidence of the TV show's 'acute insight into the disability experience' (Pulrang, 2013), and *GoT* won a Media Access Award in 2013 for its portrayal of characters such as Tyrion and Bran (Winteriscoming, 2013). Disability is significant in strikingly positive ways in *A Song of Ice and Fire* (henceforth, *ASOIAF*) and *GoT* – with injury and impairment shown as a means by which to make sense of the self (Kozinsky, 2015). Both Tyrion and Jaime Lannister evolve into more sympathetic characters because of their disabilities: Tyrion as the marginalised 'Imp' and Jaime as the warrior who loses his sword hand (Harvey and Nelles, 2014). In fact, Tyrion attributes his compassion for others to 'a tender spot in my heart for cripples and bastards and broken things' (Hovey, 2015).

Because of this it has been argued that *GoT* is an example of what popular culture can do well, featuring social rejects – with a bastard as the key heroic figure (Harrison, 2018) and gender non-conformists, disabled and gay characters taking centre stage. This approach – derived from a long-standing tradition of thinking about media in terms of positive or negative images – is further clarified in discussions about the representation of women in *GoT*. The female characters have been the subject of much lively debate in terms of their status as archetypes or stereotypes – are they inspirational and powerful figures, or are they are victimised, objectified, sexualised and included primarily for titillation, merely the subject of the male gaze? In this vein, the characters have been discussed in relation to motherhood (Eidsvåg, 2016), as maidens, crones or seers (Frankel, 2014b); as warriors (Tasker and Steenberg, 2016); as queens (Finn, 2017a); and as the 'monstrous feminine' (Evans, 2017), the abject (Patel, 2014) and grotesque (Gresham, 2015). How well women and feminism are represented in *GoT* has been widely debated in academic writing, as well as in newspapers, magazines and online commentary (see, e.g., '*Game of Thrones* failed Stark women' (Pantozzi, 2015); '*Game of Thrones* is suddenly all about powerful women getting their way' (Vice, 2016); and 'Season 7 is feminist but only for one kind of woman' (Bustle, 2017)). This is indicative of how critical-academic and popular debate have strongly influenced each other.

Elsewhere, writers have explored how *GoT*'s female characters relate to women of the medieval period (Alesi, 2017); how they can be compared across the novels and series (Jones, 2012); how they are located within the context of HBO and quality TV (Wells-Lassagne, 2013; Gjelsvik, 2016); and how they relate to contemporary issues and politics, with a particular emphasis on how sex, sex work, sexism, sexual violence and rape are represented (Rosenberg, 2012; Frankel, 2014b; Ferreday, 2015; Larsson, 2016; Genz, 2016; Young, 2017; Elwood, 2018). Sansa Stark has emerged as a key figure in discussions of rape culture, feminism, the #MeToo movement, women's broader relationships with media, and the relations between gender representations and women's position in society.

Adaptation

Another approach to *GoT* has been to consider the series as a form of quality television alongside series such as *The Sopranos*, *The Wire*, *Breaking Bad*, and *Mad Men*, part of a 'Golden Age of Television' (see Schlutz, 2016; see also Jancovich and Lyons, 2003; McCabe and Akass, 2007; Leverette *et al.*, 2008; Akass and McCabe, 2018). These TV shows are considered to be innovative, complex and multilayered productions; challenging 'viewing habits and genre expectations by breaking taboos, violating television customs, and expanding narrative rules' (Schlutz, 2016: 101). Such TV shows are ambitious and demanding of viewers, conferring the status of literature and the pleasures of 'curling up with a good book' on their audiences (Schlutz, 2016: 101). This contextualisation of the series is presented as important in understanding the changes that are made in the adaptation of Martin's books and the series' appeal to an 'explicitly upscale and (crucially) adult audience' (Hassler-Forest, 2014), which is violent and eroticised in line with HBO's production style.

The complicated processes of adapting *ASOIAF* are discussed, not simply as what happens when books become television, but as including the production of elements such as games, fan fiction and memes. The concept of 'transmedia' is adopted in a number of articles to refer to the way that the story unfolds across multiple media, expanding the story-world (Schröter et al., 2015; Shacklock, 2015; Steiner, 2015; Fathallah, 2016). With this kind of treatment, *GoT*'s story-world is presented as containing a range of texts including Martin's fantasy novel series, his prequels to this and his history of Westeros, the TV series, games created to promote the series, and games and fan productions based on both *ASOIAF* and *GoT*.

Of course, the risk inherent in this kind of work is the privileging of those particular audiences (fans) who like to play across a range of media and materials. Our study addresses other kinds of audience or fan who show much less interest in these opportunities.

Tourism and *Game of Thrones*

Tourism studies is now a well-established field in its own right, sitting at the intersection of human geography, leisure studies, business and marketing studies, and, because of filming locations' attractiveness (Tzanelli, 2010), media production studies. Unsurprisingly, much discussion surrounding *GoT* and tourism has focused on the tours' design (e.g., Irimiás et al., 2017), their impact on tourists' plans and experiences (e.g., Bolan et al., 2015), as well as the sources of their attraction (see, for instance, Depken et al., 2017; and Markelz, 2017), including the distinctive 'dark tourism' pleasures of sites associated with death and torture (see Murray, 2016; Mathews, 2018). Very little of this goes on to consider the *kinds* of fandom that might be attracted to site tours or the *kinds of involvement* that tourists have with the places that they visit (see, for instance, Reijnders, 2015), or the ways that tourist experiences are caught up in *new* definitions of the host countries' proclaimed national identities, and into reconfiguring the 'possibilities of travel experiences' (Frost and Laing, 2017: 166). Perhaps the most striking work in relation to *GoT* comes from Celik Rappas (2019), who exposes the paradoxes in the excited promotion of a transformed Belfast as, first a *Titanic* site, then a *GoT* site, when neither was of much benefit to older working-class communities undone by the collapse of shipbuilding.

However, there is little that deals directly with the virtual experiences of visiting production locations, although Waysdorf and Reijnders (2017) do discuss the role of 'imagination' in fans' experience of such locations. Drawing on a study of visitors to the Dubrovnik *GoT* site, Waysdorf and Reijnders distinguish three broad kinds of imaginative work: hyper-diegetic (adding to the overall complexity of the series' world); production-related (allowing fans to sense the processes and challenges of making the TV show); and historical (sensing local histories behind the filming, and the possible parallels between the series' histories and our own). What we hope to add to this is a sense of which *kinds* of viewer favour different forms of imaginative work.

The politics of fantasy

The past two decades have seen many publications which rethink the role of 'fantasy' more generally as a resource within political thinking and action. A whole series of books have come out in the past fifteen years, either setting out new approaches to fantasy generally (see, for instance, Mendlesohn, 2008), or looking anew at the nature and place of fantasy cinema (see, for instance, Butler, 2009; Fowkes, 2010; Furby, 2011; Walters, 2011). Much of this was prompted by the enormous success of the *Lord of the Rings* film trilogy.

But the new critical work was boosted in 2002 with the publication of a special issue of the Marxist journal *Historical Materialism*, edited and introduced by China Miéville, a major fantasy author. The volume assembled ten essays questioning the until-then prevailing view of fantasy as, in principle, reactionary, connecting instead with theories of *hope* and *utopia*. Until this point, with a few exceptions, the major theorisations of fantasy had come out of literary studies, particularly driven by a will to draw a line between the Fantastic (a proper literary genre) and 'fantasy' (popular Tolkien pastiches not worth studying) (on this aspect, see Barker, 2009).[1] As a sign of how ideas were shifting more widely in this period, see Attebery (1991 and 1992).

The rise of new theories of fantasy was partly a reaction against the recent appearance of José Monleón's (1990) major thesis, that fantasy constituted the dark repressed side of the Enlightenment's 'dream of reason', the bursting out of the repressed and instinctual aspects of humans. It is surely no accident that among those rethinking the field were writers defending their field, as indeed they were in the period that saw the rise of the 'New Weird' (see Vandermeer and Vandermeer, 2008). This new wave of writing constituted a shift from the dominant form of Tolkien-esque worlds. On the back of this, new theoretical approaches also came into existence. It is only possible to sample them here, since many address only the *general notion* of the role of fantasy in political life (see, for instance, Goodwin *et al.*, 2001; Duncombe, 2007; Ormrod, 2014; and Ryan and Bells, 2019). (Alongside these, and founded in the 1990s, is the heavily literary-critical *Journal of the Fantastic in the Arts*.)

In addition to these Anglophone developments, there has been at least one important other tradition, now centred around the bi-annual journal *Zeitschrift für Fantastikforschung*, which emerged from a major conference in Germany in 2010, and alongside which sits the volume *Collision of Realities* (Schmeink and Böger, eds, 2012). Together these demonstrate a particular combination of literary and philosophical approaches. One essay in the book stands out for its relevance to our project: René Schallegger's exploration (2012: 29–48) of the shifting political associations of fantasy since the 1950s.

Sedlmayer and Waller's (2016) edited collection asserts as a general criterion that *all* fantasy is necessarily political – and different authors pursue this idea in local contexts. Their volume contains one particularly relevant essay: Rainer Emig's study subtly explores the ways that power relations are complicated in Martin's books, but half-concludes (he hedges his bets against what the last two books might reveal) that they will end up still functioning 'in accordance with imperialist ideology' (2016: 93). As so often happens, it is seen to be enough to decide, on formal grounds, whether the texts are progressive or reactionary, without saying anything about what this might mean for audiences who enjoy and participate.

Dan Hassler-Forest (2016b) explored a range of science fiction and fantasy story-worlds as part of a larger thesis about social transformation, holding that science fiction and fantasy story-worlds must be understood as expressions of the rise of 'cognitive' or 'fantastical' capitalism and associated with the rise of transmedia production systems, where audiences are involved in doing much of the work building and sustaining media brands. He draws heavily on the arguments of Michael Hardt and Antonio Negri (2001). 'The Wall' in *GoT* comes to signify capitalism's required 'outside/other' which awaits colonisation. His argument is that, in the end, *GoT* proffers an apparently radical message: that the world is fundamentally unsafe and ordinary strategies will not aid survival. Hassler-Forest goes on to propose that, like so many jobs today, to survive, one must be flexible in a precarious world, but is virtually doomed to find a solution at the end which will blunt this by 'solving' the problems of succession. While having almost nothing to say about reception, Hassler-Forest walks shaky ground when he writes that series like *GoT* 'operate as an expression of global capitalism' (2016b: 84), and that 'popular fantasy is adopting the paradigm of cynical reason that appears increasingly hostile to the genre's traditional idealism', calling it 'ideology at its purest' (2016b: 74).

Holliday and Sergeant's 2018 collection takes a very different tack, focusing entirely on the ways in which fantasy and animation are interwoven. Ben Tyrer draws on Lacanian psychoanalytic approaches to understand the achieved realism of *GoT*. His argument is that fantasy can become *more realistic* through its (well-used) devices than simple 'realism' can. What this means for audience participation, individual or collective, is left unconsidered. These are varied and inconclusive, but perhaps important for precisely that.

The rise of this new kind of questioning is another indication of the tectonic shifts in the way that fantasy is experienced and thought about. In a way, it mirrors the sheer sense of *surprise* and the *shock of the unexpected* that many of our participants report. But how it might *matter* can be seen in the vitriolic critique by Sam Kriss (2015) of a light-hearted and speculative Paul Mason *Guardian* article, which asked how *GoT* might properly end from a Marxist perspective. A lot now appears to be at stake – fantasy is creeping under the skin of the theorists.

What about the audience?

Given the intensity and spread of interest in everything to do with *GoT*, it is not unreasonable to expect to find a fair number of attempts to investigate the series' audiences – thanks in part to its longevity. However, as best we can determine, there has really been surprisingly little to date. There have of course been regular releases of publicity-boosting overall viewing figures – records for just about every season, encouraging yet wider media coverage and speculation. There have been interestingly ambivalent reports on the extent of its digital pirating (the makers sometimes appearing to wear it as a badge of honour, especially since piracy appears to be compatible with later DVD sales). One fascinating essay by Kate McNeill (2017) explores the responses to Jeffrey Bleich, then US Ambassador to Australia, denouncing Australians for having the 'highest levels of illegal sourcing'. McNeill analyses the reasons given by series fans, when they responded angrily to Bleich's criticism.

There is little doubt that other kinds of research will have been conducted but kept confidential, or only released strategically when the figures could be used to good effect (e.g., Berg, 2017). Nielsen, for instance, released data about the gender proportions of viewers in 2011, which were seized on by *Wired* magazine to challenge the dismissal of the series as 'boys' fiction' (see Watercutter, 2013).[2] An equivalent thing happened with a news release on LGBTQ+ audiences' enthusiasm for *GoT* (Dry, 2019). And the communications giant MediaCom ('We help people, brands and businesses unlock their growth potential') conducted research for Sky on how to boost viewing figures for the series, by investigating reasons for not watching, and then organising 'watch-a-longs' for people who said that they were put off by the scale of what they had already missed (see MediaCom, 2015). Meanwhile, fan sites have had a go at gathering responses in simple but interesting ways (see, for instance, Dan Selcke's (2017 and 2018a), reports on the 'Winter Is Coming' sites' survey of its followers, which reported, among other things, the varying responses by gender, sexuality, ethnicity and political affiliation to particular events and characters within the series). Fan sites have also, from time to time, complained about the desire to please mass audiences as marginalising those with *proper* interests in the series (see, for instance, Desai, 2017, in attacking the rise of the 'casual viewer'). Fans themselves meanwhile have been the object of close study by commercial bodies (see, for instance, Latitude's (2014) study of 220 American series fans regarding what keeps them coming back to the TV show).

And what of academics? Here, the picture is decidedly thinner. As already noted, there have been studies of queer fans' engagement with queer characters (Dasgupta, 2017); female fans' responses to depictions of gender (Ferreday, 2015; see also Naylor, 2016); fans and the broader story-world of *GoT* (Schröter et al., 2015; Shacklock, 2015; Steiner, 2015; Fathallah, 2016; see also Klastrup and Tosca, 2014; Kustritz, 2016; Spanò, 2016; Finn, 2017b); fans in particular regions and contexts (Bourdaa and Delmar, 2015; Alhayek, 2017); fan debates about history (Matthews, 2018); race (Young, 2014); authorship (Sarikakis *et al.*, 2017); and fans' responses to spoilers in *GoT* (Castellano *et al.*, 2017). Aside from work specifically by and on fandom, there appears to be very little academic study. Pérez and Reisenzein (2019) studied online responses to the death of Jon Snow from the perspective of cognitive psychology (in relation to surprise structures and how audiences cope with them). Sarah Florini (2019) explored the ways in which black fans in the United States played at ethnicising the series (by, for example, calling it 'Dem Thrones' and affiliating strongly with its rare characters of colour – or granting honorary 'black status' to characters that they approved of). While these offer valuable insights into particular audiences, there is not a great deal out there.

There is one kind of research, however, of which we must be much more critical: the work of Anthony Gierzynski (2018; Gierzynski and Eddy, 2013). Gierzynski's work is, we would argue, a paradigmatic example of how *not* to study TV shows such as *Game of Thrones*. Intensely 'American' at a plethora of levels, it signals the resurgence of a terribly outdated 'effects' research in numerous ways. His first book focused exclusively on the *Harry Potter* series and its millennial audiences. In his second book, Gierzynski presents case studies of research into a series of TV shows and films, including, among others, *Game of Thrones*, *House of Cards* and *The Hobbit*. His aim with *GoT* is to demonstrate the ways in which the series might be impacting on audiences' 'belief in a just world'.

His approach is set out from the beginning: either such fictional TV shows are 'just entertainment'; or they might subtly and silently transmit 'values' (i.e., 'lessons and implicit messages' (2018: 12)) which might play a role in people's political attitudes and decisions. These 'effects' can work in only one direction: a direction predictable in advance by a specialist analysis of each TV show's values. Each chapter begins with a sort of narrative analysis of the particular TV show under discussion from which such 'values' can be adduced – and the research is designed to discover whether it worked as predicted. Gierzynski describes this process as 'making visible' (2018: 1) the TV shows' persuasive content, which will operate on us 'non-rationally'.

Gierzynksi can be seriously inconsistent in his accounts of these 'values'. The earlier book celebrated *Harry Potter* as an embodiment of all things liberal – possibly even contributing significantly to Barack Obama's US election victory – because his 'analysis' of the films displayed (among other good things) Harry being kind to other species and unwilling to use violence, even against Voldemort. But in the later book, a different 'analysis' groups Voldemort within a canon of all-out-evil villains, for whom 'exposure to villains who were portrayed as pure evil and motivated by solely evil causes would elicit harsher, more punitive attitudes about how to deal with crime and terrorism' (2018: 111). This is not simply an inconsistency, it shows the risks of media critics 'knowing in advance', as the result of simplistic methods, the supposed potential 'meanings' of such materials.

The theory that drives the account is outlined in Chapter 4 (see section discussing 'media psychology') – and it is another sign of the 'Americanism' of his research that his (extensive) bibliography mentions not a single example of the alternative approaches which have particularly characterised European research (including substantial critiques of the linear effects tradition to which he belongs). He is trapped within a fixed list of ideas, including transportation (that we get carried away as we watch or read and lose a bit of our rational personhood in the process); identification (that we strongly associate with particular characters and absorb their ways of thinking and behaving as 'our own'); and cumulative cultivation of effects (doing or encountering something repeatedly increases its influence over us). These three are the pivotal taproots of media psychology. They coalesce in the standard use of terms such as 'exposure' (which hints that watching *GoT*, or another such TV show, is not all that different from getting a virus – on this, see Barker, 1998); 'immersion' (which is bizarrely individualised – Gierzynski does not see the inconsistency between noting that the most common reason people gave for starting watching *GoT* was a recommendation from a friend, and his assumption that, as they watch it, they do so in a kind of mental isolation); and 'internalisation' (those sneaky values come and get you – he even suggests that such TV shows' fictionality means that people 'may not be aware of, and thus cannot counter-argue' (4) the values being transmitted).

Gierzynski then moves on to some highly artificial methods. Groups of students are recruited via friends – in many of these kinds of study, politics and communication students stand in for all Americans, even for the whole of humanity. The student groups were 'assigned to watch' various episodes or series, and then to fill in questionnaires made up of key standardised questions to measure a viewer's 'degree of transportation' or 'tendency to identify' – now taken to be completely unambiguous. 'Fannishness' is measured by another question. An intense artificiality is produced, in which people's *real* encounters with the various TV shows are completely sidelined and their voices and lived responses are never heard. While various levels of statistical significance are claimed, it is interesting to see that on the occasions when the results failed to turn out as predicted, they are effectively set aside as 'puzzling' (e.g., 62, 88), and – in a wonderfully revealing phrase – are 'not as strong as we might have hoped' (2019: 117).

What also needs noting is the intensely 'American' nature of the 'values' supposedly identified and tested for in the various TV series, none more so than the 'belief in a just world'. This is claimed to be a pre-ideological value, meaning that an individual, by and large, believes that people get what they deserve in the world, and are therefore 'less likely to support government action to address societal ills and more likely to support harsh punitive approaches' (Gierzynski 2018: 15). This is a perilously close mapping of the long-standing ideological divide in the United States surrounding hostility to government *per se*. The idea that it might be a 'value' which can be divorced from such a history is not something we agree with. Far from being an 'acceptable and measurable tendency with stable variation among individuals' (2018: 49), it is a multifaceted political discourse with deep roots and a long history. Our study is, in every respect that we can think of, the opposite of Gierzynski's, including in its theory, concepts, methods and ambitions.

Of course, all the work that we surveyed earlier – on everything from the use of *GoT* as a metaphor, to tourism research – is in one sense also about audiences: marketers, business and brand builders, public opinion profilers, and academic researchers taking up positions on and making claims about the series. Using *GoT* as a metaphor involves examining its presence in the public sphere and estimating its potentials: that is a kind of 'audiencing'. Critiquing its implicit politics, whether on women or race, among others, involves watching the series with a preparatory eye to judgement: again, a particular way of watching. Theorising its place within broader histories of 'fantasy' involves yet another specialist mode of attending; something that we have also been doing. Our research has involved us in some very odd ways of watching – for example, watching the series as it unfolded, and wondering what kinds of response might be sparked off by events or moments, or looking at the responses of our participants, and looking or thinking back to the TV show, to clarify to ourselves what the participants were responding to, and what that might help us understand. Being an audience researcher is damned complicated …

Notes

1 Barker must admit that he is partly wrong on this account. While it is largely true that literary scholars were set on this, within the speculative fiction world itself this distinction, and also the distinction between 'science fiction' and 'fantasy' (which has been codified by Darko Suvin as an opposition between the 'logic of the possible' and the 'logic of the impossible'), had been under challenge for a considerable time – nowhere more perhaps than in the thoughtful and wry writing of Ursula Le Guin, herself a prolific author, who wrote extensively on the misunderstandings that both literary scholars *and* many traditional fans worked with. See the glorious (1979) collection of some of her (otherwise difficult to obtain) early writings.
2 'According to statistics provided to Wired by Nielsen, approximately 2 million women were tuning in to the show on average each week – about 42 percent of Thrones' total 4.8 million viewers. While that isn't quite half, it's far closer than you'd expect for a show with a reputation for alienating ladies' (Watercutter, 2013).

2

Generating a 'richly structured combination of data and discourses'

The decision to research the reception of *Game of Thrones* did not arise in a vacuum. This was the third in a line of ambitious projects on audiences for contemporary fantasy. In 2003, the first such project – gathering responses to the films of the *Lord of the Rings*, with funding support from the United Kingdom's Economic and Social Research Council – managed to gather just under 25,000 responses from across the world to a complex survey, recruiting participants mainly online, but also on paper outside cinemas in some countries. In 2014, a second, follow-up project – this time focusing on responses to the *Hobbit* film trilogy, with funding support from the British Academy – managed to attract more than 36,000 completions of its (entirely) online questionnaire. But these projects had much more in common than simply a shared interest in contemporary media adaptations of fantasy works; they also shared a strong international reach and a common, experimental methodology, of which this chapter tells the story.

The *Game of Thrones* project was first conceived in early 2016 by Martin Barker, Clarissa Smith and Billy Proctor.[1] The first call for possible participants was sent out in June 2016. The invitation went to everyone involved in the *Hobbit* project, and to many more besides (including the considerable number who had written about the books and the TV series). It was made clear that on this occasion it would be an entirely self-funded project, and anyone joining would have to contribute (the equivalent of) £50, to help fund the website, questionnaire and database – with hopefully (if enough people joined) some money left over to offer brief employment for help with publicising the project. In return, all participants would be part of the final discussions on the shape of the questionnaire and would receive the complete database, after closure, to use in any way they chose. This invitation eventually attracted forty-two researchers in fourteen countries. Following a period of intense discussion regarding the details of the questionnaire, the project went live in October 2016 and remained open until mid-2017. Three publicity assistants in different countries (the United Kingdom, Greece and Australia) were recruited to work for three months, to spread the word about the project.

The invitation to join had made clear that the questionnaire would only be made available in English (because of the costs of setting up multiple language streams), but that people coming to the website would be told that they could answer the questions in whatever language they chose – some, although not that many, took advantage of this invitation. Subsequently, colleagues in Spain were able to create their own Spanish-language version of the questionnaire, the results of which were successfully amalgamated with the main database after closure. After manual cleaning for accidental duplications, we found that we had attracted a total of 10,636 completions. The total word count for all answers to our qualitative questions was impressive, at more than three million words.

Founding questions

While the final shape and contents of the questionnaire were settled only once the network of researchers was in place, the driving research questions were declared from the outset, as part of the invitation to participate. Five overarching questions steered the whole project:

1. What is the significance to different kinds of audience of this distinctively dystopian series? How, generally, do people relate the series to their own lives and to their sense of our world?
2. How do they situate their responses to *Game of Thrones* among other recent major fantasy offerings? In what ways is this leading them to think about the significance and value of 'fantasy' more generally?
3. How does engagement with characters, narrative and pro-scenic elements work with such a 'predictably unpredictable' dystopian story?
4. What distinctive languages of pleasure, meaning and significance do people deploy for the series? How is interest and involvement sustained over a multi-year series? How do other activities (from debating and blogging, buying merchandise and visiting filming locations, to producing fan fiction or videos) interact with and shape responses to the series *per se*?
5. How do audiences set their responses to the series within ongoing controversies, in particular (but not only) over the presentation of nudity, sex and sexual violence? How do they negotiate with issues of this kind that have accompanied the TV show and the talk that surrounds it?

These are clearly not questions that can be put, as such, to audiences and answered directly. They are powerfully informed by the cultural studies-based tradition of audience research, with its focus on the combinations of meanings, pleasures (or displeasures) and discursive communities, along with our awareness of recent development in scholarship on such topics as fandom, transmedia production, and the role of fantasy in people's lives. Given the ambitious and largely open nature of the questions (there is not a hypothesis in sight!), the detailed design of the questionnaire was the key issue to be addressed.

Our methodology

The design of the online questionnaire was the outcome of a two-decade-long development and testing of what we believe to be a substantively new way of researching audiences. Although the rise of cultural-studies-influenced audience research connected strongly with a critique of experimental research procedures, based on near-linear models of communication, from the early days some researchers expressed concern that this had resulted in a wholesale rejection of quantitative methods (see, for instance, Lewis, 1997). Small-scale qualitative studies might be interesting and insightful, but there were real problems with generalisation. Plus, as Deacon *et al.* (2007) pointed out, acerbically, qualitative researchers were prone to making weak and ungrounded quantitative claims (writing of 'many', 'some' and 'a few') in their research accounts. The challenge that a number of people recognised was one of combining quantitative procedures (with their larger numbers and procedures for validation) with sensitivity to local contexts and discursive concepts that qualitative methods aim to capture – in short, a 'qualiquantitative' method.

This book is not the place for a full account of the development of this method, which has now been tried out and improved in a considerable range of projects. It is one among a growing number of attempts to develop such combinations (see, for instance, Barker and Mathijs, 2012; Barker, 2018; and Michelle *et al.*, 2018). One obvious feature is to ask research participants several different *kinds* of question. A first kind asks them to choose from among a range of cultural categories, as appropriate to themselves, generating multiple-choice (quantitative) responses. But then they are given opportunities to express their understandings of these in their own words, producing open-ended (qualitative, discursive) responses. A third kind of question invites them to talk about key aspects of the films, TV series or whatever is under investigation, so designed to get participants to reveal their operative criteria for understanding and evaluating. A final set of questions gathers some basic, desired demographic information (e.g., age and sex).[2] (Our full, final questionnaire is included as Appendix 1.)

None of these responses can be mechanically generated. For instance, even the apparently simplest questions turn out to be context dependent. Take gender, as an example. In the *Lord of the Rings* project, it was felt to be enough to work with a simple male-female divide. By the time of the *Hobbit* project, this was retained, but a number of people protested at being offered only this choice. For a survey mounted in association with a 2006 project funded by the British Board of Film Classification (BBFC), which looked into audiences for screened sexual violence, the distinction between male/female was vital – both to what the BBFC wanted to learn, and to ongoing debates at that time regarding the depiction of rape on screen. In a 2011–12 project on viewers of online pornography (see, for instance, Smith *et al.*, 2015), the male-female distinction was supplemented by a six-part question about sexual orientation, and was well received. In a project on people's memories of watching *Alien* (see Barker *et al.*, 2015), the basic male–female distinction was deployed, producing a few complaints from people uncomfortable with this. So, given the evolution of debates in many countries regarding sexual identity, we saw it as important that the *GoT* project should add an additional option – 'identify differently' – to our binary gender classification, even though the numbers that ultimately chose this option were very small. The point is that even very basic categories become loaded with meaning, and researchers must take this into account.

It becomes especially complicated when researchers are consciously targeting audiences around the world. Although in important ways the Internet has produced a cross-national culture, and set of debates, such debates are still heavily informed by local and national differences and, of course, concrete circumstances. This makes any research into the role of class and wealth particularly complicated. If these things are true of the relatively 'simple' demographic data, they become ever more complicated for any issues where cultural understandings are the direct focus of research. In the *Lord of the Rings* project, a significant variable was the length of Tolkien's books and ease of availability in different countries, and the ways in which this might inform debates about the shifts between books and films. In the *Alien* memories project (Barker *et al.*, 2015), the different age-classifications of the film could clearly have an impact on its availability to various age-groups, and the challenges that they might have to overcome to get a sight of it – as could the circulation of various kinds of associated merchandise and other paratexts.

Whatever the complications and challenges, the declared goal was to generate a *richly structured combination of data and discourses*. The crucial tests of the method's usefulness would be twofold: in reaching different kinds of audience who would respond willingly and extensively; and in developing and following clear procedures for analysis of the resulting materials.

Three overarching principles underpinned our questionnaire's design.

Principle 1

It should contain and couple within the single implement a structured mix of quantitative and qualitative questions. This is, in itself, a distinctive characteristic, and one on which some eminent research methodology writers have thrown doubt (see, for instance, Alan Bryman (2006)). Why was this so important? First, and most obviously, it allowed us to capture in one 'space', a body of data that would hopefully disclose patterns and categories, and the relations between these; along with a dense body of talk in which people explain to us how and why they take certain views and make certain judgements. Second, and of equal value, having them in the one structured place meant that we could circumvent the central challenge of 'triangulation' arguments; that quantitative and qualitative research produces *different orders of knowledge* which, while they can of course be set alongside each other, cannot easily expand, clarify or test each other. In principle – and providing our decisions about the two kinds of question were as productive as we hoped – we should be able to use each side of our materials to flesh out and explore what its opposite half seems to be revealing. That in turn presented a fundamental challenge – how exactly to conduct and sequence our probes into the database in ways that would enable us to link our quantitative and qualitative materials?

Principle 2

There are important implications from not 'sampling'. The database, as we hoped, contained a great spread of answers to all our questions, both the quantitative and qualitative kinds. We did not proceed with a fixed order of people that we wanted or needed to recruit, not least because we went in considerably ignorant about who watches, let alone in what ways, and with what consequences, among other things. There was no way to know the overall 'population' of *GoT* viewers from which we might seek a sample of answers for investigation. As a result, we very deliberately recruited widely and opportunistically, using the research team's collective intelligence regarding where and how we might reach different kinds of viewer. No doubt we would have some serious imbalances – some kinds of viewer are inevitably much harder to reach than others, with older audiences the most obvious case in point, as they were not only generally less likely to watch the series, but they are also harder still to reach via online recruitment. The principle behind this is important: we have not been seeking *any* kind of a sample, be that random, quota or purposive. Rather, we wanted to *richly populate all the categories* within our questionnaire, in order to be able to interrogate the relations among choices and answers. We were therefore interested in having a sufficiency of all kinds of answer to be able to explore with confidence the interrelations among them, and the kinds of interest and judgement that are made (e.g., ratings, importance, favourite characters and attitudes to spoilers, etc.).

Principle 3

Crossing the 'qualiquant'. This clearly led to questions: what counts as 'richly populated' and as a 'sufficiency'? When are we entitled to have 'confidence'? At this point, we hesitated. There are, of course, many tests of significance, both simple and complex, within statistics. These indicate to what extent variations between groups are of a magnitude not to be explicable by purely random factors, and they are, of course, closely interwoven with sampling scales and procedures. The fact that our raw numbers are large must help in this regard. But estimates of variance among uncontrolled non-sampled populations are still risky. This, however, is not the prime reason why we abstained from using such statistical significance tests. For this project, and others like it, patterns, groupings and differences within our recruited population are, before anything else, *invitations to look across the qualiquant divide and ask: what discursive patterns might become visible* – from the very simplest (e.g., length of answers or frequencies of word use) to the more complex (e.g., summoning of discursive frames or suggestions of explanatory frameworks)? And what might these suggest about broader hopes, fears, commitments and orientations?

There is a principle at stake here – if we take seriously our research design, then before any substantive enquiry can be considered to be complete, *it must have crossed between our quantitative and qualitative materials, in ways which allow the one to query, and inform the other*. We had to continue any analysis until we made use of the combination of kinds of question. The *point* of any investigation of quantitative patterns and variance is to generate questions whose answers will be found on the 'other side', about the *kinds of talk* that might throw light on the meaning of those patterns – because we believe that, in an important sense, people are experts in their own lives. They, and only they, can tell us what we need to know. The *point* of any examination of kinds of talk in the open-ended answers is to generate questions about the *location* and *distribution* of these kinds of talk – questions which can be answered only by looking at the quantitative evidence. Why? Because while people can, in an important sense, be experts about themselves (and display this through their talk), they cannot fully know who else is like or unlike them. What *kind* of person they are awaits discovery. Our aim must always be to cross that breach that we have designed in the 'wall' between individuals and kinds.

How the three principles drove our analytic tactics and stages

So, how did these three principles drive our analytic tactics and their stages? We began with first-level maps of several kinds:

a) First, we mapped who we had managed to recruit. This map needed to cover all of our multiple choice/quantitative questions. It told us what *spread* of answers we received to each and all of these. Even such raw data can provoke questions – when this was done with the *Hobbit* database, a wholesale refusal to characterise the films as 'children's stories' emerged. Lars Schmeink has made excellent use of this as the starting point in a (2016) essay in *Participations*. One equivalent for us was the discovery of the vastly discrepant numbers of those declaring themselves 'fans' and those who say that they choose to read fan materials. This ultimately challenged us to rethink so-called 'lurking' (see Chapter 3).

b) But these raw figures became much more interesting once we cross-tabulated responses between different questions. It was a laborious but necessary step, and in its turn it provoked many further questions. Pragmatically, we have given prime attention to focus on the largest and strongest patterns. This is similar to the way, in the *Lord of the Rings* project, that a strong relationship was noticed between pleasure, importance and a 'spiritual journey' orientation to the films. The equivalent here would be the strong relationship between engaging or not engaging in other activities around viewing *GoT* and praising the series – with the highest praise coming not from the 'fans' but from 'lurkers'.

c) We also sought ways of analysing our qualitative responses, which could then be combined with the results of the cross-tabulations. A key example of this was our exploration of favourite characters. Using the approach of seeking and counting 'mentions' (see Appendix 2 for a discussion of the principles undergirding this), we identified the most commonly named 'favourites', isolated groups of participants doing this naming, and then sifted these carefully for the features most regularly nominated as the *grounds* for choosing. This is the work of Chapters 4 and 5. The resulting portraits of the main favourite characters reveal much about the *kinds of relations* that their choosers are building with the series.

d) There is of course another kind of portrait, which homes in on *interesting individuals*. These are generally characterised as having a lot to say about their responses. They cannot, of course, be judged as 'typical'.

But they are, in their own right, richly illustrated individuals. A detailed portrait of the ways that the various aspects of their answers interweave can be fascinating and valuable. They are generally found *either* by scanning answers to key questions for length and density, *or* by using keyword searches on topics that we know are likely to interest us (think how 'Donald Trump' might point to interesting cases, for instance). Something like this led to the location, within the *Hobbit* database, of a Syrian refugee now living in Russia who proved a quite remarkable case study in the complexities of 'nation', and the roles of films and of language within these (see Barker, 2017). What is involved here is a form of *symptomatic discourse analysis* – drawing out key concepts, criteria, reference points, and the like, and seeing how far it is possible to *model* the person's responses overall. This makes it particularly valuable if the individuals chosen for such close exploration have been identified through pattern searches – they can then be seen as *exemplary cases of a kind of response*. See Chapter 7 for two examples of this kind of portrait.

e) There is no exact equivalent to the cross-tabulations which we can use to take the quantitative investigations to their second stage. However, it is possible to identify *key terms and expressions* that such portrayed individuals use, and to turn those into search terms. Deploying these terms in searches can mean that we are able to see the kinds of association and semantic frames within which those key terms operate. An illustration of this was the capacity, in the *Lord of the Rings* and *Hobbit* projects, to identify a series of characteristic terms used to describe the exceptional impact on some viewers of the films: in particular the word 'amazed'. Against a 'steady state' for most groups of around 5 per cent, it was discovered that among a very specific segment of younger viewers this rose to more than 25 per cent (for the details of this investigation, see Barker, 2020). Detailed discursive examination of those using the term 'amazed' in this age band revealed a powerful sense of the *transformative* impact of the films. In a similar way in the *GoT* project, it was noted that only a small number of our participants answering our 'Winter is coming …' question, included within their answers what *might come after winter*, 'hope' for spring and renewal. But this small minority was found to be particularly concentrated within one specific kind of viewer (see Chapter 6 for more details).

Recruitment

Our recruitment was particularly helped by three superb assistants, Elizabeth Beaton (Australia), Briony Hannell (United Kingdom) and Sophie Nika (Greece), who (among other things) were successful in getting our website publicised via a number of important online players. Over a period of several months we recruited good numbers, eventually closing the questionnaire in mid-July 2017. By that time, along with our Spanish colleagues' separate recruitment, we had managed to attract 10,636 completions. Our hopes – that we would have filled all our categories plentifully, so that we could analyse the patterning of differences – were largely fulfilled.

A quick summary of our raw results – with gender, we managed to attract almost equal proportions of females and males, with only a small number choosing the third option 'identify differently' (48.3 per cent; 50.6 per cent; and 1.1 per cent). Ages were widely spread but peaked among the 16–30 year-old age group (a combined 61.1 per cent) with very small numbers for participants over 65 years old. Our class proxy question (where would you fit in the *GoT* world – between Smallfolk and Pretender to the Throne?) perhaps inevitably skewed to the middle three (of seven) options (6.1 per cent; 10.6 per cent; 25.6 per cent; 30.7 per cent; 22.1 per cent; 3.3 per cent; and 1.6 per cent). Political affiliations show a strong skew to 'moderate left', with 43.8 per cent in this category, while a very small 1.1 per cent chose 'extreme right'. On 'importance as enjoyment' we had recruited high levels of enthusiasts (just over 50 per cent opting for 'extreme' – but that enthusiasm was not so strongly repeated on 'importance as commentary', with just 12.5 per cent opting for 'extreme' (with the largest proportion (38 per cent) attaching 'moderate importance' to this). A very similar spread showed in participants' attitude to the debates and controversies accompanying the TV show. Attitudes to spoilers differed widely, with more disliking than liking them, but with still quite substantial numbers 'quite liking' or 'positively seeking them out' (a combined 20.6 per cent).

This plentiful filling of most of our categories gave us confidence as we approached the next stage: cross-tabulating between the categories. Obviously, we cannot reproduce all these in this book, but various key examples are considered in subsequent chapters. We close this account of our methodology with a consideration of three key questions and how we approached them.

From multiple choices to ideal types

Not all questions in a questionnaire perform the same function. In our questionnaire, three in particular were crucial in enabling us to identify patterns and groupings among our participants:

- Q10. Which of the following come closest to capturing the *kind* of series *Game of Thrones* is for you? (People were invited to choose up to three from thirteen options.)

- Q14. Which of the following come closest to your view of the role that fantasy stories can play in contemporary society? (People were invited to choose up to three from ten options, including the option of 'no particular role'.)
- Q17. Have you taken part in any of the following activities in connection with watching the series? (People were invited to nominate as many as apply to them, from a list of nine options, including 'none of the above'.)

These three were distinctive in several ways: how they were developed; their structural design; and the analytic steps that they permitted.

Question 10 hinged on the notion, developed by Rick Altman (1999) among many others, that the vernacular 'labels' that people use to categorise *kinds of media* are valuable for capturing qualities that they recognise and respond to (whether positively or negatively). But it also turns on a realisation that, especially for a series as controversial and much debated as *GoT*, that there may be competing ways of labelling it. Accordingly, we attempted to construct a list of summary expressions – while, for safety, offering short descriptions of what we understood and intended by each one – from which our participants were asked to select. These were intended to capture all the main aspects of possible orientations to the series. So, for instance, we offered 'cruel TV' (hitting the audience hard with its violence and sense of doom); 'dystopia' (in the tradition of, e.g., *Brave New World*, *1984*, and *The Hunger Games*); and 'moral fable' (a warning about power and its consequences). Our list was based on surveying ongoing debates around the series and related materials.

The challenge that these questions poses is this – their purpose is to tap into people's (variable and evolving) awareness of the different main possibilities. But to do that, we ourselves must be thoroughly *au fait* with current debates. However hard we tried, it is not difficult to miss one – especially if it is quite recent. And we did miss one. In our list of possible 'vernacular labels' for the series (Q10), we failed to offer one expression that is now gaining ground among some fantasy followers: 'Grimdark'. This composite expression emphasises the anti-heroic, flawed and hopeless nature of stories such as *GoT*. In our final chapter we reflect on its emergence and the debates that are accompanying it.

Question 14 was more philosophical in intent, aiming to capture how far participants were bringing with them any broader conceptions of the meaning, purposes and potentials of 'fantasy' as a mode of thinking and storytelling. Accordingly, we had to develop a sufficient range of possibilities, without in any way privileging those which, for instance, value fantasy more deeply.

Question 17 sought to tap into the much-discussed phenomenon of fan engagements – from debating to creating – but in a way that could provide manageable numbers of options (requiring us, for instance, to create one heading for fan fiction, fan videos and fan art, and then another for game-playing, role-playing or cosplay, despite the considerable differences among each of these groups).

Tactically, we had to decide on the total number of options that we could reasonably offer, and what limits to put on the numbers of choices that we would ask people to make. For Questions 10 and 14 we invited people to indicate *up to three*, but without enforcing this electronically, for fear of irritating transgressors who were forced to go back and alter their choices. (A check on responses showed that more than 90 per cent of our participants respected the limit.) Question 10 in the end offered thirteen options, while Question 14 offered ten. Question 17 offered only nine options, but with the invitation to 'please choose as many as apply to you', since we needed to learn about both the range and extent of people's associated activities.

The deployment of these self-sorting questions brings our approach quite close to another qualiquant tradition: Q Methodology – a research tradition with a history reaching back to the 1930s (see, for instance, Watts and Stenner, 2012). This tradition has been given a new lease of life by the rise of computer-based research methods, which have made their (and indeed our) kind of research significantly easier. Typically, in its contemporary form, it works by offering respondents a table of sentences that they are asked to sort along two dimensions: agreement; and importance. These sentences are constructed from a 'cultural trawl' – that is, a wide search of circulating materials for main issues and debates attaching to the topic. Sorts are then subjected to statistical cluster analyses to disclose patterns. It is clear that in some respects our work is quite close to the ambitions of Q Methodology. There are, however, several ways in which we would mark a difference between the two approaches. First, there is a strong tendency within Q Methodology to search for *psychological universals* in a lot of recent work (typified by the 'Composite Model' developed by Carolyn Michelle (2007)). We are interested instead in exploring the operation of circulating cultural discourses, and how these are understood and responded to by different groups. Second, although such research does commonly gather qualitative responses alongside its quantifiable Table Sort, those qualitative responses are essentially used to *illustrate* conclusions reached purely statistically. This allows no independence to the potential richness of discursive materials – either in terms of *methods for examining them* or in terms of their *contribution to our understanding*. We have committed ourselves to conducting close analyses on *both sides* of the materials divide, and to crossing the divide in both directions.[3]

A 'richly structured combination'

We can best illustrate this by looking ahead to our exploration of answers to our final question, about the saying 'Winter is coming ...' (see Chapter 6). Our investigations of these answers began with a close examination of 100 randomised answers, to see what range of kinds of answer we had gathered. These, we concluded, could be coded into six distinct kinds, and the general frequency of each counted in the sample. But those frequencies were not in themselves revealing, except as a point of comparison with particular groups isolable within our overall population. This became possible when we had completed our quantitative analysis of answers to Question 17, which revealed seven separable 'kinds of viewer' (see Chapter 3). We could then random-sample sets of answers per orientation, to discover which *kinds of answer* were most likely to be given by people within each of those orientations, and to use insights from this to flesh out our understanding of how each of those orientations works. In this case, therefore, we began with qualitative materials, coding them so that they could be examined quantitatively, mapping those quantities onto an emergent set of categories of kinds of viewer, and then – the ultimate purpose – using the discoveries from this to return and flesh out the discursive models.

Stages of analysis

Four sequenced steps then were followed for these key questions.

Step 1

Step 1 simply meant drawing out the relative frequencies of all the different options. This told us what kinds of people we had managed to recruit, as well as their 'common ground'. So, for instance, it was important to know that, from among the choices made for Question 10, 'world-building fantasy' was by some margin the most commonly chosen (at 50.9 per cent of all participants), and that 'blockbuster TV' came next (at 37.3 per cent) – but not, at this, stage knowing to what degree these choices overlapped. Similarly, it was important to know that, under 'other activities', one choice 'debating the merits and faults of the series' attracted exactly 75 per cent of all respondents – but while 47.9 per cent opted for 'enjoying other people's fan productions', a mere 7.3 per cent claimed to be making such things. (As we explain in Chapter 3, this led us to re-examine the tendency to call such enjoying non-producers 'lurkers' – with its derogatory overtones – and provisionally rename them 'fan watchers'.) As ever, our hope was to have recruited sufficiently to each category, even the minority choices, to make us feel secure about doing further analysis. So, under 'roles of fantasy', although the most ambitious 'hopes and ambitions for changing the world' only attracted 11.8 per cent, that still amounted to 1,252 individuals – sufficient for us to do further analytic work on this category.

Step 2

Step 2 involved systematically exploring the *interrelations* among choices. This required us to cross-tabulate responses within our database, thereby discovering not only the various degrees of overlap and connection, but also the *spread* of such overlaps. So, for instance, while within 'roles of fantasy' 'enriching the imagination' displayed quite a low range of variation (highest interrelation at 53 per cent; lowest at 41.8 per cent) – suggesting that this was an option pretty much equally available to anyone – 'viewing our world from a distance' displayed a substantially increased range (highest at 60.9 per cent, with 'hopes and ambitions for changing the world'; lowest at 24.8 per cent, with 'grand story-telling') – suggesting a significant clustering at the high overlap, but a serious disconnection between the lows. The resulting tables allowed us to identify emergent *groupings* and *oppositions*. Some of these were hardly surprising, perhaps even mainly confirmatory of the successful workings of our approach. For instance, it was no surprise that 'making fan productions' coupled strongly with 'enjoying others' fan productions' (although nothing like so strongly in the reverse direction). But it was more intriguing to learn that 'buying merchandise' and 'visiting locations' showed a two-way strong connection. Similarly, it was somewhat startling to discover that 're/reading Martin's books' had by far the largest number of low interrelations with other categories – hinting that we had recruited a body of respondents for whom the book stands apart, and that the TV series is an inevitable second best (and whose wider responses to the series therefore need separate, close scrutiny).

Step 3

Step 3 was the riskiest methodologically, and the most complicated. Its aim was to move beyond the spotting of tendencies (groupings and separations) to accentuating these by designing search-strings for the database which would isolate these from each other. So, as the simplest example, isolating those who said 'none of the above' in response to our 'other activities' question, then asking what ranges of other responses this reveals (e.g., evaluations of the series, favourite characters, most memorable and most uncomfortable moments, and meanings attributed to 'Winter is coming …'). This was easy to do since this was an already isolated group. But their responses become considerably more interesting and meaningful if we are then able to compare their responses of those, say, who evaluate the TV show from the perspective of their adherence to Martin's books. A search-string which selects only those opting for 're-/reading Martin's books' sets up a potential contrast with all other responses. That becomes more meaningful again if we are able to do this for all the main groupings that have emerged from our cross-tabulations. So, for instance, we had noted the sheer contrast of numbers between those choosing 'making fan productions', and those expressing 'enjoyment of others' fan productions'. To be able to separate these from each other allows us to develop what we came to call 'ideal types', after the work of sociologist Max Weber.

The concept of an 'ideal type' is defined by Max Weber thus:

> An ideal type is formed by the one-sided accentuation of one or more points of view and by the synthesis of a great many diffuse, discrete, more or less present and occasionally absent concrete individual phenomena, which are arranged according to those one-sidedly emphasized viewpoints into a unified analytical construct. (1997: 90)

It is thus the opposite of an average. Instead, it is a deliberate focusing and sorting of features that can be seen to mesh together to constitute a meaningful whole. It was his solution to the challenge that cultures are messy, and that the individuals within them are even messier and prone to combining bits from different tendencies, therefore muddying their appearance. 'Reality' *needs* concepts applied to it to make its tendencies visible. Weber is cautious about their use, insisting that they cannot guide actions, nor are they ideal in any moral sense. They are, rather, *logical constructs*. One of his most famous examples is bureaucracy. Elements of this are found in many situations and organisations, but we never meet a *pure* version of it. To understand the inherent tendencies of bureaucracy, it must be thought about in its pure form. Thus, he argues, an ideal type of bureaucracy (as something like 'rational organisation for its own sake', with a dominant focus on 'procedures' and 'records') needs to be developed. No *actual* bureaucracy will be quite as untainted by interfering factors, but the *tendency to bureaucracy* is a force in its own right, he believed (on this whole topic, see, for instance, du Gay, 2000).

In Weber's account, the construction of ideal types is very much the analyst's task, whose insight allows them to see things that are not immediately obvious. For Weber, this made it the most 'subjective' element in social science. We hope to amend this by working from the *signs of patterns within the evidence*. Because of the design of our questionnaire, we were then able to isolate *those answers which most clearly embody those signs*. This in turn allowed us then to construct contrasting empirical portraits of each 'ideal group'. So, the key was to identify *emergent kinds*, to identify

Table 2.1 Proportions of all respondents covered by three 'ideal-type' searches

	Number of groups	Numbers covered	% of overall population
Vernacular categories	6	3,787	35.6%
Roles of fantasy	5	1,930	18.1%
Other activities	7	5,253	49.5%

their 'markers', and then to search the database in a way that separates those marker-features from each other. This meant that we could (to use Weber's term) 'purify' the samples and explore their distinctive emergent shapes.

This was for us a decisive methodological step. The ambition was to create strictly separate groups, with no overlap, emphasising the tendencies that we had found in our three tables. This meant that we were setting aside, for now, the many individuals who spanned and mixed orientations. As individuals, of course, they remain just as interesting as anybody else, but their combinations tend to conceal and muddy the possible groupings. The viability of this as an analytic procedure is, in part, warranted by the results that it produces. So, for instance, it is at least striking that the *type* we dubbed 'fan watchers' (rather than 'lurkers'), whom we isolated as a *group* via a search-string which captured their tendencies to a typifying wide range of activities (thus ensuring their strict separation from not only the fans, but also all the other orientations), displays particularly high engagement with the series on a range of dimensions – including (see Chapter 6 for this) giving distinctively different answers to our question about the meanings of 'Winter is coming …'.

A series of search-strings was developed, trialled and amended. They had to ensure absolute separation while maximising coverage. We wanted to include as many as possible, but only providing that there was no overlap of populations. What emerged from these efforts was the tentative identification of a number of distinctive, isolable groups, of varying sizes, expressed in Table 2.1.

These results indicate very clearly that one of the questions – 'other activities' – is substantially more effective as a guide (and its isolating search-strings were, by some distance, the simplest), and we therefore spent much more time tracking the consequences of its categorisations than the other two (see Chapter 3 for the fruits of this). 'Role of fantasy' in the other direction proved the hardest to develop isolating search-strings for its five emergent categories. This suggests that while the world around *GoT* is quite heavily stratified in terms of the kinds of 'other activities' that its audiences wish to participate in (and these are fairly indicative of other aspects of their engagement), things are much messier and less sedimented in relation to the ways those audiences *name and classify* the series, and *attach wider significances* to their watching of them as a 'fantasy' series.

This does not mean that we did not find interesting indications in the other two arenas. For instance, in our investigation of the 'role of fantasy' types, we distinguished five kinds: a 'modern genre' group, who appear to be interested in fantasy primarily as a storytelling mode; a 'political' group, who want to take fantasy seriously as commentary on our world, and diverge from focus on its scale and depth as a story-world; a 'relaxed entertainment' group, who just like stories of this kind; an 'emotional' group who like to sink themselves into a series such as this, but do not see it as just a matter of *feelings*; and a 'no role' group, for whom a series like this means nothing much beyond itself. What is striking is that when the final step was enacted it became clear that the modern genre group showed markedly higher levels of enjoyment, while interest in commentary belonged very strongly to the political group.

Take a case in point – analysis of choices for our 'kind of story' question brought up a curious result: a strong (if minority) interconnection between 'dystopia' and 'moral fable'. Further exploration revealed that the 136 people adopting this pairing stood out for their conviction that *GoT* should be regarded as an important commentary on our world – in fact, *doubling* (60 per cent versus an average 30 per cent) the proportions for our overall population. The proportion choosing 'extreme enjoyment' rises too, from 51.1 per cent (overall population) to 60.3 per cent. They also display high association with one particular option in our 'role of fantasy' question: 'exploring different attitudes and ideas'. Sensing that this might indicate a form of *dual* relationship with the TV show – a perception that its negativity might be making an important point – we were forced to ask where and how to look, in the answers to our open questions, for further evidence on the meanings of this.

In fact, our first open question brought a great deal to light. A considerable number of answers directly reflect on the relations between the TV show's *darkness* and its significance for us – nowhere more overtly than in this striking answer:

> I like the Show very much. As commentary the most important part is to consider the Sparrows, as an example of extremist believers. Another point is Arya's journey, to find her place in this cruel world. I find it interesting how she handles stuff. This is an inspiration, because I haven't found my place in this cruel world too. (#10502)

No one else makes quite such explicit personal connection, but many reflect on their appreciation of the sense of brutality and hopelessness in *GoT*. Other typifying comments include: 'commenting on the class system, corruption, petty politics and war' (#987); 'Nobody is purely good or purely evil, and being "good" can be just as dangerous as being "evil" (take Ned, for example – his honesty and mercy for Cersei and her children triggers his undoing)' (#1283); '*GoT* provokes a debate about right and wrong in a brutal world full of war, murder, betrayal, lust, bigotry, greed – that is both entertaining and worthy of discussion regarding its implications for real world' (#1519); 'bloodshed and conspiracies and lots and lots of innocent victims' (#1892); 'Takes our own world, makes it unrecognisable, yet highlights truths, explains why things are, and hints at how to change for the better' (#2345); 'through his criticism, you can see glimpses of what today's society is and how corrupt it is ' (#5214). Finally, 'the characters have to make their own choices and live or die by them. There is no good or evil, only very broken souls ...' (#2384) – this last one, part of a 500-word answer which ends with a stark 'Winter IS coming ... and we all know what's coming with it... !!' Some give a knowing wider context:

> Usually in fantasy the good guys are obviously good, and the bad guys are obviously bad. Good guys win, bad guys don't. However, normal fantasy doesn't distinguish what qualities make a good person or a bad person, or even if reputation comes in. You can be a good person with a bad rep, or a bad person with a good rep and gain, let's say, the presidency of a powerful country. *ASOIAF* explores this duality, and just like the real world, some people aren't as good as they seem, while others are good hearted with good intentions that go south quickly, and others are competent, but due to bureaucracy they are blocked at every turn and get smeared. (#3387)

We believe several things are clear from this. The qualitative materials can and do interact with our quantitative results to intensify meaning. But the steps to locate these cannot be fixed and guaranteed in advance – there is a role for hunch and intuition, provided only that these can then be tested against the contents of the database. Methods must therefore be open-ended and subject to emendation and elaboration. But findings like this surely warrant our calling our materials 'a richly structured combination of data and discourses'.

Step 4

Step 4 therefore involved taking, in particular, the search-strings used to isolate the seven distinct patterns of 'other activities', as well as running a full set of cross-tabulations of our other quantitative or quantifiable questions. The results of these provide the basis for much of the rest of this book.

Overall thoughts

Contrary to quite a few other approaches, we do not believe that research of this kind can follow fixed, or automated, analytic stages. Rather, progress in analysis depends on a number of things:

1. Reminding ourselves of our initiating questions, thinking hard about where and how in the database insights and answers might be gained, and then developing tactics to extract the relevant materials.
2. Examining raw results, asking what questions these pose, and then pursuing these down various avenues within the database.
3. Reflecting on ongoing claims and debates, and turning to the database for the distinctive angles that its materials can offer on these.
4. Not being afraid to follow hunches and intuitions, running test enquiries into the database, then refining these in light of preliminary results (or of course abandoning those which lead nowhere – and then reflecting on the meaning of those failures) in order to be sure that the results are strong and meaningful.

Above all else, we believe that the overall design of our project invites and encourages progressive, stepped analytic queries, building on first-level enquiries, and pursuing the implications of these across the 'bridges' between the two kinds of material. We have been involved in devising a fascinating series of checkable hunches, solvable puzzles and testable insights.

Notes

1 Sadly, Billy Proctor was unable, for complicated reasons, to continue his involvement with the project. Martin and Clarissa wish to record their thanks to him for his important contribution to the early stages of its development.
2 A sixth foundational research question indicated one further ambition: to gather data about 'class' in an experimental way. This has long been a particularly troubled issue in social scientific research (see, for instance, Connelly et al., 2016), especially where international comparisons are necessary, but information can only be gathered via a single question. We tried to do this via a single novel question: 'Imagine you are transported to the world of *Game of Thrones*, but you are no richer or poorer, stronger or weaker than in our world. How would you describe your place in society in terms of ranks within Westeros?'. This was accompanied by a seven-point scale, between 'Smallfolk' and 'Pretender to

the throne'. Sadly, we have to be honest and say that this experiment has not produced a great deal in the way of interesting results.
3 There is a third curious component to Q Methodology which is less relevant to our discussion here. This is its willingness to draw strong conclusions from very small numbers. Although no doubt warranted by arguments within statistics, to anyone outside their approach this does appear very strange. For a more elaborated account of these points, see Barker, 2018, looking particularly at the Q Methodology study of responses to the *Hobbit* film trilogy. See also the reply to Barker by Michelle *et al.*, 2018.

3

Distinguishing different kinds of audience

How can we most usefully talk about the many different kinds of people who have watched *Game of Thrones* in ways that go beyond simplisms such as 'everyone is different'? What groups do they fall into, and what labels best capture the nature of these groups?

The trouble is that all our vocabularies for naming them come heavily freighted with implications and judgements. 'Audience', 'viewers', 'watchers', 'spectators': these words sound fairly neutral. But even the most neutral terms, when we look at their uses, carry colourations. Talk of 'the audience' almost invariably attracts speculations about possible 'effects', even 'dangers' (e.g., Murphy, 2015) of the series, and easily extends to talk of 'vulnerable audiences' (a Google search of this expression pulls up more than 25 million references, including – intriguingly – a considerable number on how to make use of people's 'vulnerabilities' for marketing purposes). The term 'viewers' meanwhile often links to discussions of numbers, ratings and the general measures of commercial success. 'Watchers' couples more readily with interest in gathering clues (e.g., information leaks or rumours) and predicting next steps in the narrative – as, of course, in the major *GoT* website 'Watchers On The Wall'. 'Spectators', on the other hand, has strong links with a whole body of high ('spectatorship') theory in relation to film in particular, a whole approach that has been resistant to any notion of researching *actual* audiences (for a recent example of this sort of work, see Campbell, 2015).

Go beyond these terms and an array of more obviously normative ones appear: 'fans', 'enthusiasts', 'aficionados', 'cognoscenti', 'nerds', 'geeks', 'freaks'. These carry their judgements on their faces, even if some of them are happily adopted by people for themselves. When journalists sniff a phenomenon and realise that they need to discuss it, they reach into this bag of labels and think 'what's appropriate?' – 'Is *Game of Thrones* for nerds? Of course it is! Of course it is. But is it for nerds only? That's what Neil Genzlinger suggests in today's *Times*, that *GoT* only appeals to "Dungeons & Dragons types"' (Lyons, 2012).

Fan scholars have, without doubt, done sterling work on the valency of these – including reflecting on their position as 'aca-fans' (see, for instance, Henry Jenkins' ongoing blogsite 'Confessions of an aca-fan' and a good deal of the work published in *Transformative Works and Cultures*). There is also now a strong body of scholarship on what have variously been called 'figures', 'presumptions' or 'myths' of the audience, both vernacular and academic (see, for instance, Cronin, 2009; Hagen, 1999; Schoenbach, 2001; Schiappa, 2008). We need to remember that these terms, and their connotations, change over time and by location. Butsch and Livingstone (2014) have drawn together a fascinating array of essays from rarely considered countries, to show the differing ways in which ideas of 'audience' have been developed and used. Butsch himself (2000; 2008) has explored in great detail the history of audience discourses in the United States over two centuries.

Beyond these, ways of describing kinds of audience bifurcate between categories generated by theories and those generated out of empirical evidence. Examples of theory-driven classifications are the famous triad derived from the work of Stuart Hall (1973) and David Morley (1980) – 'hegemonic', 'negotiating' and 'resistant' – and, more recently, the proposed 'composite model' update on those by Carolyn Michelle and colleagues (e.g., 2007; 2012). In such approaches, *all* audiences must fall within one of their categories. In the other direction, recent years have seen influential moves towards methods of audience segmentations, closely tied to arts and media marketing strategies. The UK Arts Council, for instance, funded a major project to classify people's interests in the arts. Its ten-part scheme tries to encapsulate people's interests and motivations (Arts Agency, 2011). More widely, demographic segmentation has become a highly professionalised predictive marketing field, with two major software packages, MOSAIC (which focuses on likely consumer behaviour according to their demographic 'type') and ACORN (which begins from population locations and lifestyle patterns).[1]

In this chapter we are attempting something different, using our distinctive methodological device. We wanted to see how far it is possible to locate distinct *ways of relating* to the series, among our 10,000-plus participants. Our ambition was, as we explained in Chapter 2, to go beyond simply finding differences in the ways people responded to *GoT*. Moreover, we hoped to locate and distinguish *patterns* of responses. More than particular judgements or choices (although they might prove to contain these), these are, we believe, *overall orientations* to the series, tying together a string of connected tendencies. This includes reasons for watching, and – because of these 'reasons' – hopes and expectations, as well as consequential evaluative criteria; ways of watching – including both with whom one watches (real

Distinguishing different kinds of audience

or imagined), and preferred ways of encountering the series; particular associations, preferences and judgements – tied together by the *grounds* for them as much as their outcomes; associated activities – any ways in which watching the TV show spills out into other activities; and dominant feelings and attitudes, emotions and responses. They need not all be as serious or as committed as each other, casual viewing is as interesting and important as dedicated viewing. They are not like denominational doctrines, with small scope for variation. However, they are, we believe, patterned – and it is these patterns that we aim to disclose.

Here, the project's qualiquantitative design came into its own. As we explained in Chapter 2, our questionnaire included three key 'sorting' questions: on 'naming' the series; the roles of fantasy; and associated activities. Each one asked our participants to make choices from among a set of options, which sought to capture the main possibilities for how people might relate to and understand *GoT*. The accumulated answers allowed us to draw out tendencies, and then (in our crucial methodological step) to *accentuate* these tendencies and *isolate* those who most unambiguously expressed them. In this chapter we explore in detail what proved the most effective of these questions.

It is the answers to the third of these sorting questions that we focus on here. Question 17 asked people to pick as many as they wished from a list of nine options describing any other activities undertaken in association with watching the series. The full list offered:

- debating the series' merits and faults with other viewers;
- writing about it online;
- buying/collecting merchandise;
- visiting filming locations;
- reading/re-reading George R. R. Martin's books;
- producing fan fiction, fan videos, fan art, etc.;
- enjoying other people's fan productions;
- game-playing, role-playing or cosplay; and
- none of the above.[2]

Although some of these are composites, it felt reasonable to combine, for instance, different *kinds* of game-playing, in the interests of keeping the number of choices under control.

Table 3.1 presents the overall percentages of choices, and the degrees of interrelationship between them, with a note on the proportion in each case of single choices. The table also indicates highest and lowest interrelationships; the total numbers choosing each option; the degree of variance (separating 'very high' (exceptional difference), 'high' (highest interrelationship = more than double the lowest score), 'medium' (highest approaches double the

Table 3.1 Interrelationships of responses to Question 17

	1	2	3	4	5	6	7	8	9
1. Debating merits and faults		**88.1**	82.8	<u>76.9</u>	79.3	82.7	80.6	**83.6**	0	L
2. Writing online	35.0		40.3	36.7	*33.6*	*59.6*	37.1	44.6	0	M
3. Buying/collecting merchandise	<u>39.4</u>	48.4		53.9	41.1	55.9	42.7	<u>58.6</u>	0	H
4. Visiting locations	7.0	8.4	<u>10.3</u>		6.7	8.1	*6.4*	8.8	0	L
5. (Re-)reading Martin's books	77.2	82.5	**83.9**	<u>71.4</u>		80.7	80.1	83.4	0	L
6. Producing fan fiction, videos, art	<u>8.0</u>	14.6	11.6	8.7	8.5		11.5	<u>16.0</u>	0	H
7. Enjoying others' productions	51.5	59.7	57.3	<u>45.0</u>	52.5	<u>75.6</u>		64.9	0	M
8. Gaming, role-play, cosplay	<u>17.5</u>	23.4	25.8	20.3	18.0	<u>34.5</u>	21.3		0	H
9. None of these	0	0	0	0	0	0	0	0		–
Totals	7977	3167	3800	724	7770	774	5094	1673	558	
Single choices (%s)	7.9	1.2	1.6	3.6	6.4	0.4	3.0	1.3	100	VH
Numbers of high-lit relations	4	2	2	4	6	4	1	3	0	

Bold/<u>underline</u> = highest; **bold** = next highest; *italics*/<u>underline</u> = lowest; *italics* = next lowest. (Where there is a clear standout highest or lowest, we have not marked next cases.)

lowest) and 'low' (the remainder)) between highest and lowest choices; and for the proportions of single choices (an indicator of the extent to which a choice can be a stand-alone choice). The table needs to be read from left to right.

This complicated table revealed a great deal. All the options are well-populated, giving us confidence in making comparisons. A good number (558) said that they did nothing alongside watching the series (and thus constitute an entirely self-contained category). Those 'debating merits and faults' showed the highest levels (7,977 = 75 per cent of our total). With a low level of variance, this constitutes what we might call entry-level participation in other activities – for example, something that may be done in and for itself, or perhaps done alongside and through almost all the other choices. Thereafter, 'reading/re-reading Martin's books' shows the next highest overall total, but it also reveals two additional features. It has the second-highest level of single choices, and the largest number of highlighted cross-relations, all of them italicised, marking *low* interrelationships. 'Reading or re-reading', therefore, *tends* to be a rather separate or disconnected activity.

One striking result concerns the huge contrast between the numbers saying that they *enjoy looking at* other people's fan productions (5,094), and the number *producing* these (724). A related point can be made by looking at the penultimate line, which records the percentage of single-only choices. This clearly shows that two response-sets – 'debating the series', and '(re-)reading' – have markedly the highest levels of single choices. Again, this emphasises their greater tendency to be self-sufficient activities.

At this point, the theory and tactics outlined in the previous chapter were brought into operation, to identify and then isolate ideal types of the emergent patterns in the data. We have made the precise methods available on the book's associated website (see www.manchesterhive.com/watching-got-resources). Here, we focus on the *outcomes* of these methods, which resulted in our locating seven distinct kinds of *GoT* audience.

Our seven 'ideal-type' groupings

We shall introduce each briefly in turn.

1. **Just the Show:** Most obviously, our first group marked itself off by its choice of 'no other activities', and was isolable on that basis. Of course, as we will see, saying that they do nothing other than watch does not necessarily mean this in an exact, literal sense. Rather, it is that *by their own estimation* nothing else counts beyond watching. We dubbed this group 'Just the Show' (N=558).

2. **Debaters:** There is then a large group for whom taking part in debates on the series' merits and faults is salient. It is a common denominator for many other orientations, although not evenly so – intriguingly, its *lowest* association is with 'reading/re-reading Martin's books'. Because the numbers of this group outrun all the other groups, there are clearly a considerable number who *only* do this. It was simple to isolate those who *only* chose 'debating the series'. Hence, our title 'Debaters' (N=630).[3]
3. **Classic Fans:** There is a strong group for whom *doing things around the series* – be it producing fan fiction or fan art, etc. – is a substantial motive. But, strikingly, this is for a good number that were *marked off* from *debating* the series and thinking about its value and achievement. Plus, although not incompatible with (re-)reading Martin's books, it is not strongly associated with that. It therefore looked sensible to isolate a fans group. This is particularly important since, reading down the columns in Table 3.1, those involved in 'fandom' generally display the overall highest relationships (four highest scores, three of them being stand-out results). While fan theory has recently diversified to separate different kinds of fan, we dubbed this group the 'Classic Fans' (N=585).
4. **Contented Consumers:** There is, by contrast, a group marked by having *low overall figures* but also *low relations* with other groups. These people picked 'visiting locations' and 'buying/collecting merchandise'. The first of these in particular appears to stand alone more than any other dimension (having no high relationships, and four low relationships). There is low interest in debating the series, and the lowest relations with (re-)reading Martin's books. It seemed fair to wonder whether this might be a group more engaged with the immediate public presence of *GoT*, and less interested in public debates about its value. Although there is a high relationship for merchandise with fan activities, fannish interests are explored through a different grouping. Ensuring isolation of this group required the most complicated search-string of the seven groups, but the resultant total was still the second highest. This group became our 'Contented Consumers' (N=1,055).
5. **Fan Watchers:** We were intrigued by that unexpectedly large difference between the totals for engaging in fannish activities and enjoying looking at the fannish activities of others, and their one-way relationship. Consequently, we sought to isolate a group typifying the latter – but what should we call them? We cannot ignore the significance of existing names. The kind of response that we are isolating here frequently comes under the label 'lurking'. Lurking labels the activities of people who supposedly hang around on the Internet watching – and sometimes rudely intervening onto – *proper* fans' interests and activities. Lurkers have been the subject of a considerable amount of research and debate, mostly negative. At best, they are seen as a puzzle (see, e.g., Nonnecke *et al.*, 2004; and Preece *et al.*, 2004), not quite committed enough and therefore to be considered as seeking the 'triggers to active participation'

(Rafaeli *et al.*, 2004: 1), or, at their worst, as potential trolls (for a critical exploration of this, see Bishop, 2013; for a critical reconceptualisation of these ideas – moving from 'lurking' to the idea of 'listening' – see Crawford, 2011). Our decision to name this orientation differently is a conscious attempt to shed those negative associations. Who then are these 'Fan Watchers', as we provisionally renamed them, and how could we isolate them? One curious feature appears to be that they made more choices, overall, than other groups, and a sample scan of the database indicates that two particular combinations are particularly common.[4] These became the basis for our search-strings for this group (N=767).

6. **Players:** Our next group focused around kinds of *playing*. As with Fans, our question for here was a composite one, combining some very different kinds of play-relationship, from board-gaming to cosplay. Even with that risk, Table 3.1 indicates some curious tendencies that we needed to pursue. Much like Fans, Players display quite low interest in debating the series, both in general and online. Although it would have been possible to work with a group that *combined* fan and gaming interests, surprisingly, searches for combinations of these options produced very low results. In another direction, although the proportion of people engaging strongly with books is *low*, the proportion of Players interested in the books is *high*. We therefore decided simply to name this group 'Players' (N=1,160).

7. **Book Followers:** Finally, there are those participants associating most strongly with George R. R. Martin's books. It was impossible to ignore the fact that book-reading had the second highest number of choices, and that a higher percentage made this their single choice. With the benefit of a simple isolation procedure, therefore, for those who *only* add book-reading to their series viewing, this produced a small but clearly distinguishable group, the 'Book Followers' (N=498).

Cumulatively, these groups offer a total of 5,253 (49.5 per cent of our total population), with no overlaps at all among the groups.

The first thing to note is that there is a fairly consistent *scaling* of responses across a series of indicators. Just the Show respondents display markedly lower levels of engagement, closely followed by Debaters, and – more curiously – Book Followers. At the other end, Classic Fans compete with Fan Watchers – and occasionally Players – for the highest response levels. Contented Consumers occupy the middle ground throughout, as Table 3.2 indicates.

While there is clearly something important connecting levels of investment in the TV series with engaging in further activities, we think the discrepancies also deserve attention. Note, for instance, the way that Players come top on 'enjoyment', but fall to third on 'interest in the series' commentary on our world' – hinting that this orientation is more self-enclosed, and interested in the story as a 'thing in itself' (a point which is confirmed by other findings).

Table 3.2 Scaled responses among the seven 'ideal-type' audiences

	Just the Show	Debaters	Book Followers	Contented Consumers	Players	Fan Watchers	Classic Fans
Enjoyment[1]	7	6	5	4	1	3	2
Commentary[1]	7	5	6	4	3	2	1
Debates[1]	7	5	6	4	3	2	1
Repeat viewing[2]	7	5	6	4	3	2	1
Binge watching[3]	6	3	6	5	2	1	4

[1] Enjoyment, Commentary, and Debates are each measured by the proportion of respondents attaching 'extreme importance' to these.
[2] Repeat viewing is measured by the proportion of respondents using the word 'repeat', in answer to our question about how they watch.
[3] Binge watching is measured by the proportion of respondents mentioning either 'binge' or 'marathon' in answer to the same question. (NB: Just the Show and Book Followers recorded identical proportions.)

Notice also how Debaters – mostly competing with Book Followers for next to bottom position – jump several places with regard to binge viewing – an indication, surely, that these viewers, like the Fan Watchers, compose and prepare themselves for their engagement – while the Classic Fans may *need to watch as soon as possible* in order to enact their kind of engagement.

We found further indicators of differences in our other quantitative measures – some fully expected, others more surprising. Classic Fans were the youngest of our groups (35.4 per cent under-20s, versus Book Followers at 11.6 per cent – the latter also had the highest proportion of over-45s at 22.8 per cent (Fans recording just 4.2 per cent)). Players were the mostly-male group (65.3 per cent, versus Contented Consumers at 42.6 per cent). Less expectedly, Fan Watchers recorded the strongest left-wing slant (at 62.9 per cent, versus Book Followers at 50.4 per cent, who veered to the right) – while Contented Consumers showed the highest proportion of middle-of-the-road/ apolitical (35.6 per cent). Just the Show viewers showed the strongest rejection of spoilers (57.7 per cent recording dislike or hatred of spoilers, versus Fans at 44.8 per cent). Here, a seriously puzzling result – Book Followers, who had presumably high levels of predictive knowledge of the TV show from their reading, still recorded high levels of dislike of spoilers (49.4 per cent disliking or hating these).

In light of all these results, we examined sets of open answers, choosing people's explanations for the value that they set on their enjoyment of the TV show and its role as commentary. Randomised sets of fifty answers – all indicating 'extreme enjoyment' to ensure that we were comparing like with like – were isolated and examined. In certain respects, inevitably, the answers overlapped – anyone could say 'Because I loved the Show, it is the most fantastic series in the world' (#4306), or (with adjustments for age) 'It's a brilliant series that I've been following since I was 14 years old. It is simply perfect' (#1494). Short, general declarations of admiration are easily shared. And there are of course disagreements within each of the sets. But what follows is an attempt to mark out some small but striking differences between them.

Just the Show

The primary characteristic of answers in the Just the Show mode is that they are predominantly short and assertoric (and the word count for the overall fifty answers is considerably below all the others). So, 'Best TV Show ever!!!!!!' (#10138), and 'Although enjoyable it's a fantasy' (#3025) are characteristic. Interestingly, having indicated that they do not do anything else in association with watching, a number talk about discussing the TV show with relatives and friends (e.g., 'All my family watch it and we love to talk about the episodes, so we cannot miss one!' [#10070]) – meaning, presumably, that to this group home conversations do not *count* as 'debating its merits and faults'. One interesting indicator not found elsewhere is displayed in this answer:

> Not only is it highly enjoyable to watch but it also seems quite realistic. Every time something important happens I keep thinking of what I would do if I were in the same situation. I think that it is very essential to me because it triggers my mind with all these questions, decisions, the complicity of the characters' relationships etc. (#2562)

The strong sense of the personal and unshared here is distinctive to this orientation. However, the overwhelming sense taken from this group who did choose 'extreme enjoyment' is in effect *not caring* that much beyond the viewing moment: 'It's very well produced and acted. The story is interesting, but I haven't really thought about the commentary. It's entertainment for me' (#433).

Debaters

With the Debaters, the modality of response shifts to commentary being considered a possible 'extra'. By no means the point of the TV show, but an additional possibility: 'I want it for the entertainment value but have noticed aspects of social commentary within the writing' (#5440). What is also added is a happy recognition of the 'high production values' of the TV show, and the fact that it has broken new ground with its complexity and risk-taking:

> I think the Show has high production values, and the fate of the characters keep me engaged so I enjoy it tremendously. I only think it's a reasonable commentary on our world though, in terms of the ways in which the characters all manipulate truth or information to their (political) benefit. (#3525)

Now there is the bonus of the role that it plays among friends: 'part of my social relations as many people in my entourage watch it' (#6194). The TV show is an additional component to ongoing connections: 'The Show is one more thing that I have in common with my friends, and we enjoy spending time together talking about it' (#10159).

Contented Consumers

The Contented Consumer group does not readily distinguish itself from those other groups around it. There are odd and striking elements, such as a willingness to acknowledge sheer physical attraction ('Kit Harington is a joy to look at' (#2298 – this as the entire answer)). Indeed, there appears to be a bit more attention to *characters* in general: 'It's not really relevant to today's world other than some characters' (#1652 – again, the complete answer). Or again, 'Because there are so many characters in the Show it makes it like an epic soap opera that is fun to watch and theorize about' (#2155). The issue of *GoT* being a commentary on our world divides this orientation as much as most of the others, but there is a hint of a particular way of addressing it: 'I enjoy the story. I love how deep it goes and how much there is to learn about it. How everything just kinda connects in unexpected ways. I don't look for anything like social commentary. If I wanted commentary I'd look for it somewhere else' (#10576). *GoT* has been put into a place where it can be safely enjoyed simply as entertainment.

Classic Fans

Two senses of the word 'follow' are important when looking at Classic Fans: first, the sense of 'following the series', caught up in its unfolding and keeping up to date with it; and second, the sense of being 'part of the show's following, its devotees'. Being part of that can mean being caught up with 'fan theories', taking its strongest form here:

> It's extremely important to me to follow and enjoy because as a result of becoming a *Game of Thrones* fan I have made several new friends and become much more involved on social media than I was before. It feels significant to be a part of a fandom as large as *Game of Thrones*. (#794)

There is a strand of liking being part in a cultural event: 'I like liking things. Especially good things. I like things that challenge what you call entertainment or story-telling. I don't like watching Shows passively, every minute should be important and engaging. This is *Game of Thrones* in a nutshell' (#6580).

A curious feature of this group, something that is not found in the same way elsewhere, is an emphasis on *morality* and 'being human': 'I just wish good will win, in the series and to our world' (#2702); and 'The characters are very human. Flawed and real and sad and human' (#528). These read like a less intellectualised or political version of what Fan Watchers tend to do.

Fan Watchers

In small ways the Fan Watchers betray a greater *intellectualism* than the others, marked by the use of terms such as 'cognitive'. While there are certainly those who are happy to see the series simply as a story, others extend this in striking ways:

> *GoT* is one of my favourite series of all time. I've watched the Show through multiple times, I've read all the books, I read tons of discussion about it online. It's one of those series where there's so much happening in it that it's possible

to get into hours-long discussions about it with other fans. As a commentary on our world, I think it helps people to think about stuff they otherwise might not. In particular, politics. The series is so focused on the interplay of different factions with competing ideologies, and it can help people understand how things work in the real world. (#4093)

There is a particular kind of interplay between watching others, debating the meanings, and building a potential understanding of 'different factions with competing ideologies' which is found only in this group. Others say the same sort of thing with less completion: 'To recognize multiple, valid points of view which are at once both all-consuming yet totally futile' (#7301), and 'I've found myself smitten with the storylines, how most characters are grey rather than black and white. It's less important to me as commentary than story, but good stories do say something about the human condition' (#446). A lot of emphasis is placed on the moral complexity of Martin's world, 'grey' rather than 'black and white', its quality as conception and as writing, 'well thought out' (#5411). It is the 'realism, grit, and humour' (#6187) – indeed, a strong recognition of 'multi-layered' levels within the series.

Players

Regarding Players, there is a hint in the above answer which becomes a clearly defining characteristic in this next orientation: a fascination with the 'depth' of the story, its 'details' and 'nuances'. The scale of the world and its complexity are things worth attending to in their own right:

> I've read both the books and rewatched the Show several times. It is the first series for which I read up on theories, lore and similar. It has also introduced me to role playing games based on the series which I quite enjoy. It is clear to me that certain elements of *GoT* reflect the real world: power balances, human behaviour etc. though this is not the main reason I enjoy it. (#5948)

There is no resistance to the notion of *GoT* as 'commentary', but that is not the prime focus. This answer is admittedly unusual in making the overt connection to gaming. But in other ways, perhaps, a 'gaming' eye is one which attends to 'intricate' elements, the 'micro details' (#6845), and 'diverse points of view' (#10628) of the TV show. *GoT* can take its place among other stories in this 'world building' mode:

> *Game of Thrones* got me back into Fantasy as an adult. As a kid and early teenager I loved Tolkien and anything 'high-fantasy' related, like Warcraft or The Elder Scrolls Series (which borrows heavily From *ASOIAF*). As I grew older, most of the philosophical aspects of high-fantasy appeared very simplistic and it's often black or white characters seemed to me as only being representative

one single world-view, or mythology. So I delved into more complex literature both classic (Dante, Shakespeare) and avant-garde (David Foster Wallace, Kracht etc.), while also keeping a high interest in archaeology and history. When I watched the first Season (in one sitting...) I was hooked, as it combined my childhood love for fantasy with a pluralistic society and conflicting mythologies, it was like the half-truth, half-legend 'history' books written by medieval monks, but also generating an entire world out of equally pluralistic real existing mythologies and histories, but with a very basic human touch. That is that, every POV character is righteous by his own motives, just like in *The Wire*, yet death comes for everyone equally, just like in *The Wire*. It leaves the choice and the exploration thereof open to the reader. It's basically as real and awkward as a pen&paper game, but with way better effects and dialogue. (#4160)

This longer answer is worth quoting in full, not least since the Players gave markedly longer answers than anyone else. It displays a distinctive willingness to switch standpoints – something valuable in game-playing.

Book Followers

There is a recurrent sense among the Book Followers of literary awareness, sometimes simply expressed in single words or expressions: 'genre', 'work of fiction', 'speculative literature'. There is a greater attention to the *writers* (of both books and the TV show). Book reading does not always precede the TV series: 'I watch every episode at least twice and follow all the commentary. I just started reading the books so as to get myself off the internet constantly looking for new *GoT* content' (#10526); 'It's very entertaining so I follow but it is fiction so while some parts are based on historical events & the human condition it is from the imagination of a writer/writers & it is their perspective on life events' (#1825) – but it regularly seems to *inform* responses to the TV show. There is sometimes a slight sense of *defensiveness*:

I follow the Show, read the books, watch theory and explanation videos which all in all is about 50 per cent of my entertainment and while it does give much commentary on world affairs such as the terrors war even just wars, like Robb's campaign, it doesn't influence my views as much as my raised values. (#5108)

This mild apologia gently insists that here is an educated response, well-versed in relevant materials.

What can these mini-portraits be said to show? With great caution – these are just tendencies within the sampled groups, amid considerable overlap – we suggest that they point to the differing ways in which *people can go about the work of arriving at evaluations*. All these respondents agree that

GoT offers the highest levels of enjoyment – that is the common ground for these comparisons. But the *measures* and *criteria* against which the experience of the TV show (and books) is being judged, shift subtly between the orientations.

We return in subsequent chapters to further ways in which our seven ideal-type orientations reveal differences.

Notes

1 A good example of this kind of segmentation analysis can be seen in the research into attitudes among Americans towards climate change, which has distinguished six kinds of response: alarmed; concerned; cautious; disengaged; doubtful; and dismissive, giving percentages to each from a large survey (Maibach *et al.*, 2009). In some ways rather obvious, the groupings are clearly intended as precursors to the development of strategies for speaking persuasively to at least most of the different groups, by identifying who and what each group trusts or distrusts.
2 An electronic block on the main questionnaire prevented anyone from clicking any other options alongside this, accidentally or otherwise.
3 We debated the value of either forming a distinct group of those who *only* pick online discussions of the series, or alternatively treating them in combination with the Debaters group. But the numbers for the first option proved riskily small (N=127), while the search-string needed to isolate the combined group proved worryingly complicated. For these reasons we pursued neither option. In addition, when looking to isolate the second group from the Fans, it became clear that 'writing online' tends to be an expression of multiple choices. Looking closely at combinations which included 1, ('debating merits and faults') and 2, ('writing online'), it turns out that the proportion of those making four or more choices was *more than double* that of the overall cohort (72 per cent versus 34 per cent), suggesting that this is rarely an activity in its own right. It made sense to ensure that this option was taken up within other groups, rather than constituting its own group. Whether and in what ways engaging with the series online (other than via involvement in fan activities) makes differences to the kinds of pleasure and meaning associated with it, remains a question to be explored.
4 For detailed information on these search-strings, and much else, please visit our research materials on the Manchester University Press website, via this address: www.manchesterhive.com/watching-got-resources.

4

Favourite characters, favourite survivors

Game of Thrones offered its audiences an exceptionally rich range of characters – and, for the TV series, of actors playing them. Not simply for the mix of ages, ethnicities and sexual orientations, or of personal attributes (brave or cowardly, smart or dim, ambitious or loyal), but also for the way that the characters simply do not fall into easy archetypes or embodiments of moral attributes. *GoT* has often been compared with Tolkien's *The Lord of the Rings*, but there are such important differences between the *kinds* of character offered and the complex ways that they both belong within their cultures and are individualised. Frodo in Tolkien's world 'embodies' suffering and self-sacrifice, while Sam 'embodies' loyal friendship, in a way that none of Martin's characters ever do. Even a character like Ramsay Bolton displays complexities (e.g., personal vindictiveness, plus crawling subordination to his father) that make his 'evil' quite different from that of Tolkien's Sauron. Plus, so many of the characters must undergo major changes across the story-arc of the series. Martin's work is also remarkable for the way in which it roves across a whole series of characters, never allowing one story to dominate the narrative for long periods. For anyone following the series, it quickly becomes clear that the fortunes of many are going to be blighted. Misfortune, suffering and death are the fates of many of the characters. All the places where debate has occurred around *GoT* abound with discussions of particular characters and their actors – their qualities, their fates – making it clear that they really matter to many among the audience (including of course, for some, the differences between book and TV treatments). For people to choose 'favourites' is bound to be complicated, and any research into such choices must work with those complexities.

We asked people two side-by-side questions, inviting them to tell us who their favourite *characters* were, and their favourite *survivors*, and why. Some responded briefly, with single or multiple character names, while others gave us long discursive answers, in a few cases reaching as high as 1,000 words of intense commentary. How does our work on these answers situate our research in relation to existing work?

Theorising 'favourite characters'

There is a long and broad tradition of thinking about fictional characters, approaching the issue from many angles (see the compendious Eder *et al*., 2016, for a useful survey of many of these approaches; see also Eder, 2006). There have been substantial *ontological* debates, involving such questions as what kind of 'entity' are characters? What rules apply to characters? How can 'true' and 'false' claims be made about characters? What does it mean that characters can 'exist' across and beyond particular media incarnations? *Histories* of characters have explored their various *types* (from archetypes such as quest heroes, and generic figures such as vamps, to highly individualised personae with rich inner lives) and *media* (e.g., how character is differently generated in novels versus films). Work has also been conducted on the cultural and psychological roles of characters. While all these bear on our research in varying ways, it is the strand of potential influence that is most germane. Here, we must address a significant split. While in literary studies work on audience relations tends to focus on processes of *comprehension* (e.g., how readers can assemble a 'sense of character' from a novel), in relation to popular media (e.g., film and television), the focus – until recently heavily dominated by work in the American moral-psychological studies tradition – has focused on possible *residues* (i.e., what traces might be left inside viewers through processes such as 'identification').

More recently (since the 1980s), an emergent tradition of cognitive film scholars have theorised how films, with their complex narrative structures and presentational devices, can guide and train audiences into complex (both cognitive and emotional) relations with characters. It is not possible to examine either of these approaches in the detail that they deserve here, but a short examination of each is necessary since the approach taken in this book is so different.[1]

Media and moral psychology

The difference here is essentially between one predicated on a model of individuated audiences, still clinging to modified notions of linear transmission of effects, and one which approaches audience affiliations through all the complexity of their historical, social and cultural milieux. The general problems with the experimental psychological tradition have been long rehearsed: its results are hard to replicate outside the laboratory; research subjects are asked to respond in ways which deny their responses any social or cultural placement; and responses are reduced to checklists of researcher-devised measures, without any reference to audiences' understandings of situation, materials or meanings.

For a long time, the key concept deployed within this tradition was 'identification'. Although its roots are much older (see Barker, 1989), this concept particularly took shape between the 1930 and 1950s (see especially Maccoby and Wilson, 1957), when popular Freudianism combined with emergent commercial research and with public scares over 'bad media influences'. 'Identification' proposed that in the act of engaging, audiences might surrender to materials like films, becoming less self or context-aware, and – by associating with the 'point of view' of characters (the notion of their being favourites or not was strangely absent) – take on their feelings, attitudes, evaluations and even *in extremis* repeating their actions. 'Identification' remained the concept of choice until the 1980s when, as part of the wider turn against Freudianism within American academic life, some key people sought to retheorise the domain.

In 1980, Dolf Zillman had been a key source for theorising 'identification'; by 1994, he had renounced the concept, instead proposing 'empathy'.[2] The key difference was of course that 'empathy' did not presume adoption of the specific point of view of a particular character. What became important instead were the *emotions* that we experienced.[3] A number of theorists then proposed a second concept alongside 'empathy', that of 'transportation' (e.g., Green *et al.*, 2008), to capture the ways in which people become *absorbed* in what they are reading, watching or listening to – thus, virtually reintroducing 'identification', since it was again all about becoming 'vulnerable' to a transmitted point of view. Other researchers sought to defend and maintain 'identification', trying to separate it from 'transportation' (see, for instance, Tal-Or and Cohen, 2010). But what all these variations retained was an interest in 'narrative persuasion' (e.g., Appel and Richter, 2010) – crudely, how audiences might be being 'got at' by the media that they chose to watch.

No matter what the concepts' names, there has always been the problem that these are essentially invisible processes. Researchers cannot *see* a person 'identifying' or 'empathising' or 'being transported'. The history of this research tradition is therefore marked by repeated attempts to construct checklists and scales for processes where the only real check – what the people *think and say they are doing* – is refused as a source of evidence. Curiously, with just a few exceptions, because they will not generally ask people *who* their favourite characters are, and *why*, the focus of the research falls on the *general idea of attractive characters*. Take as a direct test case the work of a stalwart of such psychological approaches to our topic, Jonathan Cohen, author of one of the strongest recent defences of theories of identification (see Cohen, 2001 – see also the extended critique in Barker, 2005). In 1999, Cohen published a study of Israeli teenagers' choices of favourite characters from the then popular TV show *Ramat-Aviv Gimel* – a series set among fictional inhabitants of one of Tel-Aviv's real and most wealthy suburbs. The essay is an interesting inquiry but it is set entirely within a frame of 'theories of media effects' (Cohen, 1999: 327), asking about signs of good or worrying impacts on socialisation. Cohen allows for four possible explanatory concepts, all of which are derived from the psychological literature: parasocial interaction (sought intimacy); identification (sensed likeness); wishful identification (wished-for likeness); and affinity (choosing the closest from a range) – all concepts that hint at moralistic concerns that proximity to characters might leave good or bad traces behind. Teenagers, Cohen asserts, may be 'most vulnerable' because of their age, and be unable to 'separate fact from fiction' (1999: 328). In the end, Cohen concludes that there are in fact no signs of harmful effects on future aspirations – albeit he does pause over the odd fact that hardly anyone in his sample has anything to say about the wealth and status of the characters.

The giveaway is his working definition: 'A favourite character is the best-liked character, the character with which the viewer feels closest' (1999: 329). We will see that this would make a nonsense of a great many of the indicated favourite *GoT* characters that our participants named. Nevertheless, Cohen needs a definition of this kind, focusing on how 'close' we come to characters and inviting moral deductions. Proximity hints at risky intimacy, at invasion of the person or personality (we would not allow a slide from 'best-liked food' to 'one to which we feel closest'). It is this assumption that we want to do away with here, instead allowing our participants' explanations to point us towards a far wider range of ways of relating to 'favourites'.

Cognitive film studies

Cognitive approaches within film studies effectively took off from the critique of psychoanalytic approaches developed by, in particular, David Bordwell (see, for instance, Bordwell, 1991). But it took a particular shape with the publication of Murray Smith's *Engaging Characters* (1995), which combined close philosophical critique with textual examination to propose a three-level distinction regarding how audiences connect to characters: recognition (in its most basic form, ascribing characteristics to figures within a film); alignment (the results of a film *tracking* a character, allowing us to see as they see); and allegiance (taking sides and adopting a character's point of view). This was part of a wider critique of notions of identification begun by Noël Carroll in his work on horror films (1990). Smith argues against psychological accounts of identification, saying that they conflate two distinct kinds of imagining: 'imagining that I am X'; and 'imagining what it would be like to be in X's situation'. For identification to have force, the former must happen. But, argues Smith, the ways in which films call upon viewers' knowledge and emotional responses indicate that actually the latter is taking place. However, as one of us has argued (Barker, 2005), while there is real critical value in Smith's account, it falls short in its explanatory power by turning audiences into *perpetual novices*. His text-centred approach effectively requires that we know nothing about a film (e.g., its director, genre, quality, storyline and character types) before we begin watching it, awaiting its cues and guidance. The very substantial growth of cognitive film studies since such a start has not changed this. There continues to be a real unwillingness to deal with *actual* audiences and the complexities that they bring to any viewing.

There are, however, wider strands and tendencies within cognitive film theory connecting it with recent developments in neuroscience (including the re-emerging fascination with brain localisation – see, for instance, Hasson *et al.*, 2008; Elliott, 2010), and even with evolutionary psychology and its search for ahistorical 'universal' patterns in human behaviour (see, for instance, Grodal, 2009). Some of this is welded to revealing normative, judgemental positions. It is neither possible nor relevant to attempt to characterise this whole development, but one recent set of connections has impinged sufficiently closely to make a brief visitation necessary. In an essay in the Italian journal *Corporatismi*, Simone Rebora has drawn on cognitive science to argue that deep fascination with *GoT* might constitute evidence of 'maladaptive daydreaming'. This supposed condition was first 'identified' by psychologists around 2002, elaborated upon (with possible treatments) and put forward to the American Psychiatric Association for possible inclusion in the next revision of the *Diagnostic and Statistical Manual of Mental Disorders* as an example of an overlooked mental-health disorder. Maladaptive daydreaming is apparently different from ordinary 'mind-wandering, because it is characterized by increased richness of fantasy and absorption in imagination' (Somer *et al.*, 2017: 177). It does not involve confusion between fantasy and reality, rather, it is primarily that people devote 'too much' time to 'fantasising' and come to regret this. Maladaptive daydreamers are not marked by any history of trauma, only by their deep following of 'worlds'. In short, they have an addiction (Bigelson *et al.*, 2016). Rebora takes the argument one stage further, drawing on cognitive science as his warranty.

His essay unfolds an argument that (a) fantasy is the most transmedial of genres; (b) this tends to open neural pathways that are 'simulation-driven', and hence encourage 'passivity', and therefore; (c) the development carries dangers of 'addiction' – exemplified by fans excitedly saying things such as 'I can't wait for the next bit' or 'what am I going to do without this now it's finished?': 'the field of cognitive science offers a hint of the possible negative consequences of this phenomenon' (Rebora 2019: 223). Rebora borrows from cognitive science the notion of an 'extended mind', and 'lampreys' this onto Henry Jenkins' quite otherwise characterisation of fan productions as 'collective intelligence' – supposedly made worse by 'the possibility of exploring it through its most advanced technologies' (2019: 223). This is given extensive grounding in the terminology that we have seen driving media psychology – 'transportation' and 'immersion', which play an 'insidious role' (2019: 224). An instance of the kind of evidence adduced shows the extent of the dependence on claims about localisation of behaviours in specific regions on the brain: 'In a research by Malia Mason, a maladaptive daydreamer underwent a functional magnetic resonance imaging (fMRI) while fantasizing, showing "great activity in the ventral striatum, the part of the brain that lights up when an alcoholic is shown images of a martini"' (2019: 224 n. 33). All this leads to his conclusion that 'The data gathered through those three questions confirm the existence of a possible connection between transmediality, narrative transportation and addiction in fantasy fiction' (2019: 228).

Rebora cites his evidential basis for this claim in the fact that a lot of reviews of fantasy works on the site GoodReads mention some transmedia aspects and world-building in arriving at their judgements and then go on to talk about their devotion to these worlds. There is no trace of acknowledgement that phrases such as 'couldn't put it down' or 'can't wait for the next' might operate rhetorically, rather than literally. They *can and do* put it down, and they *do* wait, but gather a kind of discursive credit from their claims to be 'real devoted fans'.

Once again (as with Gierszynki discussed in Chapter 1), we feel these accounts are historically blind, normatively driven, and psychologically reductionist.

Taking a cultural approach

The big difference between these approaches and ours is the attitude to social, cultural and historical processes within people's viewing. To make this concrete, consider a few of the many ways in which those processes might enter into people's thinking about characters – these include:

- knowing (or knowing *about*) the books as precursor or source, and thinking about the relations between the books and series;
- navigating conversations regarding actors, their qualities, opinions and private lives, as well as seeing echoes of other incarnations in their performances, and being aware of issues about *kinds* of character (e.g., in relation to attitudes to women or people with disabilities);

- planning one's time to watch *GoT* in a particular way (e.g., scheduled viewings and marathon catch-ups) and choosing particular company for viewing;
- taking part in discussion communities, both local (with friends and workmates) and distant (online), which will require some level of *close noticing* of the series in order to join in;
- recognising or borrowing notable sayings or phrases from the series as signs of 'knowingness';
- managing awareness of publicity and commentaries (and of course spoilers), and through this, taking part in the building of expectations and fears, among other things, about the fate of particular characters; and
- in their participation in our project, 'performing' the making of choices, towards us (the 'clever' academics) (e.g., this is how I want you to think of me).

For all of these, there will be highly distinctive, organised versions and other, more partial and casual versions.

These are not just interferences with some basic psychological process relating audiences to characters. They are, rather, structuring elements *within everyone's* engagements with fictional characters. All of them are interwoven with the ways in which the series and its characters will *matter* to different viewers. We deliberately stress the complexity, alterability and unpredictability of responses. The one early generalisation that we might offer is this: the more that watching the series *matters* to people, the more their mode of participation in all these cultural aspects will tend to be *structured and managed* in clear ways. The more it matters, therefore, the less individually 'vulnerable' they will be – which is the precise opposite of the model offered by psychological researchers. Our task as researchers is to try to sift the *cultural patterns* from the *more individuated* involvements with particular characters.

Understanding the ordinary complexity of responses

Consider some randomly chosen answers to our 'favourite character' question and consider what we learn about people's relations with their nominated character:

> Bran! He was a favourite of mine in the books too, something about that incredible knowledge, yet the inability to act makes me like him. Like if Bran and Arya worked together they could really get some stuff done! (#13)
>
> Olenna Tyrell. A wonderful, wonderful character, such a witty and wise woman. Stands up for herself and her family and lets no one stand in the way of their

> happiness (or power). And also, it is marvellous to see such a brilliant older woman in a biggish role in TV. (#414)
>
> Ramsay Bolton and Roose Bolton were both very high on my list, I enjoy 'evil' characters who actually have an impact on the universe. (#221)
>
> Jorah. I like tragic (especially unfortunate in love) characters. (#4020)

In just two sentences, #13 points to a curiously paradoxical characteristic as his grounds for choosing Bran – his powerlessness alongside his knowledge – and then hints towards an ideal solution – a virtual fusion of characters between Bran and Arya (who are, for most of the narrative, continents apart). Olenna is chosen by #414 not simply because she finds her a wonderful character, but because she is an exception to a general cultural rule: the invisibility of older women. The Boltons are chosen by #221 as embodiments of everything that is effectively evil (and they join a longer 'list'). Jorah meanwhile is chosen by #4020 as a *kind* of character, in this case, a suffering kind. Already, we see not just wide and unpredictable choices, but complex reasons structuring such choice. Consider a second group:

> I like Beric Dondarrion a lot in the books, although he is less interesting in the Show. I like him mostly because of the complicated feelings he has about being resurrected and about his new God. I also enjoy the uncertainty he adds to the Azor Ahai prophesies. (#5575)
>
> Mance Rader. His devotion to his people, loyalty & ethics. (#7619)
>
> Thoros of Myr – he is an adventurer as it can be found in a RPG. I like RPGs. (#376)
>
> Brother Ray ... Because it's Ian McShane. As he said, '*Game of Thrones* is just tits and dragons'. You just have to love this guy. (#5468)

Beric Dondarrion is picked (with a preference for the books' treatment) for his narrative role, but also for his uneasy inhabitation of that role. Mance Rader is chosen for a much more traditional 'moral' stance – although of course he is a 'rebel leader'. Thoros of Myr is selected for his fit with another genre: role-playing games. Brother Ray is chosen by someone who clearly shares the self-mocking attitude to the TV show that McShane (also named in the quote) has evinced.

These eight brief quotations make clear what a wide range of kinds of reason motivate choices. Just listening to individual voices putting into words their thoughts and feelings, reveals differences and complexities unavailable by other means. The implied relationships with characters vary greatly, but it is important to note that these eight were all distinctly minority choices – ones where *individualising* factors were likely to be at their most prominent. The lowest is Brother Ray, for whom this was our *only* mention!

Table 4.1 Favourite character and survivor 'mentions'

Favourite character mentions					
Tyrion	Jon	Arya	Daenerys	Jaime	Sansa
2768	2273	1910	1020	799	729

Favourite survivor mentions					
Petyr	Tyrion	Varys	Cersei	Jon	Arya
1887	1672	1320	1016	679	594

The test for us has been to find a way of locating the most widely chosen characters and to determine what shared cultural tendencies might be at work in their selection. For this we adopted the tactic of counting 'mentions' of names within answers to our two 'favourites' questions (see Appendix 2 for a general discussion of this tactic). Assembling the top six for each question gives these names:

This gave us nine names. In exploring these, we asked several questions: What qualities do audiences appreciate in their favourite characters? What makes them stand out? What do our participants reveal about their relationships with their chosen characters? And are there any notable *silences* or *absences* about particular characters' qualities or narrative roles? The following 'portraits' are based on random-sampled groups of 100 for each question.

Tyrion Lannister: 'The guy is brains and style incarnate' (#10606)

Tyrion is the most frequently mentioned in response to our 'favourite character', and second highest to our 'favourite survivor' questions – and 234 people chose to mention him under both headings, suggesting that the grounds of his popularity are pretty consistent. Top comes a mix of the character's intelligence and humour. Tyrion is repeatedly described as 'clever', 'smart', 'wise' and even 'cunning'. While at the same time he is also 'funny', 'cheeky', 'hilarious' and (with doubled meaning) 'witty' – he has his 'wits about him'. Here, one small divide shows. For some, with its hint of quite low involvement, his humour is 'light relief' (his saying 'I drink and I know things' is lovingly repeated). He 'has good lines' and 'great dialogue'. A striking version of this comes from #4829: 'I love that guy, the only character who can get away with monologuing without dying'. For others, this penchant for snappy asides became irritating – but now it is the 'showrunners' who are to blame for 'letting him down' (with the interesting implication that the character/actor deserved better).

That melding of wit and wisdom ('brains and humour, what's not to love?' [#1461]) provides the common template upon which deeper accounts (including some remarkably long answers – #4265 managed 872 words!) could be built. Many of these take delight in the character's complexity. Tyrion is certainly capable of cruelty, but he is also humane. He displays courage and endurance but is also self-aware: 'a rogue but honourable' (#3284). He is 'complex', 'flawed', 'unselfish' and 'all shades of grey which makes him interesting' (#5921). He is 'round and not flat' (#4005). And for a good number of participants, he is rare in combining playing the game well while trying to do the right thing: 'one of the few who are not totally evil and want power at all costs' (#494). This is made all the more attractive by virtue of his starting position as an underdog. He is 'misunderstood', 'looked down on', 'despised', yet curiously, only a very few identify the causes of this in his dwarfism. He is instead just 'a man discriminated against by the world' (#6563). Indeed, more people see Tyrion as exemplifying disability more generically, for instance, the two who say identically that they 'have a soft spot for bastards, cripples and broken things' (#10256 and #7051). There is a sense of something not needing to be said.

Only a few answers hint at the relationships that viewers are building with Tyrion. A very few – themselves feeling outcast in some way – claim direct kinship:

> I like him for the reasons everyone else will tell you – he's funny, he's smart, all that, but I like him also because he has gone through a lot of suffering and has been looked down upon by most. I was made fun of a lot growing up, so to see a person like that be an adult who is so strong and who takes things to the chin, drinks and laughs, and tries to make the best of the situations he is in, it's really inspiring for me. I like other characters, but I think he is the one I would love to have as a best friend or mentor the most. (#7653)

> [T]he most complex character, and moreover, he is some sort of hero in his own way, despite the fact he is not the typical handsome and ethical warrior; those heroes are boring since no reader would feel identified with them. Additionally, he can be cruel, but he has the warmest and most sympathetic moments too and I find that very appealing. Finally, I feel identified with him; I also have a 'handicap' that has affected me throughout my life and which I want to overcome. Just as he tried to be the hero during the Battle of the Blackwater and he wants to be loved by other people, I want to be successful in life despite my defect and I have to confess that I also like to be recognised by others. To watch him 'win' would be the same as watching my 'reflection' win. (#802)

Complex vernacular accounts are evidently being built in these.

Another striking strand sees something distinctly *contemporary* in Tyrion: 'the most human with emotions and ideas that most fit today's standards' (#6158); and 'the one modern thinker' (#5874). Tyrion is here almost a *transplant* from ours into *GoT*'s world. Few particular scenes get picked out. Instead, more see Tyrion as having a 'character arc', becoming both more 'ethical' and more interesting across the series. But this arc leaves the early Tyrion almost untouched. Just one mentions his penchant for whores, while only three mention his drinking. These 'flaws' become symptoms of his outsiderhood, to be overlooked in light of what he later becomes. Tyrion just 'deserves more recognition and respect' (#2155) for those who favour him. It is perhaps for this reason that among all the answers mentioning Tyrion, one term is hardly ever used of him: 'the Imp'. This is the dismissive term used of him by his enemies – not to be used by those who value him.

Jon Snow: 'the hero we should all see as role model' (#377)

Jon Snow ranks behind Tyrion as the second favourite character. But he drops to fifth place in responses to our favourite survivor question. The basis for this difference might ostensibly be related to ambiguity around his 'survivor' status due to his death-then-resurrection spanning the fifth and sixth series. Yet an exploration of our randomly sampled groups of 100 responses naming Jon reveals a more complex picture.

Across both sets of answers, admiration and approval for Jon Snow is most commonly linked to his hero status. He is 'a pure hero', 'the hero of the whole story' and 'embodies the hero archetype'. For some, this makes their choice of Jon (as their favourite character in particular) an obvious one. This might be demonstrated either by offering his name and no other clarification (giving the sense that no further explanation is necessary), or by the use of terms or phrases that refer to this obviousness: 'of course', 'pretty standard really' and 'self-explanatory'. There are some answers that apologetically note that their choice will be a common one: 'I wish I was more interesting but I cannot tell a lie … Jon Snow' (#442). One even hints at the choice being almost against their will, as they had 'for the longest time resisted' because he was 'one of the ones the books wanted us to like' (#7283). A further explanation is, perhaps not unexpectedly, his physical attractiveness. He is 'hot', 'nice to look at', 'very cute', 'damn good looking' and has 'broody good looks'. These answers in the main make very little mention of other character qualities and are frequently written in capital letters, accompanied by exclamation marks and smiley-face icons, or with letters repeated so as to elongate words (e.g., 'sooooooo dreamy!!!' and

'JON SNOW BABYYYY'). Barker (2005) noted similar responses to the character of Legolas in the *Lord of the Rings* international audience project, reflecting on the number of mentions of the good looks of the actor (Orlando Bloom) rather than the character. The actor Kit Harington is similarly mentioned in two answers of this kind: 'But I find Kit Harington's performance quite hypnotic' (#3417) and 'Plus I think that Kit Harington is a PHENOMENAL actor and he excels in his role' (#7075) (but in these answers it is to draw attention to his performance skill and talent). The relationship between appreciating the physical appeal of the actor/character and admiring his acting talent thus seems to be an intricate one.

While mentions of Jon as the 'hero' of the TV show provide the predominant framework, within this there are a number of strands throwing light on how this heroism might be seen differently and distinctively. For some, it is his plain 'goodness' that makes him heroic, particularly in a 'not very nice world'. He is 'a rare really good person', 'a good human being', the 'real good guy of the Show' and 'a pure person' who 'fights for the good'. Other answers are constructed as long lists of his heroic traits. Jon is 'honourable', 'compassionate', 'courageous', 'selfless', 'loyal', 'noble', 'humble', 'brave' and 'decent'. A significant number of answers directly link his heroism to his love for his family. He 'is doing everything because he loves his family' (#2847) and is 'always attempting to make the right decision to keep the ones he loves safe' (#3795) (striking for someone marginalised as a 'bastard' by his family). For a good number though, Jon's heroism comes not from inherent, inborn qualities (although his 'noble bloodline' is occasionally alluded to), but from how he has conducted himself in significant situations. It is his 'whole path of struggle', 'his journey' or how he has 'grown from a whiny boy to a serious and clever young man' (#7432).

As with Tyrion, Jon's 'hero arc' is made even more appealing because of his 'underdog' or 'outcast' status at the beginning of the series. Indeed, many answers draw a parallel between these two characters, their stories within the TV show, and the reasons why they are both favourite characters. In Jon's case it is his bastardy and early childhood 'disadvantage' that demonstrate how far he has 'risen'. He has 'everything going against him', has had to work hard to 'get things done', 'fought his way to the top' and done so 'only because of his reputation, his honor, and the trust others have in him' (#1568). Watching Jon's struggle across the series means that viewers 'want to see him succeed', to 'see it pay off for him' and are 'waiting with great anticipation for him to find out the truth about himself' as he 'deserves the truth'. His 'classic hero' status has set up particular hopes, expectations about how his story will end. Perhaps it is this that accounts for his slip in the rankings between 'favourite character' and 'favourite survivor'.

Arya Stark: 'Because she's a tough little girl' (#81)

Arya has the third highest overall level of mentions, but with a smaller proportion of overlap – just sixty-four – between the favourite and survivor questions. Nevertheless, in both categories, adjectives such as 'badass', 'independent' 'resilient', 'fierce' and 'clever' are used to describe Arya, showing how much her ability to persist through adversity is admired by respondents. Equally, Arya's refusal to be constricted by the *GoT* story-world's gender norms is often approvingly noted, her strength as a female character making her 'a role model for young girls to be your own person' (#1825). Some viewers see in her a template for life:

> I consider Arya Stark a kind of girl I would have admired a great deal when I was a kid myself – and I still do! I like the character very much for being a strong and independent role model for girls, yet being a 'real human' with faults and weaknesses as well. Together with Tyrion she is one of those I'd really like to see more of in the future. (#2931)

Yet Arya is not simply a plucky girl, a potentially feminist heroine to be admired for the lessons that she can teach girls. Her storyline, like her personality, has been tough and unpredictable, as one respondent summarised: 'Arya is obviously a total badass but also an extremely tragic character. The juxtaposition with her is amazing' (#4797). Those contrasts were not so positively noted by others. For some, Arya had been their favourite character during the early seasons, but not as her story progressed. One respondent wrote:

> I really liked Arya, because she is very like myself. As a child I also never wanted to be a girl, I was more like a boy, well it was mostly cause I didn't like to play with dolls and I preferred to be outside and play knight with my brother, I never wanted to be a princess, rather a knight who saves the princess. After Arya got back to Westeros I started to like her less, 'cause the only thing she knows is her revenge and death, and I have the feeling that she can't rest anymore, and that she must kill or do something and so she treats others very bad (especially Sansa). (#10511)

Displeasure was felt at the way that revenge had become so central to her motivations. One respondent wrote: 'I used to support Arya Stark, because of her "riot" character, but I think that the character lost her way since she went to the Faceless Men. Revenge is not the only reason for living for a sensible human being' (#651).

Yet as we also found with Cersei, Jaime and Petyr Baelish, there are aspects of Arya's dark turn which are central to the ways in which she is appreciated both as a character and as a survivor. While Cersei and Baelish perhaps revel in their amorality and viewers can appreciate them as narrative villains, Arya occupies a more ambiguous space: 'Arya, her storyline is very interesting to me. Not in Westeros so much until now, that was boring but in Braavos it was somehow intriguing to me. Good dramaturgical development of character' (#2988). A will to revenge has become one of her defining traits – 'Arya Stark. From runt of the litter to murderous pack leader with no goal other than revenge' (#6042) – but like her sister, Arya's change is a product of her experiences, and audience members seek to explain her moral blankness through reference to the traumas she has survived. Thus, she was described as 'an interesting overlapping child hero and trauma victim' (#5137), as well as 'the plucky innocent child who has seen and experienced too much trauma – like a child soldier' (#4406). In these justifying responses, there is the suggestion of viewers caring and worrying about her as a child forced, by trauma, to find her own path.

Daenerys Targaryen: 'sold, but turned things around, kicks ass ... has dragons!!' (#558)

The most repeated component of people's descriptions of Daenerys is that she is a 'strong woman', 'fair', 'kind', but 'not flawless'. Her story arc is immensely important, coming from a past where she was sold as a bride and effectively raped on her wedding night, she won the love of Khal Drogo, lost her child but gained her dragons, and emerged from the fires to be a potential Queen of Westeros: a 'badass queen' who 'makes mistakes and tries to do her best' (#5727). A number of people comment on her having the 'best scenes', the most 'fantastic political moments' (#205). The strength of her story arc leads to some disagreements. For some, the pleasure is in not knowing: #7133 loves 'speculating what she will do'. A few find that her constant changes diminish their interest in her, while others worry about what she will become: 'so afraid she's being set up as the villain' (#4565). Occasionally others go the completely opposite way: 'Dany, but only if she goes Mad Queen' (#10503). Whichever way around, the unifying feature is a powerful recognition of a character trajectory.

There are curious tensions around how to name her. For more than a quarter of our sample, she is 'Dany', a consciously informal term for such a powerful queen. She is simultaneously so much *above* viewers, yet *felt to be close*, this allows her to become exemplary ('her arc is a kind of testimony of how a woman overcomes life's hardships, abusive relationships, etc' (#7443). This informality contrasts with awareness that she is accruing endless titles. #10612 just lists twelve of them, while another notes that she has 'way too many titles and nicknames because of how accomplished and badass she is' (#5716). But a good number choose to name her by what she *becomes* – Khaleesi – as here: 'The Khaleesi would be my favorite character because of her arc in the story … and dragons' (#1598). There are also tensions around character and actor – a good number name-check Emilia Clarke, commenting both on her acting and her looks, her tender beauty alongside an inner strength. And 'of course' (a phrase from many answers) she has 'her dragons!'. These constitute the *extra* that transforms her from ordinary to extraordinary.

There is a strand in here about a *kind of power* that some audiences – especially women – want to celebrate. For some it is almost self-evident what this amounts to: 'Because I am a feminist. It's nice to see a Show with a woman who has the most power' (#2653). One young woman expressed this most eloquently:

> Daenerys is my favorite by far. She had no power over her life, she was exiled, running away from the usurper's knives, had a lunatic brother Viserys who tried to take her virginity the night before she was to wed Drogo. She was sold like a piece of meat, yet she adapted and lived on as a Khaleesi of the Dothraki. Her first contact with a man was rape, she fell in love with Drogo, she was about to be a mother of a savior, and lost it all and gained dragons instead who gave her life a new meaning. She is the dragon Viserys always warned her she would wake, and her magical rebirth proved it, she is fierce, ruthless to the ones who wronged her, yet kind and loving to the ones she holds dear. But the only thing she ever wanted is to feel loved, safe and to be home and happy with no one trying to kill her, she wanted her childhood back. Basically she is a vengeful and yet a good person, she just wants what is hers by right and I'm exactly like her, very bold, proud and impulsive but on the other hand a good person with good intentions. (#7485)

This sense that Daenerys is a kind of ideal/fantastical woman-become-leader enables some to forgive both her mistakes, and the TV show's occasional slippage into political discomfort (e.g., a white woman freeing 'black' slaves). She becomes and remains the 'ultimate display of female power' (#4176).

Sansa Stark: 'she seemed to get a fair bit of criticism, I wanted to be on her side' (#91)

Sansa was the sixth most mentioned favourite character and the seventh most mentioned survivor. The scene of Sansa's rape was also the most frequently rated 'most uncomfortable' moment, with 1,070 people nominating this. A recurring pattern in the accounts of those who talk about Sansa as their favourite character or survivor is an emphasis on how she grows and changes from 'a naive and powerless child' to 'a full player in the game' (#3120), a 'young immature, superficial girl' to 'independent, empowered woman' (#7267). It is easy to relate to Sansa, because she is 'undervalued' (#1487) not only within the TV show but also outside it – she's 'ignored and derided by a majority of the fanbase' (#627) 'everyone hates her' (#5595). Her relatability is firmly connected to her vulnerability and suffering which make her seem a more human, complex and realistic character.

As a character Sansa has 'changed the most' (#3144) and 'grown the most' (#9783). The theme of growth is used in more than one way – growing up, growing with and growing on – 'she really grew on me over time. She's very interesting because we sort of grow with her' (#3942); 'She kind of grew up with me' (#2119). Some liked her from the start of the series, but Sansa's growth as a character is also marked by others who describe changing their stance towards her – from finding her uninteresting or unlikable to begin with, then feeling pity for her suffering – and finally moving towards admiration for her perseverance and developing strength. Sometimes her growth is likened to that of other female characters who have all had to learn to survive in a man's world. At other times it is her difference that is emphasised; she is 'a traditionally feminine character, in contrast to some of the more stereotypically "badass" female characters' (#1487) and has to manage with the 'very limited scope of skills/behaviors she was given' (#6054) – she 'doesn't have Ned's strength, or Robb's courage, or Catelyn's will' (#3069) and she cannot rely on special skills such as 'fantastical powers' (#1487). Sansa's strength seems to come instead from endurance – 'one of her deepest character traits is that she never gives up or gives in, she keeps going and finds a way through whatever obstacles are in her path' (#3120). There's a sense of her power developing in response to events rather than being something she is driving. She undergoes 'ridiculous amounts of suffering and slowly learns from her mistakes and the awful situations thrust upon her by the men in her life' (#2924) – and her suffering is significant in itself because it enables her to become strong.

While Sansa's survival and strength are emphasised – she becomes 'the director of her own life, eventually, becoming a skilled player on her own right' (#2996), she has 'a different kind of strength from all of the other characters' (#3724) – it is her 'demure attitude' that 'allowed her to survive Joffrey' (#449) and she has a 'unique skillset (intuition, empathy, seeing through others, recognising lies and manipulation and using manipulation herself)' (#9608). 'This makes her less stereotypical as a female character – she is "strong but feminine"' (#2292); she is neither a 'fighter' or a 'seductress' (#640) and she is 'one of the female characters *not* defined by motherhood' (#2924), nor by 'the trope that a strong female needs to be boyish' (#10431). She has 'compassion' and 'intellect' (#528) and she's a 'tender, loving realistic depiction of what a feminine strength can be' (#467).

Petyr Baelish: the 'Renaissance man in the feudal world' (#1336)

Often likened to Machiavelli, the key unifying comment about Lord Petyr Baelish or Littlefinger is that he is the best at playing the game. He is smart, skilled, clever and ambitious, but he is also 'a snake', 'crafty as all hell' and a 'devious clever bastard' (#2675). He is often compared with Varys – both are considered to be strategists but with Littlefinger more duplicitous; a 'jackass', 'scumbag' and 'kind of sarcastic and a little annoying at times' (#5661) in comparison to the Spider. More generously he is 'wise, dangerous and unexpected' (#3149).

Baelish has an interesting position within the narrative, many people referenced him as the instigator of the game, although he is a minor character he 'shake[s] the balance of the world (#7447). For some he is a great *type* of character:

> I have always liked villains in TV Shows, movies, and books and I personally think that often times stories fall flat or feel average if you don't have a good villain. Littlefinger is a very interesting villain who plays along with anyone who will help him move ahead and gain more power. This puts him on different sides of any given conflict and makes for a more dynamic and dangerous adversary because some of the other characters don't even realize he is one. The 'Chaos is a Ladder' scene between him and Varys is one of my all-time favorites as it encapsulates perfectly what each of those characters represents. (#5966)

Or they admire his *role*: 'Littlefinger seems to be at the heart of most things without even being there most of the time. I love to hate him! He is so sneaky emphasised by a lack of screen time, yet he is so important; always changing what side he is on' (#4238). Some even ascribe him a kind of omnipotence – 'He's basically George R. R. Martin. He is writing the story' (#7101), the 'author' of events whose motives and intentions are unknown. Favouring Petyr is about *admiring his scheming*, not liking him.

Most striking are the answers which show grudging or amused respect for his gamification of the Game: 'Petyr Baelish you conniving BASTARD. Now keep going' (#7241). Like Tyrion, Baelish is understood as a very modern man, 'baller as fuck' (#5241), and his game is 'running a too big to fail scheme' (#3469). While his motives remain unclear, many make reference to his rags-to-riches story, highlight that he is a climber and a survivor, and that those attributes make him the best player, his is 'an extraordinary combination of willpower, strategy, and an ultimate instinct to survive' (#5599). He ought to be likeable, but this response enthusiastically explains some of the complexities of his character:

> I love love Petyr Baelish! He is my favourite character in the books by far and Aiden Gillan knocks every episode out of the water. I love simply how he doesn't deny who he is, he uses his personal skills to better his own life. He is a horrible person who has done, is doing, and will continue to do terrible things. But ... he is not without goodness or decency or even his own sense of morality. He saw a system that was determined to keep him down simply because of his birth and decided to fight against that. I also love that he has taken the fact that he is not classically *GoT* masculine, he can't fight with a sword or charge head first into a battle or win a one on one fist fight, he has used this to his advantage. (#419)

His survival is tied to the ways that 'he represents the underdog story, but he makes you hate an underdog which is going against the classic archetype that everyone LOVES the underdog' (#5318). He is 'an establishment outsider, who uses the establishment's own game against them' (#3609), so for some, he represents the potential for changing the game, 'I would love if he came out on top and installed some kind of meritocracy :D' (#4274). Thus, favouring Littlefinger is as much about his ability to survive as it is about his character, 'he doesn't give up' – no wonder then that he scores highest as 'survivor'. There is no indication that Baelish is a character who could be redeemed, nor do viewers want him to seek redemption – 'Let Baelish wreak havoc a little longer, please! And then a disastrous big impact finale!' (#1664).

Finally, although there are plenty wanting him to survive and thrive, there is a sense amongst many that his end is inevitable, and that Sansa will play a part in it. Just as his relationship with Catelyn is 'tragic' and 'doomed', so his feelings for her daughter will seal his fate.

Lord Varys (the Spider): 'because his game isn't self-aggrandisement' (#273)

Only 280 people mentioned Varys as their favourite character, while 1,320 named him as their favourite survivor. Varys is interpreted as 'smart' and 'savvy' and 'probably both good and sinister' (#1226); 'quiet [yet] powerful' (#6498) and 'Machiavellian' (#9742); he is a 'spymaster ... certainly the top conspirator in the game' (#7691), someone praised 'for his calculated cunning that goes hand in hand with veiled compassion' (#5207) and his 'unwavering professionalism' (#4780). For others, Varys 'seems to be the most level headed and sensible one of the lot – well, him and Tyrion' (#5940); 'someone really acting in the interests of the state … one of the most selfless and sympathetic characters' (#1446). His climb up the class system is noted – 'while the nobles think they are the ones controlling the seven kingdoms, it is Varys (and also Littlefinger) that truly play the Game of Thrones and pull the strings that causes the events in the world to unfold' (#10331); similarly another explains how 'Lord Varys … is not a lord, yet everyone calls him one. That ought to say enough right there but, the idea of him playing a mummer's farce for the good of the realm endears me to him greatly' (#5778). There is a sense in these quotations that we never see all his character – he has hidden depths, more than he or the narrative will ever reveal.

Respondents couple Varys with Littlefinger, drawing attention to their shared, even complementary, cunning and plotting, describing them as 'game specialists and master manipulators … the story of the Show happens because of them' (#10014) and appreciating both 'because of all their chess maneuvering' (#6217). Some 'can't separate the two as they have both been puppet masters during this entire game. They're smart and cunning and creepy and mysterious' (#5372). Even so, Varys has virtues, he 'plays the game for the good of the realm', whereas 'Littlefinger plays the game for the good of himself' (#4176); 'I admire Varys, because, despite being unreliable as a friend or ally, he has a very intricate plan that I'm sure goes far deeper than has yet been explored. He is sly and untrustworthy, a Spider, but I don't find him unlikable or evil, like Littlefinger certainly is' (#4846); 'Varys is pretty cool … there's just something I really like about his way of playing the game. He's just so calm and smart [while] Littlefinger's way of playing is sometimes cool, like sometimes I like his strategies, but I feel like too often he is too … slimy' (#2720), as well as 'I am also fascinated with Varys – he's just plain interesting, but the layers on layers of his "Spy v Spy" game is really impressive … and unlike Littlefinger, he's not been stomping around getting arrogant and broadcasting/gloating over his successes' (#6543). Elsewhere, we see a different account of them – #5976 suggests that he 'love[s] them because they are small, unpredictable, kinda funny characters having a HUGE impact on the actual main story'. They are also 'incredibly smart and ten steps ahead of everyone else. But one's evil and one seems like an alright bloke with the best intentions' (#6365).

Cersei Lannister: 'I love to hate Cersei' (#68)

Cersei is seen as 'one of the best bad guys of TV' (#762); a player like Varys or Littlefinger, although perhaps more complex than either of these – as the sheer volume of adjectives piled up to describe her suggests. She is a 'lioness' – 'strong', 'proud', 'determined', 'brave', 'sexy', 'dynamic'; 'clever', 'cunning' and 'intelligent', but also a 'bitch' – 'cruel', 'evil', 'ruthless'; and for many, as a result, she is 'interesting', 'brilliant', 'admirable', 'fascinating' and 'intriguing'.

Her dynamism and villainy are hugely enjoyable for many – they relish the fact that 'she gets things done' (#9875), 'does whatever it takes to achieve what she wants' (#10217), is 'brilliantly devious' (#3244) and 'not afraid to take huge risks and make bold moves' (#205). So while she may demonstrate 'evil without limits' (#1191), be 'an absolute horror of a human being' (#4522) and 'batshit crazy' (#4094), her flaws and storyline offer a great deal of viewing pleasure – 'she just makes being evil look so good' (#2972), 'she's always wrecking things up in the most entertaining way possible' (#1731), 'it has been immensely pleasurable watching her degenerate morally and emotionally as the Show has gone on' (#5270); 'Every moment on screen is gold' (#2827).

In some instances, Cersei inspires a real sense of devotion – 'She's my queen until my last day' (#3728), but that choice is explicitly expressed as going against expectations:

> My friends think I'm a terrible person for loving her so much, but I don't care. I like mainly two things about her: she recognises that the world is not fair and she actively tries to hold the world in her image. She knows people are scumbags and that she cannot truly trust anyone. On top of knowing this, she ACTS on it … She is someone who recognises how the world is, and takes action to set in motion what she wants to accomplish. She's unapologetic and fierce and I love her for it. (#6096)

Another emergent theme highlights the tragic aspects of Cersei's social position, as well as the impact of her own actions. Although she might be 'the toughest motherfucker on the Show' (#10569), for some commenters it is the fact that Cersei 'does everything for her love' (#7918), driven by the desire to protect her children and to defend her family's power is what makes her so compelling. She is less of an enjoyable villain here, 'shown both in her terrible cruelty, and as a helpless juvenile pawn in the family's schemes' (#4406), 'the mother, the queen, the monster, the abused woman, all there' (#1728). Her tragedy is ascribed both to the limitations of her position (as a woman and as a character whose future has been foretold) and to her own actions. In her determination to succeed and her pursuit of power she becomes self-destructive, making things worse by trying so hard to control events, striving to protect her family yet behaving in ways that bring about their destruction.

Jaime Lannister: 'from delusional asshole cuck to self-aware honourable man' (#1309)

Of course, the person most affected by Cersei's drive for control is her brother and lover Jaime, who comes fifth in our favourite character category. Very few suggest Jaime is playing the game of thrones, rather that he is a bit part player in other people's strategies, particularly his sister's. Although there are complaints that the character loses his way in season 5, Jaime is appreciated as the grown-up's choice of hero:

> I enjoy adult characters rather than teenage heroes nowadays (#170)

> He is simply the greatest and most realistic, complex character. Characters like Jon are too idealized, not realistic, too traditional/standard and boring (Jon is basically Harry Potter, I think he is the most boring one, only dumb teenagers are attracted to him). Daenerys is simply annoying. Tyrion is okay, but not as great as Jaime. I love Jaime's romance with Brienne and I wish it wasn't this subtle and slow-burning, and I wish they would survive instead of boring king Jon and his queen cliché. (#1622)

The most frequent word used to describe Jaime is 'complex', but he is also described as 'a real person' (#6484) despite being an 'egomaniac' (#7753), 'a pompous prick' (#4614) and an 'arrogant butthole' (#6065). Some describe him as 'tortured' (#4273), 'a tragic hero' (#4976), 'haunted by his choices' (#6952); Jaime is 'a good man despite his family' (#6789), a character who is taking a journey into the soul: 'At the end of season 6, when Jaime sees Cersei sitting on the iron throne, Jaime's expression portrays a man conflicted that has grown to choose better moral decisions despite his personal feelings' (#6789). Despite being described as complex, most responses about him are fairly short and their predominant concern is once again with his 'arc' – the possibilities of character development and storyline sometimes seeming to outweigh interest in Jaime the person:

> Though I do not like him as a person, I really like the idea of his character. He is someone we have imagined as conceited and arrogant all along, until we get to hear him tell his story. (#5753)

> Jaime Lannister because he has the best story arc from a disgraced knight to a totally redeemed character and that says a lot after attempted child murder and incest. (#5658)

At times, respondents seem to understand him as an archetype, an anti-hero – 'He is the perfect combination of self-loathing, ironically honest, and conflicted' (#6947). Even so, in their descriptions of his complexity and the enthusiasm for his arc, there is plenty to suggest that for those choosing him as either favourite or survivor, Jaime exceeds the type:

> He's clearly playing the chevalier but despite his brutality, he has compassion. The love for his sister is a brilliant twist on the shining knight and damsel in distress narrative. (#4372)

> ... both [Jaime and Stannis] feel like real (pseudo)medieval men, who live by their medievalish code (compared to some other characters who practice too modern politics or ethics). I really like characters who are a product of the culture they live in. (#170)

Many people choosing Ser Jaime also comment on the excellence of the acting and on the writing of his scenes, some commenting favourably that 'he's one of the characters that the Show didn't butcher so badly' (#392). Most recognise the moral, intellectual and emotional journey that he is taking, and for them this means he is the most 'dynamic' character, referencing the books and Martin's strategy of introducing Jaime through other characters' eyes before allowing him his own point of view. His journey is one that is a process of unfolding – 'he's progressively finding out that he has morality and how it handicaps him' (#7492); 'he is striving to become better through facing and dealing with his demons' (#3293). However, we should note that his morality is not one-dimensional, there is evident enjoyment of the ambiguity of the Lannister heir – 'He has so many different sides, and that go beyond good or bad' (#1091) And this is all very connective: 'I feel like I've gone on a transformational journey with him' (#2234). As #6104 articulates, the appeal of Jaime is the recognisability of being misunderstood: 'I think we're rarely fully understood by anyone, and Jaime is misunderstood by everyone. He reacted initially as one so snakebit would – live down to expectations. But his honour was in here somewhere and Catelyn, Tyrion and, especially, Brienne have managed to unearth it' (#6104).

Common threads

Amid all the variations our nine portraits reveal – in themselves far too rich to fit into the Procrustean bed of psychological theories – what common processes are visible? Clearly, for each character we found different levels of depth and detail, from exclusive mention of a single element (e.g., looks, acting, memorable moment or quotes) to much more elaborated accounts. But all nine portraits illustrate that their adherents *select* and *emphasise* what makes sense of their interest and devotion. And that means, in some way, sidestepping awkward elements to allow for 'coherent' stories of each character. Tyrion's whoring goes missing and his alcoholism becomes just a source of light-hearted humour. Jon's sexual encounters with Ygritte vanish. Jaime's incest with and rape of Cersei is backgrounded, part of a 'history' that is now being cleaned up. Sansa's repeated lying becomes evidence of her vulnerability. And so on. We cannot of course reach this conclusion on the basis of any single answer. But when the same 'absences' are noted across large samples, it is fair to see these as *patterns*.

There are also small but significant signs of patterning in the languages used to express *how* people experience their relations with different characters. Some of these are strong and emphatic: seeing Daenerys as 'magical' – almost more than human – stresses the sense that she is transcendent, almost beyond human, which in turn makes sense of the downplaying of the moments where her naked body is on display. Instead she becomes etherealised, 'beauty' embodied. Tyrion, by contrast, is touched by humour, the ordinary and the earthy, and thus open both to dedicated and to more casual audiences.[4] Sansa (as we will show in detail in Chapter 7) generates a particular closeness to her fans, being found to be 'relatable'. Meanwhile Cersei is admired for her dogged loyalty to her family – and therefore becomes loveably evil.

Perhaps the most striking feature across all these character portraits is how *unusual* they all are, how rarely for our viewers they are felt to fall into standard cultural archetypes. Instead, the most repeated trope is to talk of 'change', 'growth' and narrative 'arcs'. These terms are deployed by more than 1,000 people, typified as follows:

> Jaime. The ultimate bad boy good guy! I feel his story arc is the most complete. (#2083)

> The Khaleesi would be my favorite character because of her arc in the story … and dragons. (#1598)

> How can I choose just one? The actors are phenomenal. I love so many of the story arcs, especially Theon's and Sansa's. I love to see their character growth. I love those 'gray' characters, that aren't all bad or all good, like Jamie, but they have to make choices for their families and themselves. Nobody said war was pretty. (#1625)

> Jon Snow/Targaryen. It's been a joy to watch him grow as a character. Honorable mention to Theon because the actor is fantastic and Theon's arc was so great because I believe it's understandable why he made his decisions. (#3007)

These terms make clear that people are measuring characters against their hopes and expectations of what makes them *interesting* and *credible*.

Notes

1 There are in fact some other kinds of work on the nature of 'characters' in *GoT*, particularly from a narratological angle (see, in particular, Beveridge and Shan,

2016; and Beveridge and Chemers, 2018, who explore character centrality using the concept of networks). But, as it is hard to see what implications, if any, this work has for reception of the series, we simply note it here.

2 Compare his (1980) 'Anatomy of suspense', with his (1994) 'Mechanisms of emotional involvement with drama'. The latter appears in a special issue of *Poetics*, significant in bringing together researchers from several domains, to lay the foundations of what would become known henceforth as 'media psychology' (now with its own eponymous journal).

3 Much must be said about the ways in which 'emotions' (or 'affects') are characterised in this kind of research. We simply note the overwhelming tendency to talk about *basic* or *primary* emotions (e.g., fear and desire) as against the whole array of emotions which more obviously signal their cultural operation (e.g., curiosity, suspicion, contempt, frustration, admiration and bemusement).

4 A similar process was found in the *Lord of the Rings* project, where Gimli the dwarf was particularly nominated as favourite character by those with lower levels of engagement with the films, again on the basis of the humour that he displayed (see Barker, 2005).

5

The significance of favourite character choices

There are of course a number of ways in which characters in *Game of Thrones* are unusual, but several particularly stand out. First, their sheer number and variety: this is a story-world offering a rich array of possibilities, but also one that regularly shifts narrative focus, chapter by chapter, episode by episode. Second, they are characters in a fantasy setting, whatever bits of recognisable European history might inform it; this is clearly 'another world', with added elements of non-natural forces. This makes it hard for characters to be completely grasped and assessed against 'real' measures. The qualities and powers that they can exhibit, and the challenges they may face, are expanded. Third, this story-world quickly established itself as one where doom awaits even, or especially, the best and bravest characters. All Martin's characters inhabit a world – and (Sansa aside, perhaps) *know* this – where life is desperately uncertain, riddled with risks and threats. Pleasures and hopes are therefore small and against the odds. This comes with a double imprimatur: George R. R. Martin as widely known writer; and HBO – pushy, risk-taking relative newcomer – as sponsor and adaptor. Together, these must affect how people follow and associate with particular characters.

Several authors have valuably begun the process of thinking here. Maria del Mar Azcona's book on multi-protagonist films is a valuable introduction to the issues underpinning that first dimension. Azcona shows that there is a rich history of such films, dating back to at least the 1930s (she includes a detailed study of *Grand Hotel* (1932) as an important source, where clearly part of the producers' motivation was to put an array of stars on show), but which became much more frequent from the 1980s. Although she is properly cautious about theorising such a disparate genre (think of the differences between a caper movie like *Ocean's Eleven* [2001] and the almost philosophical *Crash* [2004]), she is convinced that this growth is no accident: 'In the last twenty-five years, this narrative structure has proliferated ... because its formal pattern has proved extremely appropriate to deal with certain sets of cultural meanings which have taken center-stage in contemporary society' (2010: 26–7). Those meanings, she argues, are centred around a 'new' set of anxieties afflicting western cultures: emotional isolation; insecurity; and uncertainty. In a reflection on her book, she goes further:

> Characters in these movies used to say 'maybe we are more connected than we thought' and the movies themselves emphasized this idea once and again. Nowadays, we know that we are all connected. It is no longer an epiphany or realization, it is something that we take for granted from the very beginning. The 6-degree-of-separation rule does no longer make sense. It is probably 1 or even 0 degree of separation now. (2018)

The implications of this are, of course, that we might expect a *decline* in this genre. That remains to be seen. But we do see considerable value in her attempt to name some of the cultural tensions pressing in on the production and reception of a series like *GoT*.

Azcona is also cautious about making claims about impacts on audiences, but in as much as any suggestion on this emerges, it is in her close study of *Short Cuts* (1993). There, she suggests several times that the shifting between characters, and the sense of their disconnection, must lead to difficulties with audiences engaging with its characters. Given that *Short Cuts* is for her something of an exemplary film of the new development, the implication appears to be that to the extent that a film (or TV programme) works with the dominant motives for creating this kind, audiences are likely to be only loosely engaged. This will just not work for the passionate connections that we find many of Martin's characters attracting. While we find her overall account useful, we must challenge her deduction of 'audience positions', however cautious.

A significant source for thinking about the distinctiveness of *fantasy* characters has to be Brian Attebery, who devoted a chapter to the topic in his 1992 *Strategies of Fantasy*; an important transitional book, embodying new approaches to fantasy generally. Although slightly hyperbolic at its end (we admire the fantasy tradition greatly, but see no need to claim that it has 'a unique ability to investigate the twofold process of constructing a self' (1992: 86)), Attebery's account of the construction and operation of 'characters' in fantasy offers striking insights. Rooted strongly within literary theory, Attebery sees fantasy as something of a test case for the choice between *psychological* (characters as richly conceived individuals with motivating inner lives) and *structural* (characters as functional necessities, driving the story where it needs to go) approaches to characters. Using Alan Garner's *The Owl Service* as his pre-eminent example (chosen because it embodies Garner's *most mature* writing), he makes the intriguing case that in well-written fantasy, characters have to learn to *combine full psychological depth* with facing up to the *large demands of fantasy narratives*. Their narrative course is a 'coming to terms' with these twin demands. This is, we think, a very valuable notion.

But for all its illumination, there is a risk in Attebery's use of exemplars which are in effect 'quest narratives': where central characters must face up to a *task* set by the world they find themselves in (although, to be fair, this was probably the dominant form of fantasy in the period that he examines). But what is so unusual about *GoT* is that, if there are tasks, they are pretty much self-defined and self-imposed. Eddard Stark does not *have* to become the King's Hand but, having done so, has to live out the consequences – to the point of dying for it. Brienne of Tarth does not *have* to attach herself to Catelyn Stark but, having done so, commits herself to rescuing her daughters. Jaime Lannister does not *have* to save Brienne's life but, having done so, is committed to further steps and to becoming a different kind of person. And so on. At the heart of the narrative operation of *GoT* are *decisions with consequences*, paths to be chosen and then stuck to. In choosing favourites among the panorama of possibilities, audiences are effectively *cheering characters on* with their choices and then living with their implications. We are watching them look inside themselves for the ability to face these challenges, in this world of endless conflicts and rising dangers.

Questions of reader-reception are not high on Attebery's agenda, but he does suggest that 'it is often unsophisticated readers who mount the most vivid mental productions' who 'come to life and continue to haunt the reader', while 'professional critics give half-hearted read-throughs' (1992: 69). This is no more than a passing observation, and none the worse for that. We believe that we can add something concrete to the reasons for this, provided that the notion of the 'professional critic' is enlarged to include those who approach a work through various kinds of critical lens.

An important context is the position of HBO within the contemporary TV ecology, as self-declared embodiment of 'quality TV' (see Akass and McCabe, 2012; and for possibly still the best overall exploration of this phenomenon, see Thompson, 1996). In a striking essay, Shannon Wells-Lassagne has used close consideration of two HBO series – *GoT* and *True Blood* – to argue that their status as 'fantasy' has allowed them to take risks with otherwise hardly imaginable scenarios, particularly around sex. HBO's 'aesthetic of excess' has meant that it can provocatively use sex to generate controversy, and 'the very controversy they cause allows for a better understanding of the workings of audio-visual narrative and the function of titillation' (2013: 421). Sex provides, she argues, both the context and the 'charge' to generate debates about wider social and political issues. She illustrates this by showing how, in *GoT*'s season 1, highly explicit sexual moments are linked with characters' commentary on the way that sex can be used to manipulate people. We are made simultaneously voyeurs, and aware of the dangers of voyeurism. This suggests a combination of complexity and controversy as a main 'atmosphere' within which reception happens. But Wells-Lassagne assumes that this co-presence of titillation and cynical talk will almost automatically 'create a distance from the eroticism', and 'any vicarious emotions [will be] deflated' (2013: 423). That's certainly a possibility, but it does not allow for what any audience researcher will tell you: the sheer variety and 'perversity' of responses in the round. The one thing that is almost impossible for any audience is not *to choose in awareness of there being controversy* and *that the series challenges us with these elements*. To adopt a character like Petyr Baelish, the cynical brothel owner, is to delight in taking a wrong side. To overlook or 'forgive' Jaime's incestuous relationship (and offspring) with his sister Queen Cersei is to map out a deliberately risky relationship with the series. On the other hand, to choose a character such as Jon Snow, the pure hero,[1] is to try to rise above it all. Choosing Sansa is perhaps the most complicated of all, and we leave full exploration of that to Chapter 7.

Our last critical resource on this is a 2012 essay by Susan Johnston, who crosses between Tolkien and Martin scholarship. She picks up Tolkien's concept (2008 [1947]) of 'eucatastrophe' – the idea that folk tales and fantasy stories commonly conclude with the painful saving of the world (see her 2011 essay on *Harry Potter*), which has the potential to release a form of grief-filled joy – and makes a strong case that in Martin's narrative Tolkien's opposite notion – 'dyscatastrophe' – is at work; effectively, a narrative driven by the realisation that 'all men must die'. Strikingly, she calls this quality in Martin's work 'the defeat of Tolkienian fantasy' (2012: 139), meaning that 'good, if it ever existed, has gone out of the world' (2012: 140). Her argument is that in the end one thing of value remains: honour. Honour becomes a contemporary version of chivalry. It is what enables people to remain strong or to rediscover strength within themselves. There is something important in this, but its problem is that it produces *lists* of honourable versus dishonourable: Syrio Forel versus Gregor Clegane; Catelyn versus Cersei; and so on. It means that Jaime Lannister becomes a possible target for affiliation, but not Cersei. Speaking of Jaime's refusal in the end to side with his sister, she writes: 'He has indeed found his honour. Rejecting the self-serving and murderous Cersei to bring some semblance of order to the realm' (2012: 151). This is analysis as recommendation – who we should and should not approve of. Johnston's valuable ideas need some reformulation to be usable in analysis of the sheer range and density of audience choices of favourites. Viewed in the light of these points, how might we summarise the 'call' of our nine prime 'fantasy' characters? We offer the following, for thought, as summaries of their various 'journeys' (assessed, of course, from the mid-series point when we conducted our research):

- Tyrion is, *despite himself, on the way to transcending his own cynicism.*
- Jon is *unwillingly facing up to his own emotions, and the requirements placed on him.*
- Arya is *having to grow up to become an 'actor'* – in which way is yet to be settled.
- Daenerys is *becoming magisterial, in the teeth of her own beauty. Plus,* she has her dragons.
- Jaime is *creating a new version of himself, as an 'honourable' man.*
- Sansa is *being, and tries to remain, a girl-cum-queen.*
- Petyr is *playing all ends, for (undisclosed) personal ambitions.*
- Varys is *following secret plans, for (half-disclosed) imperial purposes.*
- Cersei is *ever more ruthlessly refusing to let anything get in the way of 'family'.*

Individual audience members are faced with making a selection from this rich array (and of course many more), and in doing so committing to (at least some of) a project. Characters are not therefore lists of attributes that we might match with or model ourselves onto. They are arrows in flight, made and remade out of decisions, performances, goals, silences and absences.

As we will see in Chapter 6, the more engaged audiences are with the series, the more they are aware of the richness of this whole array – and that in indicating choices, they are saying something about themselves. More than anything, this turns on the *general orientation* that they take up towards the series. But one specific demographic factor certainly plays a substantial part. While we can find no discernible effects from age, class or politics, gender assuredly plays an independent role – as we might expect, given HBO's choice to play the game of controversy around presentations of nudity, sex and sexual violence. Audiences' choices are strongly skewed by gender, as Table 5.1 (recording proportions of mentions by gender)[2] demonstrates:

Females and males tend to choose their own gender (with Jon as a striking exception – on this general tendency, see Chandler and Griffiths, 2004).[3]

Table 5.1 Gendered choices of favourite characters and survivors

	Tyrion	Jon	Arya	Daenerys	Jaime	Sansa	Petyr	Varys	Cersei
F	49	56	62	68	47	73	41	44	61
M	51	44	38	32	53	27	57	56	39

And there is some evidence that females are more invested in the *idea* of character than males (the skew is clearly to their side, suggesting a combination of more females making 'mentions', and more males making minority choices). Sansa, once again, stands out as the most extreme case, and so we attend to her separately in Chapter 7.

So, what are we able to say about who chooses which characters, and why? In Chapter 3 we outlined our discovery of seven distinct orientations to the TV show. Mapping character choices onto these proves both interesting and frustrating, as Table 5.2 demonstrates.

What might we learn from these results? The fact that there is a considerable consistency across the orientations suggests, first, that factors other than the differences between these are at work. Tyrion, Jon and Arya are fairly consistently the most frequently mentioned, with Jaime mostly coming last. But then, the occasional strong exception invites closer consideration. Most notably, Sansa's leap into joint third place (alongside Petyr) among the Classic Fans is the strongest, but also noteworthy are Daenerys' plummet to last place among the Fan Watchers, and Jaime's partial 'rescue' by the Players. We need to bear these results in mind as we scope individual characters. For space reasons, we limit ourselves to just five cases of the most commonly mentioned characters.

Tyrion Lannister

The picture with Tyrion is complicated. He is, as we have shown, by some distance the most popular character overall (as both favourite and survivor). Variations can therefore easily be swamped by sheer numbers. But some interesting tendencies can still be seen, especially since a series of smallish variations all seem to point in the same direction: towards Tyrion being a character of choice for people with low involvement. The first indicator of this is Tyrion's score among the Just the Show sample. Here he scores highest, and at almost three times the lowest (at 10.1 per cent versus Sansa's 3.5 per cent – only Jon Snow is marginally higher). Cascading from that, his choosers have three lowest scores: for involvement in writing online; buying merchandise; and producing fan fiction. He also scores highest within our 'contented consumers' ideal type (at 22.8 per cent versus Varys' 15.1 per cent). Tyrion is the most gender-equal character, suggesting again a kind of neutrality. He scores lowest on interest in commentary around the series. With the exception of the very first of these, none generates a large variation, but they all point in the same direction: that Tyrion is a character with whom involvement is *easy* and relatively *undemanding*. This is also pointed to by recurrent wordings suggesting Tyrion as an 'obvious' choice – or as

Significance of favourite character choices

Table 5.2 Rank order of character mentions by ideal-type orientation (combining favourite character and favourite survivor answers)

	TOTAL	ALL	Series alone	Debaters	Book Followers	Contented Consumers	Players	Classic Fans	Fan Watchers
Tyrion	4,208	1	1	1	1	1	1	1	1
Jon	2,838	2	2	3	2	2	2	2	2
Arya	2,440	3	3	2	3	3	4	5	4
Petyr	2,105	4	5	5	4	5	3	3	3
Varys	1,528	5	8	7	6	8	5	8	5
Daenerys	1,517	6	4	4	4	4	7	6	9
Cersei	1,300	7	6	6	8	6	8	7	8
Sansa	1,215	8	9	7	7	7	9	3	6
Jaime	1,033	9	7	9	9	9	6	9	7

In a few cases, numbers of mentions were identical, hence (for example) two awards of seven among Debaters.

one person put it, after listing six (other) favourites: 'and of course everyone's favorite Tyrion' (#1806). But is it right, as another (#5578) puts it, that he is simply 'an easy choice for most people, considering that he's one of the main sources of humour'?

We isolated two groups to highlight contrasting levels of involvement, setting off those displaying the lowest interest in commentary, along with interest only in the TV show; against a group at the other extreme (highest interest in commentary, and involvement with fandom) – both, conveniently, exactly sixty-one responses! The first and most obvious contrast was in the length of answers. 'Low involvement' (henceforth, 'LI') produces an average of twenty-two words per answer; 'high involvement' (henceforth, 'HI') produces an average of fifty words per answer.

No absolute distinctions can be drawn, but clear tendencies are evident – partly, of course, the simple effect of HIs choosing to say more. Even so, there are some indicative differences, beyond the unsurprising finding that LIs give shorter, almost gnomic answers (e.g., 'Tyrion, because come on ...' (#88)):

- LIs make more references than HIs (9/3) to performative aspects (e.g., Dinklage's acting and dialogue); and
- LIs make more reference than HIs (19/13) to wit, humour and entertainment.

In the opposite direction:

- HIs make many more references than LIs (19/7) to Tyrion being 'smart' or 'intelligent'; and
- HIs make twice as many references to his political role.

The most complicated but interesting contrast, perhaps, is the degree to which LI and HI respondents reflect on the nature of their relations with characters. LIs use a series of short, standardised phrases. Tyrion is 'someone we root for' (#7012 LI), he is 'really likeable' (#9810 LI), 'the most identifiable' (#2898 LI), and 'I can relate to him' (#3064 LI). By contrast, within the greater space they allowed themselves, HI respondents think through the implications in their attitudes – none more so than #449 (HI). After devoting several sentences to Catelyn, Arya and Sansa, she offers a meta-comment on the implications of her also admiring Tyrion:

> Tyrion Lannister – I've always loved that my #1 & #4 hate each other, and yet I don't hate either of them for their hate. He is an AMAZING character, and yet like Arya, he's seen as a 'badass' but ignored for his real complexity. He is in a world that hates so much of who he is, but he continues to fight for life. GRRM does a great job writing him as a little person when that is everything about him and also not the most important thing about him. (#449)

Another respondent reflects on her nomination of Jon Snow and Tyrion – negotiating her feelings about the 'obviousness' of choosing the former:

> I suppose Jon Snow for the very unoriginal reason that I think of him as the traditional 'hero' and underdog. I suppose this choice is rather traditional and displays a lack of nuance but, screw it, he's my favorite and I won't deny it. I also really like Tyrion and Dany and it was a rather close choice, they're sort of the 'holy trinity' of characters in my opinion. The closest to 'main' characters. (#2152 HI)

Character choice is not an entirely innocent process, it involves acknowledging something about yourself to others (in this case, to us). What is really significant is that the more audience members *care about* the series, the more complicated their relations become with characters, overall TV show, and us. They situate their own choices and responses among other people's, whether known or imagined. This of course runs directly counter to transportation theory's claim (briefly outlined in Chapter 4) that the more closely we engage, the more we are likely to 'lose our sense of self'. And that is where listening to people's *talk*, rather than reducing their engagements to itemised choices, shows its lasting benefits.

Jon Snow

Jon Snow is another complicated case, again partly occasioned by his high overall figures. Attraction to Jon associates with highest levels of enjoyment, by a moderate margin (extreme = 59.0 per cent, against a lowest of 51.3 per cent for Sansa choosers). Again, by contrast with Sansa, Jon scores highest (at 46.9 per cent versus 35.5 per cent) on choice of 'epic saga' as a series label, highest on right-wing tendencies (14.9 per cent versus 8.6 per cent), and lowest on interest in debating the show's merits and faults (71.9 per cent versus 85.7 per cent). As noted earlier, the most striking thing about Jon's choosers is bucking the gender trend – he is the only character not to be more widely chosen by his own gender. This had to become our driver in separating and comparing groups. Was it as simple as Jon's sex appeal to women, as a lot of commentators have suggested (e.g., Dockterman, 2015)?

We checked to see how gender might intersect with the other variables. On two, no marked gender distinction showed: overall enjoyment of the TV show; and labelling it an 'epic saga'. These seem to be tendencies of Jon-choosers overall. But there are some striking – indeed, surprising – co-variations between gender and the other tendencies. None of these is more curious than the discovery that *male* Jon-choosers (henceforth, 'MJs') are markedly more right wing (20.4 per cent versus 10.7 per cent choosing moderate or extreme right) than females ('FJs'). They also, albeit not so strongly, vary by class, with MJs opting 33.3 per cent for the top three class levels, against 24.2 per cent for the FJs. But in the other direction, almost twice as many FJs indicated no activities beyond watching compared with MJs (although here the overall figures are perilously small – just 5.6 per cent versus 3.0 per cent).

Our comparative groups were formed of males, with right-wing tendencies, and higher class, numbering eighty-one; and females, indicating no interest beyond the series, numbering sixty-one. Our analysis begins with the trivial but still intriguing confirmation that our Just the Show females were less committed to the series – five times as many of them (30 per cent/6 per cent) misspelt 'Jon' as 'John', a hint that they had not seen the name written down and were very unlikely to have read the books. It is what goes with this that is important.

Our males typically deploy a language of *noble leadership*. Jon 'perseveres' with his 'duty', he is 'principled': 'dutiful, honourable, courageous' (#10525). He has an 'instinctive ability to lead fairly and justly' (#7923). He is the 'central and most essential figure' (#7551), and even 'humanity's only hope' (#3049). He is someone to aspire to, the 'most relatable' (#1190), the 'most likely person I would follow in real life' (#1098). The 'mystery' about his parentage adds to this, in hinting at his Targaryen birthright to the throne. He is on the 'journey of his life' (#3484), and he has his direwolf (something not mentioned by a single one of our female group). Jon takes on almost epic dimensions, in these kinds of account: 'Jon Snow, well he is an honourable and brave man and OMG he is the Prince who was promised and rightful heir of Rhaegar Targaryen' (#1282 Male). By contrast, among our female respondents, Jon appears very differently. He is 'caring', 'humble', 'tender', 'true to his heart', 'the most sympathetic': 'brave, gentle, fair, nice, good-looking' (#1746). Jon is 'sensitive' and 'vulnerable': he is 'decent and kind, brooding and sulky' (#3691). He is even judged 'realistic, fair and polite' (#8761). And he is to be 'loved' (a word used by eleven of the female group, but never by any of our males) – Jon is chosen by *comparison with others*:

> Love Jon Snow, he's decent and kind and brooding and sulky. A complicated and decent person. I love Brienne, too. Arya is another favorite. Dolorous Edd, don't know why. And Tyrion, everyone loves Tyrion. Oh, the Hound. Also, I see Jaime becoming a better human being. People are complex. I like that he's complex. (#3691 Female)

> At first Arya was my favourite because she was plucky and a real survivor. But I'm not a fan of vengeance and vendettas so I've latched onto Jon Snow. In a sea of delightfully terrible people, he has the purest heart. (#3009 Female)

It is hard not see in each of these emergent portraits a prototype – and we will not resist the temptation! For our right-wing, higher-class males, Jon is a perfect natural-born leader, the centre of things, whose personality commands respect and loyalty. He is an epic, mythic male leader. For our relatively uncommitted females, by contrast, Jon embodies a sort of Jane Austen-esque brooding gentleman, to be 'loved' and fancied from a slight distance. Physical attraction is no doubt part of the frame, but a wider attraction to a *kind* of masculinity is more evident.

Arya Stark

The profile of Arya-choosers is curious; and became more puzzling the closer we looked. On many dimensions they occupy middle ground, but on a few – and one in a particular – they show a marked skew from the overall corpus. Arya-choosers share the overall lowest score on extreme enjoyment (51.7 per cent versus Jamie's 59.0 per cent), and the lowest score on interest in debates (11.9 per cent again versus Sansa's 22.5 per cent). Her followers also score *lowest* overall on the series descriptor 'Cruel TV' – again, opposite Sansa. This opposition with Sansa persists. Arya scores highest among our Book Followers (10.6 per cent versus Sansa's 4.4 per cent). But the key opposition comes over age, with Arya recording the lowest results among the 16–25 year-olds (36.7 per cent versus Sansa's 49.0 per cent) and highest among the over-40s (20.4 per cent versus Sansa's 10.1 per cent). It made sense to explore the role of age in responses to Arya – first, by checking which of the other skews link with that age difference.

Here the puzzle deepened. The choice of 'Cruel TV' as a descriptor was *overwhelmingly* concentrated among the younger viewers – six times as many (15.9 per cent versus 2.3 per cent). But a check on their enjoyment ratings showed that choosing 'Cruel TV' was strongly associated with *increased pleasure* from the show: where our overall figures for extreme enjoyment were 51.1 per cent, these rose to 62.9 per cent for these younger viewers – in the teeth of the overall low enjoyment ratings among Arya-choosers. It appears that, to this younger group at any rate, what we might have presumed to be a *negative* label (and it certainly is for Sansa-choosers) in fact operates as a *positive*. Two groups were therefore isolated. A group of (seventy-seven) over-60s, non-adopters of 'Cruel TV' was contrasted with a group of (forty-seven) 16–21 year-olds, all of whom had adopted the descriptor 'Cruel TV'.

How then do these curious tendencies make themselves visible in people's accounts of their interest in Arya? It is important not to exaggerate the differences between older and younger respondents – for instance, it is slightly surprising that the same proportion of over-60s and the under-25s are happy to describe Arya as 'badass' and 'kickass' – expressions often thought of as generationally associated. Several older viewers class themselves as (being? having been?) 'tomboyish', and associate with her on that basis. Both equally make reference to her status in the books as well as the TV show. But some striking differences are visible. While not a single one of the younger respondents does this, a number of older viewers name 'Maisie Williams', or even 'Miss Williams' for her acting contribution. The flavour of these is important, as here:

> Arya is my favorite character on the TV series. I think Miss Williams does a fantastic job. I watched the first year before reading the series and I hoped she would make it home safely and the ride we have been on is so inventive and sad and heart rending and ... (#5574 Older)

There is a marked sense of *incompleteness* here, both in the tailing off of the answer, and in the sense that her destiny is uncertain. While both groups talk about her development, or arc, over the series, a number of the older viewers seem to be watching nervously, unsure of the outcome. 'The question is open whether Arya – in a sense a refugee displaced by war – will end up as a revenge-obsessed terrorist ... or have a redemptive arc' (#153 Older). 'Arya Stark. Interesting and strong female figure – can't tell from what I have seen where the character is heading' (#10443 Older). This aspect seems to be missing entirely from the younger viewers, for whom Arya just is what she is – a remarkable, tough young woman:

> Arya Stark. The fact that she saw her father's head get chopped, got separated from her sister, and got lost just so many times but managed to be self-reliant, taught herself how to survive and fight at a young age is very admirable. Also she defies gender roles given to her by society. Cool. (#2395 Younger)

> Arya because she's total badass and she does what she wants even though people think a girl couldn't do it. (#3496 Younger)

The older viewers display a more 'parental' attitude, wondering and worrying about how this young girl might turn out: 'I feel so sorry for this child' (#1348), 'Maisie Williams is a heart-tugger' (#1275). 'Arya, the against all odds character, she survives and grows, getting darker each season, I hope she can balance that and find her humanity again as well as achieve the goals she has set to balance so many wrongs' (#1484). But none more so than this respondent:

> Arya. Why? The joke is on me. I've read the books as they've been released. With each new volume, my character concern was for Arya, where is she, how is that child, she was aware of her father's beheading, she is separated from her wolf and her family, and so on. The joke occurred to me on the day

I realized that Arya would be the one to save my butt if the going got tough, at the same time, Arya needs to sit down and have a good long deep and emotional cry, in other words emotionally she needs a mom. (#9701 Older)

Older viewers appear to display a predominantly *parental* attitude towards Arya, coloured at times with memories of their own young days – and perhaps celebrating how much more is possible for young women today. Younger viewers – however unsurprisingly – seem to relate very differently to her. Arya is 'the dark justice type' (#4277), she is 'the person I wish I were, if I wound up in such a situation' (#7602):

Arya Stark. At the beginning, I loved her because we're both tomboy-ish, wild girls who prefer the company of boys. Then I grew more attached to her when all of those bad things started to happen to her. Even though we went through completely different things, I understood her mental pain of having to deal with tough things at a young age. If I lived in that world, we'd totally be best friends. (#4627 Younger)

Although it outruns our evidence, it would be fully compatible to say that younger admirers of Arya are taking uninhibited pleasure in the idea of a young woman managing to live defiantly in a world that can be threatening and cruel beyond measure to her kind. This is beyond wish-fulfilment or role-modelling. This is imaginative celebration of unrestrained – yet still completely moral – vengefulness: 'This girl faced hell and only learned and got better with it. She is good and has a pure heart. I just love her' (#10172 Younger).

Daenerys Targaryen

What Daenerys is called turns out to be really quite important. While the largest number overall (741) use her full name, smaller but significant groups use either 'Dany' (247) or 'Khaleesi' (58). This proves highly significant when we consider – by some measure – the biggest skew associated with choice of her labelling *GoT* as 'female empowerment' (36.5 per cent versus a lowest of 13.0 per cent for Sansa). It is also noteworthy that overall Daenerys-choosers rank themselves highest on our 'class' dimension, although the figures are not so striking. However, separating those naming her 'Dany' and 'Khaleesi' (just one solitary person uses both), it becomes apparent that both skews are much more heavily associated with the latter name – with an additional remarkable skew emerging in relation to political attitudes:

This is a very striking confluence of tendencies: 'Khaleesi' is associated with higher self-ascribed 'class', dramatically less political commitment, but markedly higher adoption of 'female empowerment' as a series descriptor

Table 5.3 Patterned variations in naming Daenerys Targaryen

	Lower class[1]	Higher class	Female empowerment	No political commitment[2]
'Dany'	40.7%	24.7%	27.9%	3.6%
'Khaleesi'	20.7%	37.9%	48.3%	44.8%

[1] From this seven-dimension scale, 'lower class' here combines 1+2+3, while 'higher class' combines 5+6+7.
[2] No political commitment here combines those choosing 'middle-of-the-road' or 'apolitical'.

(it also has the lowest association with book following, although the spread is not so strong on this). How does this display itself in any differences between the two groups' *talk*? The two groups were closely compared, and – while none of the differences is absolute – some pretty evident distinctions emerge.

The first thing to note is a clear difference in the way that the two kinds contextualise their choices. Both use lists, although in very different ways. 'Dany'-namers (henceforth, 'DNs') situate her among long lists of other contenders for their affection, while 'Khaleesi'-namers ('KNs') repeatedly present a set of honorific titles. Compare these examples:

> Dany, Davos, Brienne, Arya, Bran, Yara, Osha, Meera, poor pathetic Theon, Varys, Cersei, and Olenna. (#1100 DN)

> Cersei, Tormund, Dany, but only if she goes Mad Queen. (#10503 DN)

The second points towards another tendency among the DNs: their interest in her character arc, often indicating preferences for particular seasons, worrying about tendencies or pointing forward to expected outcomes.

By contrast, KNs, if they use lists, do so to list her special qualities and titles:

> Daenerys Stormborn of the House Targaryen, First of Her Name, Rightful Queen of the Seven Kingdoms, Protector of the Realm, Khaleesi of the Great Grass Sea, the Mother of Dragons, the Unburnt, the Breaker of Chains. For the same reasons I listed above. I'm also heavily attached to her dragons as well. (#10612 KN)

> My favorite character is Daenerys Stormborn of the House Targaryen because she is the First of Her Name, the Unburnt, Queen of the Andals and the First Men, Khaleesi of the Great Grass Sea, Breaker of Chains, and Mother of Dragons. Also the scene at Astapor was BADASS:) (you know the one). (#5315 KN)

The second is unusual in using a word more commonly used by DNs, 'badass', along with 'underdog'. By contrast, more KNs tend to call her a 'leader'. There is a sense of overwhelming admiration for her magical qualities, embodied of course in her dragons but transforming her into something beyond human (although still 'kind' and 'fair'). This sense is particularly captured in this short response: 'Khaleesi, mother of dragons, is my spirit animal. I also have a crush on the Khal' (#9531). There are subtle differences between the suggested simple emotions of this, and the following from a DN:

> Daenerys. She's had the most character development. She's gone from a shy pushover to conqueror of the world. I wish I could be Dany. Her struggles seem more real (well, besides the dragons and the sorcery and all that) because there is never an obvious answer or solution. She confides in those around her for advice. (#1887 DN)

And the much shorter: 'Dany, her life is a lot like mine' (#3409 DN). Space limitations debar us from exploring these fascinating differences any further. But they do suggest that a kind of apolitical feminism may underpin naming Daenerys as 'Khaleesi', while naming her 'Dany' leaves people open to note at the very least, as in this final quotation, a degree of nervousness about the *kind* of woman she becomes: 'Dany. She's a white savior, I know, but she's a lady who gets to be as powerful as the men, and I love it' (#3658 DN).

Jaime Lannister

There is a clear and striking pattern to the choices of Jaime Lannister as a favourite character. A scrutiny of the full set of cross-tabulations between character choices and all other quantitative measures reveals this: wherever Jaime's figures are highest, Daenerys are lowest; and vice versa. This occurs over reading/re-reading Martin's books (J = 88.2 per cent versus D = 67.0 per cent); seeing 'fantasy' as the creation of alternative worlds (J = 23.8 per cent versus D = 36.9 per cent); and belonging to the Fan Watchers orientation (J = 25.3 per cent versus D = 14.2 per cent). This suggests that in some significant way that Jaime and Daenerys are *opposite kinds of character for purposes of affiliation*. Sharpest of all is their separation over naming *GoT* as 'female empowerment': Jaime scoring just 13.5 per cent, versus Daenerys' 36.5 per cent. Yet while this might hint at a strong gender component driving the differences, in fact the figures for gender are fairly balanced for Jaime: F = 46.0 per cent versus M = 54.0 per cent, whereas the figures for Daenerys are F = 68.0 per cent versus M = 32 per cent. What might this reveal about the *kind* of engagement with character being enjoyed by Jaime's choosers?

A careful cross-check revealed that while three of the above four show no marked gender variation, the fourth – naming the series 'female empowerment'

– is strongly gender marked, with more than the proportion of women accepting this descriptor than men (17.8 per cent versus 8.4 per cent). This suggests that these women find no incompatibility between favouring Jaime and characterising the overall TV show as empowering women. We therefore isolated and compared two groups of Jamie-choosers: sixty-nine women who chose 'female empowerment'; and a random sample of sixty-nine (from among the overall 429 total) men *not* accepting 'female empowerment'. Analysing and comparing these groups proved tricky because, we sense, understanding them depends on *theorising things 'not said'*. In many regards, the two groups show remarkable similarity, nowhere more strongly than in the way that both refer over and again to Jaime's 'change', 'development', 'unfolding', 'evolution' or 'arc' – more than a third of each, in fact. What he *becomes* through these is clear: a complex man of 'honour', 'loyalty', 'courage' and 'integrity'. It is what he was *before* that is unsaid. Just one from each group mentions his defenestration of Bran at the outset of the TV show. *Not a single participant* names his incestuous relationship with sister, nor his later rape of her beside Joffrey's dead body. Instead, they mark simply a 'moral development' (e.g., #2703), from something hateful (intriguingly, women say they 'hated' him (e.g., #3325), men say he 'is to be hated' (#6845). It is as though something that is in our current cultural climate largely seen as unforgiveable, hereby becomes 'redeemable' (a word used by several). Several even turn this into a *gift* from another of her favourites, Brienne:

> Jaime Lannister is my favorite because he's the most beautifully flawed character, in my opinion. His redemption story has been magnificent to watch/read as it unfolds. From someone who could push a child out of a window to the man who saves Brienne from the bear pit and sends her to find Sansa, Jaime has transformed right before our eyes. Humbled by the loss of his most dominant trait (his fighting hand) and betrayed by his lover's lack of concern for him (at least in the books), I imagine we'll see the completion of his redemption arc with some noble yet terribly tragic end – probably killing his sister the same way he killed the Mad King, therefore saving millions of people. (#6086 Male)

There is another feature in here not found at all among the female Jaime-choosers: a re-interpretation of Jaime's motives and a re-imagining of his place within the narrative. He does not understand himself, it seems, and needs to be seen from another angle, through the auspices of Brienne:

> Every girl not blessed with fairytale princess attributes can identify with Brienne. I love that Tormund is so deeply attracted to her. I do hope that she is the woman in whose arms Jaime gets to die. I believe his love for Brienne is deeper than his attraction to Cersei. (#6849 Male)

Moves such as this, it seems, make compatible an adherence to the incestuous rapist Jaime, with still perceiving the show as 'female empowerment'. This surely indicates what a mobile, slippery expression this has become.

A final thought

What these investigations prove is how complex the processes are that drive character affiliation. But there are definite patterns. What is harder to determine is the extent to which such affiliations shape other aspects of people's responses to the TV show, and its overall narrative, or whether they are (as we suspect) just 'bonuses' or even 'multipliers' associated with watching, upping the stake in the dangers that ensue. An analogy to think about would be the difference that it makes to a gambler once they have put money on a horse they fancy, but in a race that is long (and dangerous) enough that if the horse falls, there is time and opportunity to check out and bet on another!

Notes

1 An interesting debate has taken place in various online fora as to whether Jon Snow should count as an 'emo hero': all dark, half-hidden emotions (see, e.g., Lacob, 2012). It is interesting to note that the expression 'emo' is not used by a single respondent to our project, suggesting that this is an *external* judgement foisted on those who do adopt him as a favourite.
2 As before, for simplicity of presentation we have omitted the very small numbers of those choosing 'identify differently', who appeared to be evenly distributed.
3 Jon stands out a little as a character associated most strongly with enjoyment of the series – and Sansa is at the other end of this spectrum. While mentions of Jon associate with 59 per cent 'extreme enjoyment', Sansa falls away to just 51.0 per cent – and has 7.0 per cent awarding the two lowest enjoyment ratings, compared with just 1.4 per cent for Jon. It looks as though Sansa is, for some, being chosen *against the grain* of the series. Chapter 7 explores this topic in more detail.

6

Winter is coming ...

In a review of the TV show on the eve of season 8, Matthew Reisener (2019), Chief of Staff at the US Center for the National Interest (a conservative foreign-policy body established in the 1980s by Richard Nixon), praised *Game of Thrones* as providing 'an excellent lens through which to examine theoretical debates and global problems facing contemporary international relations scholars'. He went on to suggest that Tywin Lannister's cruel realism contrasted with those leaders who sought to live by values such as 'justice' or by goals such as 'vengeance' in ways that enabled viewers to debate the relative merits of those forces for international politics. Reisener proposed that: '*Game of Thrones* makes the case that international institutions require greater levels of coercive power to address existential threats such as the White Walkers, a not-so-veiled metaphor for climate change that threatens to plunge Westeros into an eternal winter.' Two years earlier, *Vanity Fair* had noted the array of climate scientists who were thinking through the ways that *GoT* could work as a metaphor for climate change – with very different outcomes. Was it about the ways that politicians get distracted by trivial political concerns from the major issues of human survival? Could we usefully map attitudes to climate change onto particular characters? The connection was being widely proposed by others, via the show-defining expression, 'Winter is coming':

> What many viewers aren't talking about — and *should* be — is the overarching comparison of *GoT*'s multiple plots and subplots to climate change. The pop culture allusion of 'Winter is coming' is just one of the many *GoT* markers that are indicative of a global shift in our climate — long predicted, poorly understood, easily disregarded — that has the capacity to destroy an entire civilization. (Fortuna, 2019)

The urge to find metaphorical meanings in *GoT* has been strong and insistent. In this chapter we look at the ways that our body of evidence might throw light on this tendency. We draw on four aspects: how people pick and describe the lands or peoples that most intrigue them; the ways that different audiences think about the meanings of 'winter' in the series; how they think about the 'world' that is Westeros/Essos, and its relationship with our own; and – most broadly – how these relate to their sense of the general role of 'fantasy' in contemporary cultures.

A moderate number of our participants talk directly about connections to current real problems. Top comes 'climate change' (220 mentions), with other global conditions following (global warming = 122; nuclear/atomic conflict = 86). The common term most capturing the *scale* of people's metaphoric concerns is 'apocalypse' (182 mentions):[1]

> Once again this greater power which is coming to the seven kingdoms, a sort of apocalypse, reminds of climate change and how we must put aside our own politics and work together. (#9798)

> I think that 'Winter' is a metaphor for 'bad times'. Other names for it could be the Apocalypse, the Climate Change or World War III, for example. It depends on the phobias about the future of each person. (#7504)

The most repeated specific mention, clearly influenced by our questionnaire's timing, is Donald Trump (ninety-three mentions across various questions) – who symbolises for many a large-scale threat. An extreme but pointed example combines a whole series of 'threats' into one basket:

> It really makes me think of our world today. For example, in Brazil we're living a very serious political situation. Our president was impeached by a bunch of white-collar thieves. It was legal but never legitimate. It was a plot to take her out. So winter is coming to Brazil in a sense that we're about to live very dark times in regards to our civil rights. It makes me think of the world because every day we see terrible news. Syria is falling apart and apparently nobody is actually doing anything about it. Trump got elected in the US and it's scary not only because – whether we like it or not – POTUS is the most powerful public position in the world but because having someone like him as POTUS incites some kind of behavior. Meaning: we have a wave of far right extremists in Europe, South America and the US and it is bad. That's not to mention the situation with ISIS, Congo, Afghanistan, etc. And that's what winter is all about. (#10154)

The sense that 'winter' symbolises a threat arising from the global developments, parallels what Manjana Milkoreit (2019) found in her analysis of uses of *GoT* as a rhetorical gambit in recent climate change discourses. Deploying the idea of 'pop-cultural mobilisation', Milkoreit analyses a corpus of commentaries around *GoT*. She shows that, while not absolutely uniform, most commentators developed critical analogies, using the TV show as a resource. So, for instance, the Night's Watch are seen as akin to climate scientists – desperately trying to warn the world but ignored by self-obsessed politicians and rulers.

Thinking metaphorically

The study of metaphors has become a major field in its own right, particularly since 1980 when George Lakoff and Mark Johnson first published *Metaphors We Live By*. This book provided one epicentre for a much wider shift away from theories of language focused on its descriptive capacity. Lakoff and Johnson demonstrated powerfully that metaphors are a central feature of everyday talk, and that they come in structured groups. Typical examples are the ways that we speak of relationships as journeys (e.g., 'on the skids', 'hitting the buffers' or 'in a dead-end'); and argument as war (e.g., 'attacking and defending positions' or 'shooting down arguments'). Their emergent theory was that metaphors enable us to place items adjacent to other conceptual frames, thus making them more thinkable and communicable. As a bonus, forms such as poetry gain richness.

But what Lakoff and Johnson were primarily drawing attention to are the *most sedimented* and *near-automatic* forms of metaphoric speech. There are also other levels where novel images, and conscious analogies, can propose realignments. This is surely one of the functions of fiction generally, but particularly, we suggest, of those forms of fiction which offer differently conceived cultures and worlds for comparisons with our own. One indicator of the ways that such novel analogies might work came in people's answers to Question 13, which asked about the 'most intriguing' lands or peoples depicted in the TV show. This gave, we hoped, a space in which they could think out loud about the various cultures deployed, and the interests and issues that they were seen to provoke. We were not disappointed. Some, of course, answered the question quite minimally. They did not want to use *GoT*'s array of cultures as vehicles for thinking about our own. As a result, their answers tended to be brief and uninvolved: 'Not really, they all are great and interesting in their own way' (#2089). Even when they do single out a people, the response is quite short and their positive attributes are transparent rather than elaborated: 'The Dothraki have a very interesting culture. And they are strong!' (#11843). But for many, the way that they engaged with the 'other' cultures was a site of emotion, fascination, comparison and evaluation: 'It's really close between the Wildlings and the Dothraki. The Wildlings for their great diversity, I would like to know more about each of the cultures and clans. But the Dothraki are just viscerally entertaining to watch' (#13956). The Dothraki illustrate well the range of ways that people could relate to this 'other' culture. For some, it is shared affinities and a sense of difference that gives interest: 'Being from Finland it must be the North and the Starks that *feel closest* to me, stubborn and honest like Finns. The Dothraki people are maybe more interesting because they are so different' (#2889). For others, already held fascinations could be sparked by represented cultures: 'Having a life-long admiration and interest in Native American culture, I would love to know more about the Dothraki' (#1851). These emotional responses are not always just about feelings, they often have a critical and political element, that engaging with a particular land or people means thinking more broadly about them:

> Khal Drogo and the Dothraki. They were definitely outsiders in the world but had their own structure, customs. They stood out in the world of 'white' characters with royal clothes and formality. They were the most exotic and looked down upon from the mainstream society. Although they didn't seem to lack, there was some interesting classism in the way others look at this group. (#4693)

Others were not as content with these images:

> I'm appalled at the racist depiction of peoples like the Dornish, the free folk and the Dothraki in the show. The Dothraki in particular were very well adapted in season 1 but season 6 turned in them into savages who follow a foreign witch who burned down their holy place (complete with dirt that catches fire – what?) ... Or is it because she's white, can't tell. (#514)

But once we reach more expansive answers such as these, we are able to see *what qualities* people are seeing in the various cultures (whether positive or negative), and what these add up to, and some definite patterns emerge. Table 6.1 was formed by close examination of randomised samples of fifty 'mentions' of the six most-discussed lands/peoples in *GoT*:

Without trying to tidy up too much, there are indicative differences among these. The Starks and the North are valued for their openness and honesty, embodied in their strong sense of 'old world' traditions – and those naming them often want to claim some likeness to them. The Wildlings are almost the opposite: admirable people, perhaps, but living under such harsh conditions that it's hard to imagine being *like* them. The Dothraki are sufficiently exotic that they risk being seen as 'savages' – but some at least want to try to recuperate them. Braavos and the Faceless Men, meanwhile, are fascinating for their inscrutable dangerousness. The Dornish are identified regularly as a very 'woke' community – but curiously, with by far the highest level of complaints that their depiction has just not gone far enough. Dorne is very much measured against an ideal and is found wanting for its failure to meet that ideal. Valyria, on the other hand, definitely benefits from the air of mystery which surrounds it; it is a place and time of legend.

Given these emergent differences, it was interesting to discover that choices of particular lands/peoples show *no* meaningful relations to our seven ideal-type orientations.[2] It seems that choices of most intriguing lands/peoples have other, maybe very personal drivers. But there *are* strong associations

Table 6.1 Most intriguing lands or peoples

	Numbers	Attributed qualities (representative quotes)	Attitude indicators
The North/ Starks	1,793	Spartan but honest (#1817), hard-working (#7508), diligent and loyal (#7015), honor (#1136), 'real' and genuine (#3617), their interactions and political alignments (#7246), I like the Northern stories and people (#121), their 'Old Gods' religion (#147)	Being Scottish (#5686), Finland (#107), Canadian (#5515), identify and admire (#10367), I feel attached to the North (#25)
Dorne	1,215	Fiery, headstrong (#4799), open-minded (#2088), women more blood-thirsty than the men (#9635), bastards, women and homosexuals more accepted (#3414), open relationships (#5076), pro-LGBT (#9709)	Let down by the show (#various), failed by the show (#various) – *in all, 30% recorded complaints*
The Wildlings	769	Dedication (#5487), tenacity (#3121), hardy (#4930), respect leaders who want their survival (#2942), live hard but are truly free (#5493), not bound by a class system (#7442), considered savage but more loyal and straightforward (#1665)	Live in such a harsh place yet can still be so fun loving (#4100), like crazy dirty hippies who live off the land and I love them (#6091)
Valyria[1]	737	The ones we know the least (#40), the lost city looks cool (#5784), mystical (#2551), incest, female empowerment, genetic disorders … (#5062), long-lost advanced culture (#5361), seems to be a very advanced society (#9631), its doom is intriguing (#1574)	Works best because we know so little (#5872), it's what you glimpse but don't see (#2594), satisfying the darker part of me (#9438)

Table 6.1 Most intriguing lands or peoples (Continued)

	Numbers	Attributed qualities (representative quotes)	Attitude indicators
Braavos	560	Pretty cool with its weird death cult, and so on (#6216), merciless assassins (#7927), because of how deadly they are (#6845), the mystery around them (#6060), did they cause the Doom of Valyria? (#6922), secret city and global bank controlling the world (#4794)	Would like to know their story (#7212), deep nihilism – intrigued by how audiences have responded to this (#3319)
The Dothraki	480	Authentic (#450), closest to what the Mongols were like (#2155), unquenchable machismo and worship of strength (#9481), 'realistic'-sounding language (#3299), most exotic and looked down upon (#3670), primitive from the outside, but complex in reality (#319)	Strays away from the complexity of individuals that I appreciate about other peoples in the text (#9481), nomadic, horse-centric lifestyle (#6129)

[1] In an intriguing essay which is quite close to the issues that we are addressing here, Istvan Csicsery-Ronay has explored the history of science fiction's fascination with *empires*, alongside the re-emergence of comparative studies of their workings, and the relationship between science fiction and the post-second world war 'hypertechnological phase of European imperialism' (2015: 15):'We see galactic federations, hegemonies, United Planets, inter-galactic commercial alliances. We see grand utopian visions of violence redeemed by astronomical harmony achieved; we see almost as many slave planets and resistance movements. We see cosmopolitan affinity groups. We rarely see nations or democracies.'

Thinking about this led us to check how many of our participants speak about 'empires'. Almost all mentions do indeed come in connection with our lands/peoples question. The numbers are quite small – just 42 – and almost 70 per cent of those do so in connection with thinking about Valyria as a 'lost' world. At least in relation to *GoT* it seems that 'empires' are things of 'the past' (even in relation to such a medievally inspired history) – while concern with the *world* is a more future-oriented attitude.

Table 6.2 Proportions of ideal-type orientations mentioning at least one land/people in answers to Question 13

Just the Show	Debaters	Classic Fans	Fan Watchers	Contented Consumers	Players	Book Followers
29.9%	41.4%	74.7%	71.7%	52.4%	66.0%	42.0%

and consistent variations in *likelihood to talk about cultures*, as Table 6.2 shows:

Our evidence clearly indicates that being attracted to the general notion of intriguing cultures is strongly distributed by general orientation and the associated willingness to think metaphorically, but *not* the choice of individual culture.

The many meanings of 'winter'

Question 24 was a 'wild card' question, aiming to draw out surprise materials – and it certainly provoked a wide range. A few participants told even us that this had made them think in new ways: 'Good question!' (#8005, #7208, #132) or 'Haven't thought about it before' [#433]. In the other direction, a larger number marked their answers with expressions such as 'obviously' (seventy-one cases), to suggest the opposite. But what people 'knew' could vary greatly, from 'Christmas and snow' to 'the end of all life'. Indeed, it is what is added to the word 'obvious' that becomes especially interesting: 'It's obviously a season in the series, but also a metaphor for hard times, suffering and the darkest elements of the characters' development' (#3527).

Not everyone answered the question. A random sample of 100 responses showed 15 per cent either left it blank, or said that they were not sure how to answer the question (a rare one or two calling the question 'stupid' – e.g., #1150). The reasons for not answering were no doubt complicated, with everything from sheer weariness (this had been a long questionnaire) to lack of interest in what was being asked. To these had to be added a number of participants who gave such minimal responses as to be unanalysable (e.g., 'winter' [fifteen instances]; and 'snow' [forty-three instances]). As we sought to identify patterns in the answers, our first category had to be a combination of 'no answer' and 'not analysable' (NA).[3] While primarily an exclusion category, this proved to be of interest when we came to compare how strongly different orientation groups felt about 'winter' in the series.

Completed responses ranged from very short (often single-word) answers, up to the very long (the longest we spotted used 562 words (#7282) in which the writer regaled us with a complex and fascinating theory about George R. R. Martin's world, and the meaning of winter within it). The great majority of answers consisted of one or two sentences. When we came to try to code answers for their implied attitude and orientation to the series, we had to be very careful. Six coding categories proved sufficient to cover the full range of answers. Reworked twice and shared among the authors, the following were eventually agreed on:

- no answer or otherwise not analysable;
- 'doom' pronouncements;
- story focused;
- metaphors and analogies;
- survival, renewal and hope; and
- mundane or resistant.

'Doom' pronouncements

A considerable number of answers were very short predictions of disaster, with no markers to indicate whether it is limited to the *GoT* world or applies also to ours. Typical minimalist answers are: 'doom' (eighteen), 'death' (128) and 'the end' (thirty-five). Several dramatised their answers, as #3220's 'Dooooooooom. For everyone'. Others accumulated lists of disaster terms, as #1696's 'dark … death … doom'.

Story focused

Many answers pointed to characters or events within *GoT*. The shortest were those who simply named 'the White Walkers' (138 instances), or 'the Others' (fifteen instances). More complicated answers included a considerable number (258 instances) making reference to 'the Starks', for whom 'Winter is coming' is their House motto. Typical of these kinds of answer are the following:

> It makes me think about Danger somehow. You see, every house has its saying, and it's usually something related to power. The Lannisters, for example: 'Hear me Roar', like, 'See how powerful I am'. But the Starks, in the other hand, give everyone a warning: Winter is Coming, Danger is coming. (#10550)

> Well 'winter' is the long night, referring to when the first men and the children of the forest fought against the White Walkers and the disaster that that had brought to the land of Westeros. And since the Starks are descendants of the first men this house saying means that it is a warning that the threat of the

Whites is not over. They will return. And when they do, winter will be here. (#10318)

Beyond these are a range of other answers offering series-related answers to our question.

Metaphors and analogies

More or less explicitly, many answers offered one of two ways of reading 'winter' beyond the boundaries of the series' narrative. The first kind ranged across openly expressed notions of 'symbolism' and 'representation':

> Winter, symbolically, represents the difficult opposition that humanity faces in common that if we don't get our shit together and brace it with one another then we are in trouble. The fact that these are the words of House Stark could be used as a great analogy in real life to a sort of oral tradition a group of people, here being a family, took to be their responsibility for the benefit of mankind. (#4686)

It also included encoded warnings ('Always be prepared (for the worst), since winter WILL come, don't get caught unawares!' [#460]). The second kind are directly offered analogies with events or circumstances in our world (e.g., the earlier quote about Trump).

Survival, renewal and hope

In and among the many gloom-filled answers were a number hinting at something *beyond* winter, even 'spring' (244 instances). Hardly any answers elaborated on what this might be – it appears as a small, fugitive component. Something of this uncertainty is captured:

> No matter where you are in the cycle of the year, winter is coming. Hard times, or harder than current times, are always ahead. I guess Westerosi optimists could say 'Summer is coming'. Referring specifically to the world of the show, though, I think it refers to something apocalyptic. Similar to Dany saying she's going to 'Break the Wheel'. Some kind of long night that will end in a reset to the political system of Westeros. (#1302)

Primarily addressed to *GoT*'s world, this only hints at analogical application. Some of this ambivalence can be found again in #3958: 'In my more optimistic moments it makes me think of change, adaptation and perseverance against all odds. At other times it makes me think of death – i.e. the difficulty of survival and development in the middle of a desolate winter.' Perhaps the most recurrent word in this mode is 'hope' (199 instances). The hesitations that this brings with it can be seen in the following:

> Clearly there have been other Winters in the history of Westeros, and like our more traditional winters, it is a time to hunker down and prepare for spring. We are privileged to be visiting Westeros on the eve of a Winter of epic proportions with the fate of the world hanging in the balance. I hope this remains only a fascinating story and not a harbinger of things to come in our own world! (#265)

> Winter marks the end of the cycle, but after winter comes spring where the earth is renewed. It's a cycle, so even if winter is often synonymous with cold and death, there is always hope. To me personally that means after you hit a very low point you can only get back up, and there's always hope. In the show Winter is most likely when all hell breaks loose, and all the characters come to terms with their pasts, and while some might very well not survive, those who do survive will only grow stronger and will be instrumental to rebuilding the world. (#238)

There is a definite lack of clarity about the politics underpinning these views, and it must be said that (rather unlike those coded under metaphor and analogy) most of the answers in this mode give little indication of what critical position is generating the fears and hopes of the respondents.

Mundane or resistant

A fair number of participants wrote under this classification with a clear sense of what they believe that we were looking for – and then decline to provide it. Instead of talking about the series, or its metaphorical or other meanings, they insist on talking about their own experiences of winter. A not uncommon element in these is a reference to Christmas (85 instances) or things such as skiing and family holidays (128).

A number of answers, unsurprisingly, needed coding under more than one heading (although obviously not our 'doom' and 'not analysable' categories). We then looked to see how these answers map onto our seven orientations, as spelt out in Chapter 3. Table 6.3 shows the results of coding 100 randomised responses, and then for 100 sample groups for each of the seven orientations (along with the total word counts for each group). The results are striking and show more divergences than we had expected.

Some strong variations can be seen. Closest to the overall totals and distribution are the Debaters – who add to their viewing by taking part in discussions about the TV show's value. We have already suggested that this may constitute a kind of watching 'norm' – to view the TV show, and to

Table 6.3 Codings of 100 randomised responses, the seven ideal-type orientations

	Doom	Story	Metaphor	Survival	Mundane	NA	Totals
Random 100	19	37	23	7	16	15	1,710
Just the Show	24	14	19	5	18	27	1,160
Debaters	18	32	19	1	15	19	1,634
Classic Fans	7	44	28	6	12	13	2,571
Fan Watchers	15	43	31	21	8	10	3,352
Contented Consumers	37	40	23	9	11	13	2,007
Players	19	42	23	4	13	11	2,238
Book Followers	14	35	34	7	13	20	2,151

enjoy debating its merits and faults with relatives and friends, and perhaps with online contacts, is a kind of cultural standard. However, they do vary in one particular respect: the very low level of responses mentioning 'survival'. The following answers seem to us to typify this group:

> A really difficult period of political changes and intrigues. With a hard winter and ... the dead are coming. (#325)

> Winter is anything inevitable that you're dreading. It's your taxes. It's Donald Trump. It's the mountain of papers that I put off grading to answer this survey. It's whatever is looming over your shoulder that you can't quite prepare for no matter how hard you try. (#7928)

Perhaps because this group is the nearest to 'average', it is hard to delineate any defining characteristics to their answers – except perhaps a tendency to move with ease between seeing the TV show on its own terms, and engaging with it as metaphor:

> It's a season. For us, thank the gods it just ended. Literally yesterday. And it makes me think of cold. The general people are like 'White walkers! Death! Big Bad Ice Enemies!!' But all it makes me think about is how I want to go vacation somewhere warm. Seriously, they have like a seven year winter period? Forget that noise, I'm going off to Dorne. Who cares if they screw goats? (#6383)

> Death. Winter in the books is described as cold and dark. A lot of death surely happens during actual winter in the universe of the series. The Long Winter does sound imminent. I think for everyone, though, winter will come in a much more figurative way. (#5176)

Whether serious or jocular, this ease of transition fits well with the notion of a group who simply favour having a debate about the show.

Behind the Debaters come the Just the Show participants, who display several degrees of disconnection. They tell us the least; they are the most likely not to answer a question (these two of course are interrelated); and – perhaps most tellingly – they are the most likely to respond with mundane comparisons. Simply to watch is to watch with a low level of engagement. These short, almost dismissive answers typify this mode: 'A big problem' (#175); 'Cold, snow, ice. Christmas!' (#1424); 'Just like the normal winter season I think' (#2397).

Classic Fans show the highest levels of engagement with the story itself – but the lowest levels, by quite a margin, of willingness to reduce 'winter' to short dramatic epithets. It is its place within the world of the story, its characters and conflicts that most captures them:

> Winter means a couple of things. On one hand, it means the White Walkers and the war is coming, and along come hunger and cold. On the other, winter represents a time for wolves, and as we know the Starks refer to themselves as wolfs, so it can mean 'The time for the Starks to rise is coming'. 'When the snows fall and the white winds blow, the lone wolf dies but the pack survives' – Eddard Stark. (#2144)

> It's both a warning whose topic – the Night's King – has been forgotten, and a reference to death. In the Seven Kingdoms, among those who don't know of the Others yet, it's the Starks' version of 'All men must die'. (#6195)

This conscious referencing of characters, sayings and events typifies the Classic Fans, along with acknowledging as parallel possibilities their application to our world.

The most striking results concern the Fan Watchers. Where for all the other orientations mentions of 'survival, renewal and hope' are almost residual, for the Fan Watchers more than 20 per cent volunteered answers containing this dimension. Not only that, but the combined word-totals of their answers are considerably ahead of any of the other groups, including the next highest, the Classic Fans. They also show the lowest levels of 'not analysable' and 'mundane' answers, and (more marginally) the highest levels of reference to 'metaphors and analogies'. All these indicate that people adopting this orientation have the greatest commitment to 'reading' beyond the series' world, valuing doing this, and engaging with our research. These results comport well with our earlier discoveries that the members of this group are ahead of almost all the others in their *levels of enjoyment*, and *interest in the series' role as commentary*. We see identifying and investigating this group as one of the substantial achievements of this project. Some typifying answers are as follows:

> It has multiple meanings, including fate, doom, the reckoning, the revelation (e.g. in the biblical sense of the apocalypse), the denouement. (#539)

> Winter is basically saying trouble is coming. It can take many forms, it's meant as a warning to everyone to never forget how hard the winter is, and how they need to be prepared. It can be used as a battle cry as well if you consider the Starks used to be called the Kings of winter. This could also be a warning to the north to never forget the dangers of the white walkers. (#3461)

> The dark long nights that draw in slowly, the cold that bites you to the bone, the long wait and hope for the spring. (#1012)

In addition to the other points we have made, there is a *seriousness* about many such answers: the series is a pointed warning, not something to be lightly thrown off. And it will take seriousness on our part to get us through the winter.

Perhaps the other most striking tendency to emerge from Table 6.3 concerns the Book Followers, who show a low level of interest in answering the question, yet, for those who *do*, the highest level of engagement at metaphoric and analogical levels:

> Entombment. Death and rebirth; dying off and regrowth. Survival of the fittest. (#1148)

> Hard times, the kind of events that tests your capabilities, moral and beliefs. (#391)

> Dystopia? The wrecking of world as we know it. Something that in the end is our own doing, stems from our greed and selfishness. The ultimate test, can we ever look past ourselves? (#632)

It should be noted that although this group is built around its interest in the books, only one in our 100-sample references Martin or his books. It is less an authorial interest, and perhaps more a will to high-level re-descriptions.

Contented Consumers have the highest number, by some margin, of short 'doom' answers. They are, it seems, content to boil down their reactions to short responses: 'Hard/difficult times' (#5159); 'The end' (#3417); 'Misery and doom' (#5713). Even their longer answers have a casualness to them that it is rarely replicated in the other groups:

> Winter makes me think of both literal winter, with cold and snow and ice and soil turned hard and darkness with barely any sun, but I also see it as a more metaphorical expression meaning essentially 'these good times won't last forever'. A bit like the 'memento mori' really, a reminder that the good times won't last and that sooner or later we're all going to die so don't get too big-headed. (#108)

Players are hard to characterise. High on story-associations, they are otherwise closer to the overall mean on other dimensions. Occasional answers reference the notion of the 'game' of Westeros: 'Winter seems not only like an apocalypse of undead icy corpses coming across Westeros but a reality check for an illusion that is the game they created to take the throne. Also it can be seen as a sort of metaphor for vigilance' (#4126). But this is unusual. A little more common are comparisons of what we might call 'house strategies', a degree of *taking sides*, rather than positing the whole of Westeros as the focus:

> I think of the season of winter is approaching. I think a lot of people take it as 'The north is coming' – a threat. However I don't really see that being the meaning behind a popular expression because the Starks have been pretty non-aggressive. Yes, they attacked the south. But that is only because they were provoked by the killing of Ned Stark. Northmen historically (I think) have been pretty ... not passive, but not the initiators of aggression. For that reason I don't think it's a threat. So to actually answer your question, I am going to say it more reflects the grim outlook the northerners have. 'Don't get too complacent and happy with the way things are, things WILL get bad. And soon' is how I interpret the famous saying. That's another reason I prefer Lannisters over Starks. Starks are just such bummers, ya know? (#6096)

> I think 'winter' in this context means 'hard times'. The Starks are by and large a pragmatic, rather grim group of people, and as their house saying, I think it represents that they feel it is important not to become complacent in good times or give in to luxuries, but to prepare for when things are not so good and to endure the hardships. It's a fitting saying for the series as a whole because hard times are coming for everyone, and things can always get worse, and winter is also quite literally coming. (#5786)

The will to metaphor, as we might call it, is unevenly distributed, but in patterned ways.

Thinking about 'worlds'

It may seem an obvious thing to say, but it is surely important that 'fantasy' involves the construction of alternative *worlds*. That is to say, it is a condition of good storytelling in the fantasy mode that authors construct convincing universes of characters, living in conceivable societies, within geographies with coherent kinds of people, creatures, vegetation, weather patterns, and so on. Decisions as to variations in natural laws, powers and special capacities ('magic') must not feel arbitrary. All of these are part of what has come to be talked of recently as 'world-building'. Of course, this is not new. Science fiction has been inventing alternative scenarios from its earliest days. Fantasy, even at its most *faerie*, has suggested that there might be things beyond the immediately perceptible, where other rules apply. There are what we might call 'moral universes', such as Tolkien's self-contained 'Middle-earth', or C.

S. Lewis' 'Narnia', and (more complexly) Stephen Donaldson's 'Ill Earth' series, these two reachable through 'portals' from our world which set up challenges between powers and problems originating in our world, and the demands of the created universe (see, in particular, Mendlesohn, 2008).

In the past thirty years, there has been a massive increase and complexification in fantasy storytelling, which in some way maps onto a set of major changes in ways of thinking about our own world as a system of interdependent parts. From the late 1960s, the 'Gaia' movement sought to promote the idea of the world as a living, self-regulating system, even with rights and legal status (see, for instance, Lovelock, 2016). And the huge debates over 'globalisation' (how far and in what ways is it happening; is it inevitable; should it be welcomed, etc.?) are part and parcel of the domain (see, for instance, Ritzer and Atalay, 2010). Recent years though have brought new phases and developments to the very idea of 'the world'. Clark Miller, for instance, has deftly pointed to the way that, in climate policy debates, a signal transition occurred when between the 1960s and 1980s scientists ceased talking in terms of weather systems located in different regions, and began to argue in terms of *global* climate – with all local and regional systems interacting and interdependent. 'Only when the Earth's climate was reimagined as a *global* system, bringing views of the atmosphere in line with assumptions about the jurisdiction of international institutions, did claims about climate change begin to engage with debates about international politics' (2006: 51, emphasis in original). The resultant calls for world action and governance over climate are massively important. Similar situations have encompassed the areas of health and medicine[4] (see, for instance, Meisterhans, 2016), species loss and environmental degradation (see, for instance, United Nations, 2004), and world economy (see, for instance, Siebert, 2008). But for our understanding of *GoT*, we must point to the steady rise of writing about 'world-building'. This has taken mainly two forms. The first has been in the form of instruction manuals for writers, game-designers and the like: how to create credible characters, with languages, clothes, food and customs, among other things; how to manage 'magic' or other ideas of extended powers; and much more (see, for instance, Gillett and Bova, 2015; Ellefson, 2017; Franklin, 2018; Nelson, 2019). The second is in critical work on the topic. With just a few exceptions (e.g., Wolf, 2012), to date most critical work on world-building has attended primarily to its *transmedia* qualities – that it is built and distributed via multiple interconnecting platforms (see, for instance, Jenkins, 2008; Boni, 2017). The emphasis here has been on the skills that this requires from fans and the challenges it sets them. This is certainly important, but it seems to us to miss something significant. We are proposing a refocusing onto the *very sense of there being worlds*: complete, coherent and recognisable from where we are – but at risk or in danger. This involves building on the emerging reconnection with *utopian* thinking (what is the best that we can imagine for our world, and how might it be attained?), *dystopian* thinking (what is the worst that might happen, and what are the forces within our world that might bring that into being?), and *fantasy* thinking (how do we imagine coherent alternative worlds beyond our immediate experience?).

A considerable number of our participants were moved to talk in terms of 'worlds'. In answer to our final ('Winter is coming') question, 754 used the word. Of course, mentions might be of many kinds and have many purposes. Viewed from numerous angles, it must be said that such mentions do not appear to point to any wider differences. Checking cross-tabulations with all our other quantitative questions, it seems that along most dimensions mentioning the term 'world' makes little or no difference. There are no visible differences in gender, age or class. There are slight – but only slight – increases in the importance attached to enjoyment and to commentary. 'World'-mentioners are moderately more left wing than our overall population (63.6 per cent versus 56.7 per cent) – mainly at the expense of apolitical participants. In adopting vernacular labels, even 'world-building fantasy' shows only a small increase on the overall spread (55.8 per cent versus 50.9 per cent). There are small, interesting variations in choices relating to the 'roles of fantasy' (small increases in the more 'expansive' [ways of thinking about our world from a distance, and allowing us to explore different ideas and attitudes] and matching decreases in more 'circumscribed' choices [means of escape, and grand storytelling]). Is the use of the word 'world' then mainly just a linguistic foible?

One striking feature suggests not. When we tallied the sheer amount of writing done by matching groups of participants mentioning or not mentioning the term 'world', the scale of difference was remarkable. Counting the length of a sample 100 answers from those mentioning, and not mentioning 'world', revealed a difference of 4,933 to 1,792 words, a difference of almost three to one. How might we make sense of this? It would appear that thinking in terms of 'worlds' does not so much *alter* people's attitudes, as *expand their capacity and willingness to explain* their views. We might call this a form of 'discursive confidence'.

With this idea to hand, consider the following example of 'world-talk':

> It's the time for the peoples of the Westeros to show if they really belong to that world or if they can rule it no matter what. It's the ultimate enemy and also the nature, that must be defeated by men before they can fully rule the world. So it means a dark time, but mostly to the men. It was interesting to see that the White Walkers were actually created by the Forest people, to battle against men. So I see the Winter as nature's final way of wiping men from the face of the earth or diminish their power. It's the nature's way of

> fighting back – nature personified by the kind Forest people but also the ruthless White Walkers, because that's how nature is. It makes me think the role of nature in our world, how it does not have same kind of personified forces to fight for it but must suffer in the hands of men until it dies. [#74]

In an answer such as this, it is possible to discern a play of ideas regarding the notion of 'the world'. It is an entity structured by rules and forces, but in which we (humanity) are being tested. In the fantasy world, this is realised in the form of forces designed to test humans to the limit, perhaps even wipe them out. But that has a parallel in 'our world', where we are also being tested – will we wipe it, and ourselves, out?

> There are four seasons in everything – including civilisations. In spring they grow and branch out in all directions and their world is overflowing with raw imagination and life and hope and determination. Summer is their apex, when all the ideas and aspirations and ideologies that are destructive or self-defeating or poisonous have been left behind and they are the very best of what they are. Autumn is when those once-great aspirations and ideologies crystallise and become too abstract to be useful to them, but become the seeds of the next civilisation. And winter is when the civilisation dies back, when those seeds gather their strength and wait for the world to be nurturing again. Winter is the Dark Ages, before the Renaissance. [#86]

Here, we can see an idea of 'the world' being developed within a philosophical idea; that of cycles of growth and decay. It is a philosophy that allows a *kind* of hope: that after winter things will regenerate and find new forms. The important thing, for us, is that the very idea of 'worlds' – systems of interrelations – assists in the promulgation of such larger sets of ideas.

One further example to demonstrate that, even in a shorter and less philosophical answer, the notion of a 'world' functions as a point of aspiration:

> A static world without life. A world without that is stuck in the same state with no chance of changing towards something new, good or bad. If 'Winter' wins, the world will stop moving, stop changing, become pointless and boring. This is why the characters fight to save a world that is admittedly kinda shitty. It's the same for us. [#111]

Thinking about 'fantasy'

What then is fantasy for, and what can it achieve? Are there any functions that it is particularly suited to? What can fantasies contribute to our sense of our world, its peoples and problems? We saw earlier that in broad ways public pronouncements on these questions have been shifting in recent years. The old, dominant view that fantasy was 'just' that – self-indulgent, undisciplined, near-pointless (unless it was bad (e.g., sexual) fantasy, in which case its wild and uncontrolled nature might be a threat) seems to have faded – although it has not disappeared. But what might be taking its place is less clear. We wanted to find out what thoughts our participants had on these much wider questions, and to capture the ways in which people's broad understandings of 'fantasy' guided and shaped their responses to *GoT*.

Our mechanism was one question (14), 'Which of the following come closest to your view of the role that fantasy stories can play in contemporary society?'. We asked people to choose up to three from a list of ten options (see Appendix 1 for the full set) – one of which had to be an exclusionary 'no particular role' (although only a tiny 132 participants chose this). Our hope was that we might again be able to discern patterns and connections among the ten options. Although not enforced, the vast majority responded to our request to limit their choices (90 per cent making between one and three choices, with 3 per cent giving four options, and 7 per cent giving more than four).

There are two clear favourites: 'enriching imagination' attracted just over 50 per cent of all responses; followed by 'means of escape' at 46.4 per cent – with high interconnections between them. But we must be careful here. While the word 'imagination' tends to carry very positive implications, the word 'escape' has tended to suggest low status, undemanding material. In fact, in people's spelled-out answers to our first open question some complexities in the terms 'escape' and 'escapism' are revealed.[5] While 342 participants do use these terms, as a way of contrasting enjoyment to commentary, there are some clear ambivalences. Compare the following:

Something to look forward to, nice escape from reality. (#2217)

I don't think of the show in terms of 'our world'. I enjoy speculative fiction as an escape, and am irritated when elements of what I would consider 'our world' – the elements I seek escape from (misogyny, sexism, queerphobia, etc, toxic social constructs) – penetrate the fictional world. (#2747)

The show allows us to dream us into another world. Westeros is so perfectly explained in books and Show so we can fully imagine us there. Some of us need that escape. (#3518)

I immensely enjoy *Game of Thrones*, but for me it is more of an escape from our world. I am aware that the political machinations are not endemic to Westeros/Planetos and could take place anywhere. They are a major reason for the appeal the series has for me. Nevertheless I do not understand *GoT* as a commentary on our world. (#2253)

It is a good escape. I think during this election cycle in Europe (Brexit) and in the United States, people dislike abuse of power and people dislike abuse of religious power even more. *GoT* makes you think about: the hypocrisy of religion, gender roles, rape, poverty, rankism, people born disfigured, the inherent evil in man killing the world around it (people of the forest), prostitution, slavery, honor, courage, betrayal, and mortality – without making you think about them. (#2180)

[I]t is such a fascinating and wonderful world that Martin has created. It is almost a kind of escape from our world, which is why I don't see it as a commentary on our world at all. However, I feel that there is at least one quality in almost every character that I can relate to in myself. It makes it easy (and incredibly fun) to put myself in their shoes and understand their thoughts and actions. (#2303)

All these answers resist the notion of direct commentary, but only the first stops there. For the rest, there is no impenetrable barrier between fictional and real worlds. With caution, we suggest that there is a continuum of meanings and associations to the word 'escape', along five possible senses:

- hideaway;
- refuge;
- fun relocation;
- respite; and
- vantage point.

'Hideaways' want to forget their problems in this world, while 'Refugees' know they are only getting away for a while. For 'Fun Relocators', the driver is just the attraction of the 'other place'. Those taking 'Respite' know that they should return with something gained – whatever that might be. And for 'Vantage Point', it is the positive draw of seeing our world from a new angle and distance that attracts. 'Escape' need not be a vacuous refusal.

The third highest choice was for the rather different 'seeing our world from a distance' (39.4 per cent). But – as Table 6.4 reveals – this is strongly separated from the preceding two. Table 6.4 (which is constructed in exactly the same manner as Table 3.1, see Chapter 3) reveals the degrees of interconnectedness between all the options. Strikingly, 'seeing our world from a distance' has the *lowest* relations with 'enriched imagination' and low relations with 'escape'. But in the other direction, it has a two-way high relationship with 'hopes and ambitions for changing the world':

Consider, then, some answers from among those in this second group:

The people with authority usually have little care for the average man. (#6508)

It makes sense to me. It is a perfect blend of emotions that we as humans face in the real world. It doesn't carry a message on which the story is based upon. It seems to be like a series that is shaped by the circumstances, basically the situations in which the characters have led them into it. It seems very practical to me, especially Tyrion Lannister's quotes, they are life lessons that

Table 6.4 Interrelations among choices of answer to the 'roles of fantasy' question

	A	B	C	D	E	F	G	H	I	J	
A. Enrich imagination		45.4	<u>**41.8**</u>	51.3	44.9	48.4	47.6	42.9	<u>**53.0**</u>	0	L
B. Explore emotions	27.7		29.9	25.3	**36.8**	<u>*23.2*</u>	27.7	**32.0**	24.8	0	M
C. Our world from distance	32.9	39.7		29.1	50.0	<u>*24.8*</u>	30.5	<u>**60.9**</u>	29.8	0	VH
D. Means of escape	**47.5**	39.5	34.3		<u>*29.6*</u>	47.3	**51.8**	36.5	47.3	0	M
E. Different attitudes/ideas	27.5	38.1	39.0	<u>*19.6*</u>		19.8	26.0	**42.8**	27.2	0	H
F. Grand storytelling	32.6	26.4	21.3	34.5	21.8		**37.4**	<u>**19.9**</u>	<u>**37.4**</u>	0	M
G. Shared entertainment	22.9	22.6	18.7	<u>**27.0**</u>	20.5	26.7		<u>*17.3*</u>	20.8	0	L
H. Hopes and ambitions	10.1	12.7	<u>**18.6**</u>	9.3	**16.4**	<u>*6.9*</u>	8.4		10.1	0	H
I. Alternative worlds	29.6	23.8	<u>**21.6**</u>	29.1	25.3	<u>*31.5*</u>	24.6	24.6		0	L
J. No particular role	0	0	0	0	0	0	0	0	0		
Totals	5334	3158	4194	4934	3269	3598	2571	1252	3036	132	
Single choices %s	1.7	1.5	3.7	3.2	1.7	3.4	1.4	1.3	1.3	100	
Numbers of strong crosses	1	1	6	3	3	7	3	6	4		

Bold/<u>underline</u> = highest; **bold** = next highest; *italics* = next lowest; <u>*italics/underline*</u> = lowest. NB: where there is a clear standout highest or lowest, 'next' is unmarked.

just one can learn from watching this show. This show has made me love Tywin Lannister more than Rob Stark, it has made such a change in my thinking in which I now can think about striking a balance about emotion and reason. It has made me realize the importance of balance in this world. (#1259)

Game of Thrones to me is about struggling to survive with honor in a world full of hypocritical, political and cruel people. It's about losing naivety, seeing the cruel people as they are without becoming cruel. And it's real, people can die, even honorable heroes, just like life. (#9781)

To follow/enjoy: I watch reaction or analysis videos about *GoT* or *ASOIAF* almost every day. As commentary: realistic, inspired by some real history events, dragons can be seen as metaphors for nuclear weapons. (#3414)

To follow and enjoy: my life kinda sucks and it's too damn hard with a lot of problems, watching *Game of Thrones* make me forget those problems, I know with watching it my problems do not solve or go away but at least watching it make me feel again for some moments. (#2770)

I think it definitely relates to the real world – obviously – but maybe some people take the 'survival of the fittest' type thinking a bit too far. Do the baddies really make it further because they are tougher and don't have those pesky morals to 'hold them back'? I don't think that's relevant on a larger scale in the modern world. What the show does do, however, is perhaps give more perspective to societies which may have become 'soft' in the sense that their lives have become so safe and easy. So it's a sort of morbid fascination; a feeling of 'wow … thank God that's not me!' Who knows… maybe it's some generic interest in survival instincts. (#3387)

From one (#2770) which could almost appear in the 'escape' group – yet chooses not to – to some finding direct analogies with either specific elements (e.g., #3414) or the overall 'feel' (e.g., #9781) of contemporary society: again, there is clearly a range of kinds of answer here. And this is for convenience, choosing from among the shorter answers (#2923, for instance, gave us more than 600 words in the one answer). As with the word 'escape', we must be careful not to lose the nuances in the way people talk about 'fantasy'.

Dimensions of 'fantasy'

A sizeable number of our participants (954 in total) used the word 'fantasy' of their own accord in response to our first open question (which asked people to explain their ratings of the series' importance, as enjoyment and as commentary). A quick comparison of the distribution of these among our seven orientations as ever proves revealing (see Table 6.5).

Table 6.5 Spread of mentions of 'fantasy' or 'fantasies' by orientation

	Just the Show	Debaters	Classic Fans	Fan Watchers	Players	Contented Consumers	Book Followers
% mentioning 'fantasy/ies'	6.1	6.7	9.2	9.6	12.1	9.9	8.2
Average word count	41.4	59.5	71.2	75.0	72.9	41.6	56.2

With quite a wide spread, what is clearly visible is the low involvement on both measures of the Just the Show viewers. Contented Consumers rate very low for the length of their answers – they are, it appears, contented! Meanwhile, at the high end, Players are the most likely to mention the terms, while not quite the highest in length of answers (out-topped by the Fan Watchers).

We needed to separate out the main different meanings conveyed by 'fantasy', including how these might give rise to criteria for distinguishing good from poor fantasy narratives and worlds. This was done, first, by close inspection of a randomised sample of 100 responses from among the 954. Seven distinct strands could be discerned in people's talk (with an eighth, for a very small number of unclassifiable responses). Answers could of course receive multiple codings.

1 Limited fun

The first kind is typically characterised by barricades around the category, often with words such as 'just', 'simply' or 'ultimately'. It appears to be part of people's enjoyment that 'fantasy' is no more than inventive, but undemanding fiction. No particular criteria distinguish good from poor fantasy – unless and until it insists on making demands. This kind shows a tendency to emphasise the 'medieval' nature of the story, as a distancing factor.

Answers in this mode were often marked by their brevity ('although enjoyable it's a fantasy' [#3025]), and by demarcating the series as 'entertainment' ('To me it is a chance to escape to another world, as a lover of fantasy it is perfect for me. However it is just fantasy and I don't draw any connections to our world from it. To me it is just entertainment.' [#6310]).

2 World-building

The key distinguishing feature here is a desire for *more* and *more depth*: for complex storylines, characterisation and a well-embroidered world. The effects of this are *intensity* of involvement, *immersiveness* and getting caught up in all the rich detail. *Good* fantasy is new, varied and visibly different. For some, this is the be-all and end-all of the story:

> It's extremely important because it is one of the best and most in-depth series that is on-going right now. Not only are we provided with an amazing story, but with multi-dimensional characters and the books break away from the stereotypical 'hero vs evil overlord' pattern. As a commentary of our world I rated it 'reasonably', but only because it's not an aspect that I've focused on. I'm sure Martin has introduced some parallels between our world and the *GoT* universe, but I haven't paid much attention to that. (#10545)

For others, it is a stepping-stone to further involvements:

> When I first read the books beginning around 2003 it was purely for enjoyment. Since the TV Show began, I have discovered the fascinating depth and analysis that other readers have invested in the book series. While I do not always agree with all the theories and commentaries fellow readers have developed, I find myself seeking out these well-researched essays, and find that they have enhanced my overall enjoyment of the books and TV show. (#265)

3 Community

An addition, or variant, on point 2 (world-building) is the emphasised value of belonging to a community of like-minded people, who can discuss details without limit, and bring questions and theories to bear. *Good* fantasy is marked by making demands on understanding, leaving questions and holes whose pursuit enthusiasts can share. *Implied* participation can be marked by words such as 'theories' (as in #265's answer above), which are part of the argot of these communities:

> I really enjoy how *Game of Thrones* makes me feel like I'm part of a coherent audience community. I really enjoy talking about the Show every week with friends, engaging with online debates and memes, and the general feeling of having a shared frame of cultural reference. The show itself is frustrating and uneven, and I take most of my pleasure from these ancillary elements. I don't watch the Show for what it says about our world – while there are interesting points of reflection (no text exists in a vacuum), I don't think this is a strength of the Show. (#10568)

4 Acknowledged linkages

People may find clear and significant bridges between the TV show's 'fantasy' world and ours. These can be direct/analogical comparisons of characters or events, or more thematic revelations about 'human nature'. (We saw some of these earlier, in the connections made with Donald Trump and with climate change.) Some do this in very explicit ways:

> It is the only TV-series I can think of, that stays interesting after 3 seasons. The dialogue and political intrigues are exciting to follow. As a commentary on our world, the biggest parallel I can draw, is the dragons are Planetos' versions of atomic bombs. Seeing them be so destructive makes me think of the potential dangers of nuclear war. (#4920)

Others do this more suggestively: 'The books and the Show provide an extremely fascinating, emotional, and exciting story, while, at the same time, showcasing the complexity of human nature in a beautiful, unique, and accurate way' (#148)

5 Evolving genre

Answers may stress the *exceptional* status of George R. R. Martin's work – how it extends and maybe transcends its genre, which is otherwise seen as having become formulaic. For many, this is part of a longer career of interest in the fantasy genre:

> I read the first books as they were published. I had goosebumps while reading them, because I realised I was reading something unique. Fantasy as a genre is difficult because many writer use truisms, and to stand out from a mass of look-alikes is very difficult. GRRM [George R. R. Martin] did it, and *Game of Thrones* stands out as a truly unique story among anything else I've ever read. Not so many writers can do this. (#286)

6 New hybrid

A variant on this finds a special achievement in Martin's work, becoming a distinctly new combination of fantastical and recognisable elements. Here, the *real* becomes distinctively visible *through* the fantastical:

> It is difficult to articulate, but it is not one Show. It is 15 Shows that constantly cross over. Yes, it is a fantasy story, but it is also a romance, a tragedy, a comedy, with elements of horror and then shaken vigorously, and then turned upside down. It allows us to see the breadth of our world, mirrored in a place with a different moral compass, which leads us to examine our perceptions of our own world. (#7150)

There is often an element, as here, of struggle to articulate this idea, which is one marker of its novelty and emergence. The 'Middle Ages' also now become a thought-model for our times:

> [...] With the incredibly substantial, immersive and detailed world-building – society-building – done by George Martin, *GoT* gives us a high fantasy saga that feels real enough that we can identify and bond with it, and the people who populate that society. But it also speaks to the greater ideas, common human experiences, and values that we wrestle with, love and want to explore as humans. In this way I think it serves us in much the same way that fairy tales used to serves us in the middle ages and thereabouts. Some things we recognise as being a part of the human experience no matter the year or century, and it's in these kinds of stories that we can best access and explore them. I suppose I'm saying, the magic, fantasy, swords, etc. allow us to bypass the weight of everyday minutia, technology, restrictions, stuff and structures of our current time and pay more attention to what it means to be human, to be people. (#10485)

This was the final third of a very long answer from a woman keen to 'rescue' the importance of the potential of the story from some aspects (notably elements of sexualisation) of it as a TV show.

7 Falling short

This approach evaluates the TV show from outside, either by comparison with Martin's books or by reference to other external criteria (in terms of characters, events, narrative or presentation), rejecting the notion of 'televisual fantasy' as an excusing explanation – our world is too 'real' to be dodged in this way:

> I love high fantasy, like when female characters are multi-dimensional and shown in various roles with different strengths and weaknesses. But I do not like when gore/violence is glorified. (#3684)

> The *A Song of Ice and Fire* book series is phenomenally written, and embodies post-modern themes in a fantasy setting better than any other contemporary work. Unfortunately, the Show is a commentary on American culture, in that it eschewed a faithful adaptation and internally consistent narrative in favour of stringing together a series of scenes transparently designed to be fan service, a trap that should be avoided in the age of the internet. (#7892)

Although there are, no doubt, other criteria in small numbers, the greatest concentration of these kinds of answer revolves around the issues of nudity, sexual violence and sexualisation.

8 Unanalysable

This category holds any residual answers which simply could not be coded or classified (i.e., answers that were too short, incomplete or ambiguous). Table 6.6 shows the results for the various groups' first open answers, coding for these eight dimensions of meaning of 'fantasy'.

Before anything else, the sheer scale of the variations along each row is striking (albeit some of the totals are quite small to begin with). What do the figures indicate and, especially, what might they add to our portraits of the seven ideal types?

A lot is mainly confirmatory of things already discovered. The Just the Show viewers are confirmed in their low levels of engagement, although with the additional emphasis on the presence of critical external criteria (that 20.6 per cent for 'falling short' is highest overall, even in the teeth of their overall low responses). Debaters meanwhile are clearly much more content with the series as 'just fun', with that one score (66.7 per cent) wildly outstripping all other results – along with almost the lowest levels of critical complaints. Much more surprising, perhaps, are the results for Book Followers, which once again quite closely mirror the Debaters' views – except with a rise in what we might call 'generic interest'. This strengthens the sense that, rather than this being a *literary* preference for print in general, or Martin's particular version, this orientation sets its requirements quite

Table 6.6 Distribution of coded mentions of 'fantasy' across the seven orientations

	Just the Show	Debaters	Classic Fans	Fan Watchers	Players	Contented Consumers	Book Followers
Limited fun	44.1*	**66.7**	38.3	*8.1*	9.0	24.4	61.2
World-building	*20.6*	21.4	63.0	**68.9**	50.0	47.7	35.0
Communities	*5.9*	7.1	**25.9**	16.2	8.0	14.0	10.2
Linkages	*8.8*	16.7	46.3	**60.8**	32.0	37.2	26.5
Evolving genre	*0.0*	9.5	31.5	18.9	25.0	**32.6**	26.5
New hybrid	*0.0*	*0.0*	24.1	21.6	**25.0**	10.5	10.2
Falling short	**20.6**	4.8	13.0	14.9	14.0	5.8	*4.1*
Unanalysable	**11.7**	2.4	*0.0*	*0.0*	1.0	1.2	*0.0*
Totals	34	42	54	74	100⁺	86	49

Highest = **bold/underline**, lowest = *italics/underline*
* Figures display the percentages of total responses coding for each meaning of 'fantasy'. Because of multiple codings, all columns add up to more than 100% (with a span from Just the Show at 111.7, to Classic Fans at 242.1).
⁺ Players had the highest levels of mention of 'fantasy', at 140. For coding, 100 were random sampled.

low – *viz.*, their bottom result on 'falling short'. Contented Consumers, despite very average overall response levels, top the table for interest in 'evolving genre', and (confirming earlier findings) are low on critical judgements. Classic Fans are nearly the highest on 'world building' and on 'evolving genre' – but (as expected) easily top the poll on community interests. Players, with the most to say on 'fantasy' overall, clearly take their fun seriously (with that very low score for 'limited fun').

It is once again the Fan Watchers who stand out, in our view, with those top figures for 'world building' and 'acknowledged linkages'. We close this chapter with some indicative quotations from members of this group whom we double-coded for these two factors:

> It's an incredibly interesting show, although I'm mostly watching because the books aren't finished yet. As far as it concerns its commentary purposes, to me it seems as a fantasy allegory of how royalty always matters more than anyone else, and how humans fail to see past their egoistic and naïve short sight and miss the bigger picture on what's actually important (the Long Night/ global warming). (#10509)

> To follow and enjoy I say extremely because it's a really well done TV show, you don't get that so often, and plus, the story is very catchy if you (like me) grow up reading fantasy. For me this is like how *Harry Potter* was like for me growing up, a safe place when reality is not so awesome. As commentary to our world I say very because I think the way the show and the books reflects the wars and conspiracies for power it's very like how I perceive the politicians where I live (Argentina) and around the world. People like Baelish do exist in real life, for some chaos is a ladder. (#4931)

> *Game of Thrones* is probably my favourite fantasy story since watching the *LotR* trilogy as a child. I particularly love its incredibly in-depth lore, its constant betrayal of expectations, its political intrigue, and vast possibilities of plots that could occur in the future due to the aforementioned political intrigue and lore. I think it's an excellent commentary on a variety of topics from racism to war, and while it's not massively important to me in this regard it's something I love about them. (#5998)

When we discovered this group, we dubbed them 'Fan Watchers', as a place-holder for what had drawn them to our attention. Now, that name seems inadequate for an orientation which so emphasises the ways in which *GoT* combines rich lore with potential relevance. Very tentatively, we propose henceforth to call this group 'World Watchers'. Everything about the world of *Game of Thrones* that interests people in this orientation – including, of course, the way that fans relate to it. But their interest is more philosophical than fan-driven. They are fascinated by the *possibilities* of a narrative of this kind, and the world that it creates in front of them.

Notes

1 Not all such uses are metaphorical. Some uses parse it in relation to the horror movie tradition, and the 'zombie apocalypse', retaining it within the sphere of fiction. For this context, see, for instance, Leigh, 2008.
2 Perhaps the one slight exception to this is the case of Valyria, where the number of Just the Show viewers mentioning this mythical land is vanishingly small (just over 1 per cent), with the highest (among Classic Fans) at over 10 per cent.
3 This category also included a very small number where answers came through as digital junk.
4 And, of course, as we write this, we are – like just about everybody else in the world – caught up in the Covid-19 pandemic, where the operations of the World Health Organization and its relations with national bodies are being tested as never before.
5 The concept of 'escapism' has long been a topic of a certain narrow kind of research. As early as 1962, Katz and Foulkes introduced this as a possible kind of 'need' that people might have, leading to their seeking out 'safe' forms of media. This reductive approach to the concept has persisted for a long time almost unchallenged. A quite recent version of this from within media psychology associates TV viewing in general with a 'lower need for cognition' (see Henning and Vorderer, 2001).

7

Conflicts and controversies

Game of Thrones has been beset with controversies since its early seasons. Its sexual explicitness, various deviations from Martin's books, shock moments (especially for those who did not know the books), physical threats and conflicts (from individual acts of cruelty to battle scenes), the way that particular peoples and cultures were presented, and so on, have all generated wide and very public debates. These were reflected in many comments that we received, particularly in answers to Questions 15 and 16, which asked people to tell us about a most memorable scene (and things can of course be memorable *because* they are controversial), and then about any moment or element that had particularly made them uncomfortable or angry. As we will see, we received a great variety of responses, ranging from very personal anecdotes about responses as they watched, to wider critiques and even withdrawing from watching any more (or, interesting phenomenon, turning to watching specifically in order to condemn it – 'hate-watching'). Beyond reflecting on this sheer variety, what light can an audience research project of this kind throw on these controversial elements? We would argue that the task of research of this kind is not to take sides or adjudicate such debates, rather, to try to *unpack and analyse the nature of the 'sides'*.

Discomforting content across various media genres frequently centres on bodies (especially bodily rupture, abnormality or injury, or conventionally undesirable bodies); violence, cruelty, suffering and distress; on power wielded by the strong over the weak – men over women, adults over children, humans over animals; and on death and dying. Our responses certainly included many such elements: gruesome deaths (e.g., Ned's beheading, Oberyn's *squished* head); brutality and torture (especially Joffrey's and Ramsay's); but also more general visceral moments (focusing in on an image of dead deer in season 1, or Daenerys eating a raw horse-heart). Moments within scenes of general mayhem stand out for some people – pregnant Talisa's death by repeated stabbing through her womb at the Red Wedding was one, particularly for a number of women. Some summed up their feelings in small generalisations: 'any deaths of innocents, ie, children' (#10414).

Many participants simply recorded the aspect that had hit them. But some at least hinted at the conditions of the impact. Sometimes these make clear that it was not always just the physicality of the violence that struck home – it was its implications. Often this was for narrative reasons. So, Jon's betrayal and killing by members of the Night's Watch hurt #9805 hard because Jon's intentions had been so good – it challenged the watcher's sense of narrative *rightness*. Sometimes it was because of external resonances. Bran's cruel monologue about Hodor upset #5872 because it mocked a 'disabled' person. Personal acts of non-physical cruelty got under some people's skin – 'Catelyn insisting Jon leave Bran's bedside. The hatred she has towards him is inhumane and makes her less of a mother!' (#6949). A mini-ideal was challenged by Catelyn's action. As Mikita Brottman (1997) has argued in her study of 'offensive films', media which disrupt existing expectations, norms and conventions are seen as particularly disturbing. HBO's long-standing – and deserved – reputation for 'edginess' pretty much guaranteed that many people would find grounds for complaint. Sex and nudity bothered many respondents, in some cases because of the awkwardness of watching with others: 'I introduced my mother to the Show, watching the first episode with her. Holy shit I had forgotten how many sex scenes are in that episode' (#4093), or because of the possible reactions of others: 'it makes me feel like I can't watch with other people because they would think that's the reason I watch the Show' (#5103).

We should not overstate the level of complaints. At least 25 per cent of our respondents found nothing to complain about. The response 'not really' to our question about discomfort was dominated by males (62.3 per cent compared to 36.9 per cent females) who saw 'debates and controversies' around the series as unimportant and chose 'no other activities' alongside viewing the TV show. It was also associated with those who identified the series as 'must-see TV'. There were plenty for whom the TV show's shocks are not necessarily being criticised. While many intensely disapproved of the scene of Sansa's rape by her new husband Ramsay Bolton, some at least wanted to recuperate it: 'I found Ramsay Bolton's torment of both Theon Greyjoy and Sansa Stark very uncomfortable to watch. The degradation was captured so horribly well' (#3758).[1] The cruelty of the TV show and of reality – especially the injustices, betrayals, pain, sadness, fear and helplessness of life – was a particular theme in accounts of how difficult *GoT* could be to watch, requiring effort and stamina: 'my husband almost stopped watching several times because he's tired of seeing good guys die and bad guys win. I had read the books so knew what was coming', often causing unpleasant, painful and strongly felt responses: 'The screams from the actress which played Shireen got underneath my skin. Terrible!' (#1299); 'The Red Wedding made me feel physically sick' (#6053); 'The scene of Jon suffocating under the bodies in the battle between him and Ramsay ... was incredibly well done and made me start breathing heavy' (#6820).

Nevertheless, for everyone approving of the effect on themselves, there were plenty objecting to it – #7508 explains his response to the burning of Shireen, daughter of Stannis Baratheon, at the command of the Red Lady, comparing the treatment of the characters in the book and series:

> I have typed and erased this paragraph a dozen times, I am so angry. Not only does it destroy the best character from the books. It completely ignores everything from Stannis's conversation with Shireen earlier in the series. This almost made me stop watching the series. There is no way a man like Stannis would ever burn his daughter. In the books, he orders his men to put Shireen on the throne if he falls in battle. In the books, Shireen is protected by her father from her mother and the red woman. This one really upset me.

It is not simply the character's suffering and death, but the violence done to her father's portrayal and to Martin's work, that outrages this man. For a good number of participants, the books provide a template, a sort of biblical origin, against which to measure the TV show. Such deviations are inexcusable, or – as a number of participants say – 'pointless', 'unnecessary' and 'gratuitous'. In addition to concerns about adaptation and authorship, a long debate regarding issues such as the responsibilities of media representation and the realities of life is effectively being continued through responses to our research:

> The reality is bad things happen. Women get raped, beaten, murdered and taken advantage of just as men and children do. Free will means every terrible thing that is possible can and will happen. If that makes you uncomfortable then you still have a lot to learn about reality. There is no such thing as a 'safe space', and until you realize that good luck to you. (#4922)

Notice how this answer uses our survey to address and combat another position, and the people who adhere to it.

Discomfort with watching *GoT* took not only the form of pained responses, but also of feelings of awful tension, shock at subverted expectations, or a sense of being destabilised by the twists and turns of the series. These two responses, both relating to Ramsay Bolton's cruelty, make this sense of not knowing, being played or 'messed with' clear:

> Not knowing what Ramsay was going to do next and imagining all kinds of awful stuff was really disturbing. (#3414)

> It was Greyjoy's escape. He's running and running and then he gets jumped by all those guys, and already I was really bothered when they were trying to rape him, but then he gets saved and I was 'HELL YES!!!' (because Greyjoy has been one of my faves since near the beginning.) He gets led into the dark

passage and then we learn that he is back with the Boltons. I absolutely hated the way my emotions were played with. Hodor was sad, The Viper's death was gruesome, The Red Wedding was pretty awful, but none of them messed with me like that. I am not saying it shouldn't have been in the Show, but dang. (#7653)

This within-show imagining is not the same as the many cases where people felt the need to judge the series against external criteria:

> [T]he scene where the Khaleesi is lifted up by the people of Yunkai ... I had a problem with the combination of the visuals of the 'brown' people reaching towards this very white, very blonde girl and the triumphant music that swells around her ... it's not often I find something difficult to watch or offensive but that scene wasn't the best. (#7442)

The hesitation at the end of this answer ('I am not easily offended but ...') is carried much further in many answers – signalled by the wide use of the words 'angry' and 'angered' (857 mentions in the 'uncomfortable' answers). 'Anger' implies a pushing away, a rejection of the series, while the other most common term – 'shock' (272 mentions) – *could* be coped with. How do these answers work? We can see this more clearly if we look via the overall pattern of 'mentions' in our database.

Table 7.1 Top ten 'mentions' of most memorable and most uncomfortable elements

Most memorable	No.	Most uncomfortable	No.
The Red Wedding	1,198	Sansa's rape by Ramsay	1,056
Joffrey's death	779	The Red Wedding	890
Robb Stark named King of the North[1]	740	Nudity, sexualisation, rape culture	638
The Battle of the Bastards	465	Shireen's death	503
Hodor's death	341	Oberyn's death	374
The Battle of Hardhome	302	Cersei's incest with/rape by Jaime	279
Daenerys gives birth to the dragons	298	Hodor's death	195
Jon Snow's death	222	Ned's execution	176
Battle of the Blackwater	160	Joffrey's cruelty	147
Cersei destroys the Sept	129	Daenerys at the Bay of Slaves	123

[1] Robb Stark named King of the North: 740 – we must be careful with this figure, since a number of people, puzzlingly, appear at this point to confuse Robb with Jon Snow.

Conflicts and controversies

The evidence of a clear 'leader' in both categories warrants giving particular attention to the Red Wedding, and to Sansa's rape, to explore how and why things become memorable or uncomfortable for viewers. We want to take advantage of the Red Wedding appearing so high in both columns. To fully understand the following contrast, it is important to consider the TV show's relations with Martin's books. Both scenes involved a significant change from the books. In the books, the Red Wedding is not attended by Robb's wife (Talisa in the TV show) who is also not pregnant (and is in fact a different person, Jeyne Westerling). Her inclusion in the scene, and her horrific death (stabbed repeatedly through the stomach), is a substantial alteration. In a similar way, Sansa's marriage to, and subsequent rape by, Ramsay Bolton marks a change from the books, where Ramsay in fact marries and abuses Jeyne, after Robb's death. *Both* scenes therefore invited equivalent commentary and critiques, especially from book-savvy viewers. They could have been responded to in the same ways, but we found a distinct asymmetry between them.

The Red Wedding

In order to examine how and why particular scenes register as memorable and/or discomforting we random-sampled and compared fifty each of those mentioning the Red Wedding as 'memorable', 'uncomfortable' or both (158 in total). All three share some characteristics, the most evident being the tendency to see their choice as 'obvious', whether briefly ('The Red Wedding. Duh' (#870)) or more elaborated:

> Yep, yet another person giving you the same old answer, sorry! It just has to be the Red Wedding. Having never read the books, I just had absolutely no idea what was coming, and boy did it hit me hard. Everything about the scene, the specific moments of the scene for me start with the throat cut of Catelyn. I really don't know what it was about it, it just felt so real! I can always picture her face and the moment so clearly. The second is how the credits roll with no music. The silence made it all so much worse. I was genuinely staring into the void of my laptop screen for a good 10 minutes after the episode, bizarre experience! (#3822)

The shock of this scene is also evident throughout a range of responses: 'couldn't sleep that night' (#5157/memorable); 'completely shook' (#3780/memorable); 'I sat there in silence absolutely gob-smacked' (#4829/memorable); 'devastated and sad and angry' (#2709/uncomfortable); 'heart-breaking to watch' (#2503/uncomfortable). But thereafter a difference emerges. The 'memorables' are greatly drawn to the pleasures of watching others react to the scene, whether directly (through friends and relatives) or through YouTube reaction videos (20 per cent mention this). Not one of the 'uncomfortables' mentions this. Instead, there are strongly *personal* aspects to their viewing – notably a visceral reaction to the manner of Talisa's death. We found eight components to viewers' grounds for finding the scene exceptional:

1. The sheer scale of the carnage (overwhelmingly 'memorables'):

   > The Red Wedding ... Everyone is enjoying their meal, the bride has just been taken off for the bedding and the rest remain drinking and celebrating. Catelyn notices the doors start to close to the dining hall as the clangor of guests starts to fade and the music grows louder. The song, the Rains of Castamere. Catelyn hears this and looks to the band, confused with fear on her face. Grey Wind is seen howling and seems agitated which also does not bode well. The Hound pulls up to the gate of the Twins to be told the feast is over and the look on his face says it shouldn't be and then he sees armed men run into the castle. Frey then stands up to give a speech as the music fades. Roose Bolton who has been one of the few lords not to be drinking that night meets Catelyn's eyes and looks down to his arm in which chain mail is revealed under his jacket. Catelyn screams to Robb as a Frey steps up behind his wife and stabs her repeatedly in her pregnant belly and then the band fires crossbows into Robb. Carnage ensues, many dying until Catelyn takes Frey's wife and threatens to slit her throat if Robb is not released. Frey looks at her as if he doesn't care and says he'll find another. Bolton walks up to Robb and whispers 'the Lannisters send their regards', then stabs Rob in the stomach finally killing him. Catelyn screams, slits Frey's wife's throat, then drops the knife and stands there all emotion drained from her face. A Frey comes up behind her, opens her throat and Catelyn does not react as blood pours out of her neck and she collapses to the floor because how can she feel anything now she has lost her last (or so she thinks) son. Great scene. (#6158/memorable)

   This detailed retelling marks someone who has watched and rewatched this scene to lodge it precisely in her memory. This answer also doubles as a fine example of the second aspect.

2. Its unexpectedness, the build-up, and capture of it all ('memorables'): 'The crescendo leading up to that moment was phenomenally done' (#5854/memorable).

3. The proof that it provides that this was an exceptional series ('memorables'):

   > The Red Wedding will never be topped. As a book reader, I waited for the moment on the Show for years. I anxiously teased non-book readers about the impact of it, years before it happened. It became the moment I was waiting for. Not just because I wanted to see it, but because I wanted everyone else to see it. I felt it epitomized the series. We could

Conflicts and controversies 123

not take anything for granted – nobody was safe. It also signifies the masochistic nature of the series and books – to love something which also makes you hate it. But the thing you hated is one of the primary reasons you love it. It's a unique premise not found in many other things. (#3144/memorable)

The Red Wedding changed who I am as a TV viewer and book reader. (#2088/memorable)

4. Fascination with seeing others' reactions ('memorables'):

I couldn't stop laughing at the shocked expression on my sister's face. (#4522/memorable)

I try to convince them to watch it and then enjoy talking about it with them and hearing their thoughts. That might be why I also like watching reaction videos on YouTube. (#121/memorable)

5. The loss of favoured/loved characters ('memorables'/'uncomfortables'):

For sure nobody can forget the red wedding! I was so shocked and sad in that episode. I mean I knew *GOT* can kill your favourite characters any time but I thought the Starks had more to give! I couldn't believe a whole army and house could get destroyed in a wedding night! Saaaad, but cool. After that point i stopped having any hopes for the guys I like in the series. (#560/memorable)

Robb and Catelyn Stark were two of my favorite characters. I didn't want to see them die. I thought that Robb had a good chance of ruling Winterfell and Catelyn didn't deserve to die. (#7785/uncomfortable)

6. The intensity of reactions that it produced ('memorables'/'uncomfortables'):

The one scene I remember most is the red wedding. The scene was so shocking, it was at that point the program went from being a good TV series to an awesome TV series. Throughout the scene I was hoping for an Ex Machina to happen. It didn't come. The most haunting part was seeing Rob Stark's head replaced with his direwolves. (#5195/memorable)

Red Wedding! When I saw it I was so devastated and sad and angry and so I decided to stop watching the Show! But eventually I started again. (#2709/uncomfortable)

7. A sense of individual viewing 'failure' ('uncomfortables'):

The Red Wedding. Having re-watched the series I should have seen it from a mile away. I didn't. (#1171/uncomfortable)

The whole Red Wedding. It was so unexpected, yet made so much sense that it kills you for being invested in those characters. (#1511/uncomfortable)

8. The particular manner of Talisa's death ('uncomfortables'):

> The Red Wedding and the killing of pregnant Talisa Stark; i haven't been able to watch anything remotely related to children's suffering since my own children were born, and this scene has definitely haunted me for months. (#1645/uncomfortable)

Those choosing the scene as most 'memorable' describe their appreciation of the scale, orchestration and impact of the scene, a feeling that the scene encapsulated *GoT*'s exceptional nature and a desire to share others' reactions to it. Audience reaction videos have become an established form of online participation in media culture, and *GoT* has its fair share of recorded reactions, particularly for the Red Wedding (e.g., in Twitter threads such as 'Red Wedding Tears').[2] The sharing of audience reactions suggests that there are pleasures in being 'shocked', 'horrified' and 'disgusted' and in performing this for the camera and other audiences (Kennedy and Smith, 2012: 241). The pleasures of savouring the spectacle of the wedding are particularly evident in responses from those who enjoyed watching the audience reactions of others to the scene – sometimes simply because their shock was funny, but also as a way of reliving the emotion of the scene: as #2831 notes of watching YouTube reactions, 'It was funny, but there was a degree of empathy to it too, watching someone else go through the Red Wedding for the first time and remembering what that felt like'.

What also seems clear in the responses is the way that the ability to embrace the nature of an arresting scene like the Red Wedding is linked to the extent that its discomfort registers as acceptable. That acceptability is expressed in the sense of a reciprocal relationship between viewers and the series – sometimes expressed as an acceptance of *GoT*'s unique nature or in the developing understandings of the unfolding plot and its characters.

Sometimes respondents commented on their reactions to the scene in retrospect – 'The Red Wedding pissed me off, but it's a great end to Rob's story, and therefore I have come to terms, but at the time, I wasn't ready for it, and was pretty upset by it' (#5789/uncomfortable). This is not a simple matter of accepting the narrative flow but requires quite complex negotiation of character motivations and acceptance of consequences, including, as in the following, postponing viewing:

> The Red Wedding. I can't even watch it – I love the Starks, and while, yeah, Robb made some SERIOUSLY stupid decisions, that ... that's just a bit much. It turned me off the series for a very, VERY long time, and I'm STILL not sure that I'll be able to get past it when I finally read it. As I haven't read/ watched it, I can't really tell you beyond a lot of very good people die because a teenager was an idiot and married the wrong girl. (#10362/uncomfortable)

This is more than just refusing to watch; it involves a series of responses which will take time to process. Another respondent describes how significant were his irritations on first encountering the Red Wedding in the books and then his seemingly contrarian pleasure in anticipating other viewers' shock at the scene:

> When I was reading the books, I have never been more angry at a work of fiction than when I read the Red Wedding (read it during Season 1), I was so angry I threw the book that I rented from the library hard enough to dent the drywall in my room and didn't read from the book again for two weeks. About two episodes into season 3, I realized the Red Wedding was going to happen that season, and I could not wait to see everyone else's reactions to when it happened on screen. (#5076/uncomfortable)

We can reasonably sum up the differences between the memorables and uncomfortables as follows: while the uncomfortables are rather overwhelmed by their own responses, and reflect on their own incapacities, the memorables rather revel in this as an exemplar of 'extreme storytelling'.

We need to note something very significant: we can find hardly a trace of a *moral critique* of this scene of slaughter, nor of a summoning up of Martin's books as ur-source for complaints that the change was 'unnecessary' (just four answers among our entire corpus suggest this linkage – all relating to pregnant Talisa's stabbing). For all the depth of people's reactions, nothing is seen as *morally wrong* with having the scene. The situation could hardly be more different with Sansa's rape.

Sansa's rape

We begin with an absence. We cannot find a single example of a reaction video for Sansa's rape. Or, more accurately, we can find one wickedly well-done parody, mocking the very idea of such a video.[3] Borrowing a scene from the film *Downfall* (2004), about Hitler's last days in his bunker, the video 'shows' Hitler getting news of Sansa's marriage and then rape, and having a complete meltdown. Fake subtitles have Hitler obsessing about her 'innocence'. 'Not my Sansa! That never happens in the books! Sansa has had enough torture in her life ... and now this!' There are considerable risks in theorising from absences, but we think the absence of reaction videos in this instance is quite telling, especially when it links with many other components in our respondents' answers. The issues were too *serious* in very particular ways to allow for the sardonic pleasures afforded by reaction videos.

Individuals' reactions as captured in our database are of course framed by the very public debates over this and other scenes of violence in *GoT*. Some critics found these too much – with 'a new rape, quasi-rape, murder, betrayal, torture, or other degrading act done by one human to another' every week (Elkus, 2015), and the popular feminist Mary Sue blogsite announcing that it would no longer promote the series (Pantozzi, 2015). Almost 10 per cent (1,056) of our respondents chose that scene as the one that made them angry or uncomfortable, while a further 638 chose the more general option nudity, 'rapey' storylines and sexualised scenes. Cersei's incestuous couplings with, and then rape by, Jaime were chosen by 279 respondents. Together these represent almost a fifth of our responses and suggest that our viewers felt at least some of the same concerns about sexual violence as the many popular and academic commentators. Various writers have noted the depiction of sexual violence of the series as a key characteristic (see, e.g., Rosenberg, 2012, 2015; Frankel, 2014b; Ferreday, 2015; Gjelsvik, 2016) – focusing particularly on three rape scenes: of Daenerys by Khal Drogo; of Cersei by her brother Jaime Lannister; and of Sansa by Ramsay Bolton – and observing that the series presents sexual violence in the present and in graphic detail, unlike the novels where rape occurred offstage or was recounted as a memory (Douthat, 2015; Rosenberg, 2012). Some note that the series reworked scenes which the books depicted as consensual into rape, and that it was less likely to associate sexual violence with monstrosity (Rosenberg, 2012) or to punish rapists (Frankel, 2014b). Moreover, the TV show's writers adapted elements of the books' violence so that it was enacted against major female characters. HBO's foregrounding of sexual violence is in line with its reputation as controversial (see McCabe and Akass, 2007b; 2008a), prone to breaking conventions and intent on shocking its audience, and this 'masculine prestige channel identity' (Woods, 2015: 37) meant much more graphic, direct and central presentations of violence against women than in the novels, and with less framing as problematic.

Criticisms of the TV show's scenes of sex and violence are very much local registers of the longer and wider critical debates about the media and sexualisation. Jane Mills argues that rape is frequently presented as entertainment (1995). Sarah Projansky suggests that fictional media often use 'representations of women's rapes to tell stories about men' (2001: 12) but also as a device to turn a female character 'into an active, independent agent' (2001: 99). Rape scenes in *GoT* have a particular significance in light of the TV show's production by HBO which has become notorious for its 'portrayal of nudity, sex scenes, and prostitution' (Gjelsvik and Schubart, 2016: 4), and especially its presentation of 'sexualised violence towards women' (Framke, 2016). It has been argued that *GoT*'s sexism differs from that of other quality TV Shows – for example, Genz (2016: 257) contrasts the way that *Mad Men* places the sexism of its male characters firmly in the past with a much more visible presence in *GoT* operating 'in the absence of a moral framework', while Bruun Vaage (2015, in Gjelsvik, 2016) notes that contemporary TV anti-heroes are rarely depicted as rapists, even if they are otherwise lacking in traditional heroic characteristics, making the rape scenes featuring central characters such as Jaime Lannister especially shocking. The issue that now confronts us is who was shocked, and what *kind* of a shock is it felt to be.

Demographic variables (e.g., gender, age and class) and political associations play only a small role in shaping responses to our questions about memorable and uncomfortable viewing. However, those choosing Sansa's rape as an uncomfortable moment are distinctive in being younger (9.5 per cent for the under-16s, declining to 3.6 per cent for the 41–65 age group – although rising to 10.1 per cent for the over-65s), more female (12.3 per cent compared with 7.7 per cent for males), and more left-leaning (12.5 per cent for left politics; 7.1 per cent for middle politics; and 6.1 per cent for right politics).

Comparing a randomised selection of responses from those choosing the rape scene as their most memorable scene and as their most uncomfortable scene, we found that while both sets of responses show extreme discomfort with that scene, there is a much more frequent rejection of it as 'necessary' in the second group. For example, responses in the first group included the comments that the scene 'shows the stark, brutal reality of rape' (#6096), 'how the world is' (#3543), that it is 'pretty necessary for people to understand how bad it is' (#5797) and that 'if rape shouldn't be uncomfortable I don't know what should be' (#5996), suggesting that for some 'there is an important distinction between finding something *disturbing* and nonetheless *wanting it to be shown*' (Barker and Petley, 2001: 4). In the second group there is relatively little of this. Instead, respondents note that it makes little sense in terms of Sansa's storyline and motivation, or that it represents unfair treatment of her character compared with others – 'Theon fucking deserved what he got by all accounts and measures, but Sansa getting raped is NOT OKAY' (#7644); 'Bran&Arya&Sansa are supposed to be each in a foreign, strange location, each learning their craft, but no! arya&bran learn to be assassin & magician but sansa is just raped and beaten in her own home!!!' (#693). This more nearly conforms to Frankel's argument that while there is certainly 'a spectrum of strong women' in the series and books, their strength is undermined by the ways their 'path to power' is predicated on surviving sexual exploitation (2014b: 1).

It becomes clear that seven things are at work – each of them hinting towards wider criteria and frameworks which transcend the TV show.

1 'Not in the books'

A complaint that scenes are not faithful adaptations – because they are 'not in the books'; that they misunderstand the books; or that the producers, writers and editors are not skilled enough to interpret the books properly:

> Entire sections of the book, critically adored sections that built the world and characters while exploring PTSD and class, were cut wholesale for the sake of giving increased time to a relatively minor character (Ramsay) and further torturing Sansa Stark. (#590)

> Sansa's rape, because it was not in the books and not necessary to the story whatsoever. (#5357)

> I read a very detailed wikia about it that showed pretty compelling proof that none of the writers, directors, or actors intended for this to be a rape scene, but the editing made it look that way. (#6955)

2 'Out of character'

A claim that the scene shows characters behaving 'out of character', doing things that are illogical or create plot holes, or that they do not otherwise play by the rules of the books or series:

> Sansa's senseless rape and character flip-flopping is awful. Every time she supposedly takes control of her life and circumstances, she becomes a pawn again even though we're told she's now 'empowered'. (#805)

> In the books she's not up north. She isn't supposed to be there (yet at least). It doesn't make sense for Petyr Baelish to flee from the Eyrie and the Vale of Arryn. If he wants the throne of the North all he has to do is weather the winter in comfort in the Vale and then attack the North after winter passes. (#4385)

3 How a character arc is 'supposed' to unfold

An appraisal of the scene in relation to some harder-to-define criteria laid down by the books, or more generally by the operation of archetypes or rules of narrative structure; and focused on the way that character arcs are 'supposed' to unfold:

> It was also the end of the Ramsay/Sansa arc: a Show-only arc about Sansa being transformed in a Strong Woman by being raped and getting revenge. (#847)

> Sansa's fulfillment of that role and subsequently her subjection to rape was not necessary for her arc into a powerful political player. (#4331)

Again, it is clear that we are in receipt of echoes of ongoing debates in other spheres, as shown by this response:

> I found the outcry over certain decisions stupefying. Particularly the one made of Sansa's 'rape' on her wedding night. 'It wasn't supposed to be Sansa!' Ok, so your outcry is because it would have been somehow acceptable for the character who was supposed to be there to be horribly abused, raped and mistreated by Ramsey, but since it wasn't written that way and it's happening to a beloved character suddenly it is not? 'They made it all about Theon.' Oh Jesus, I felt more as if they were responding to earlier SJW bs about the 'sexual exploitation' on the Show by not aggrandizing what was happening to Sansa, but rather you had a little distance from it by watching it, so to speak, through Theon's eyes ... thus knowing how horrifying it was but not having to watch it and having yet one more thing to complain about. In particular much of the 'Ermahgerd! Egregious abuse against women on a consistent basis – MISOGYNY!' annoyed me because the 'fandom' of the Show was particularly quiet when Theon was being flayed and having essential parts and pieces removed, but a woman? Hell, call the UN! (#10049)

4 Scenes that are simply 'not necessary'

A rejection of the scenes as superfluous, extraneous, excess to requirements – simply 'not necessary':

> The scene in which Sansa is almost raped by the mob and when she is raped by Ramsay make me especially angry. Both scenes were not necessary to the plot of the Show, yet they included them anyway. (#645)

> She had plenty of reasons to hate that people before marrying Ramsay and I felt like it was not necessary. (#1210)

5 Gratuitous

A marking of scenes as gratuitous, meaning that they are only there to court controversy, and that they are not only unnecessary but also designed to titillate, manipulate or shock:

> [t]he whole purpose of the scene seemed to shock people. It was emotionally manipulative. (#233)

> It proved that D&D were concerned only with courting controversy (#590)

6 Adaptation and the discussion of 'rape culture'

An appraisal of the scene in ways that reference issues of adaptation but go beyond a concern about the books and the ability of the series to translate it faithfully, to talk in terms of something about the TV show/producers/televisual style that is judged to be worrying and that often shades into a broader discussions about 'rape culture':

> The Sansa rape scene made me very uncomfortable. But that was the whole meaning of the entire scene. I don't see why people think that should have been cut. It's supposed to be grim. Looking away is not going to make a problem disappear, and I think that it is high time people learned that. (#1913)

> Sansa's rape by Ramsay seems so pointless in her arc. Not because it has no relevance, but because it's a really cheap way of giving her personal stakes against him and yet another season of Sansa being helpless. Specially after they teased some Darth Sansa before the season premiere. (#3402)

7 *Scene construction*

A complaint about the scene's construction, which shifted to a camera focus on Theon, forced to watch and horrified beyond words. This was found by a good number of critics to be, not a way of avoiding the danger of viewers getting off on Sansa's (still audible) distress, but simply another example of the tired old use of male responses as the lens through which to see the world:

> Sansa's rape scene. it made me uncomfortable and angry because it was to me unnecessary. Also it was filmed in a way that told us very clearly that it wasn't about Sansa but about Theon instead. It was used to bring manpain. (#468)

> Again, Sansa's rape scene (and all the others). It did not belong in her character arc, was a regression, and the way we see it through Theon's eyes makes it look like we need a male view to see that it's horrible, after all that male gazing in other scenes. (#1721)

The common thread across these seven strands is an insistence on judging this scene against *normative* criteria. Something – or some things – make the case of Sansa's rape exceptional, a different kind of special case.

Two portraits

Attitudes towards Sansa and the rape scene do not exist in isolation from other aspects of people's responses. Here, we offer two portraits, overlapping in some respects but diverging sharply to constitute examples of the two 'sides' of the debate about the scene. Both are young women, aged 16–20, and left wing. And both are very aware of the controversy over Ramsay's rape of Sansa and its presentation. But they end up on different sides. We do not know their names, but we want them to come as 'alive' as possible, and so we have given them names from among the most popular in their respective countries in their birth periods (1996–2000): 'Hannah' (United States) and 'Jessica' (Australia).

'Hannah's' (#6073) ratings of the TV show's importance to her are different to 'Jessica's' (#10115). 'Hannah' gives extremely positive ratings both for the TV show in relation to enjoyment (1) and as commentary (1) – but only a moderate (3) to the debates and controversies around it. She indicates a high level of dislike of spoilers (1) – while admitting that it was some spoilers that got her watching in the first place. 'Jessica' gives lower ratings for both enjoyment (3) and commentary (2) – but a maximum (1) for debates and controversies. She does, however, positively *welcome* spoilers (5), expressing her gratitude at seeing leaked scripts for season 7 ('at least I am prepared for the worst now'). Their summaries of their initial ratings show a striking contrast:

> It's really easy to make connections from Westerosi history to our history, ancient and modern. It's important to understand how things have happened in the past, both real and fictional, so we can avoid the same mistakes. Also, it's really good at humanizing other people, and understanding how people and groups of people are all still people with gray morality, which is something we can all learn from. Although sometimes it can be a bit too easy to take away the impression that no matter what you do, nothing will work out for you, it can help you realize to take nothing for granted, as well as to never assume that something is inherently denied to you. ('Hannah')

> As for following & enjoying, I have an issue with some of the choices of the writers (i.e. Sansa's season 5 storyline) but still enjoy the Show for the most part & find it entertaining. It's pleasant to discuss it within the fandom. And as for commentary, I guess you could say some of the happenings in Westeros reflect modern day – but I prefer to look at it from a historical perspective. ('Jessica')

'Hannah' offers a near-philosophical account of the significance of the series to her, with a search for the positive upbeat as its outcome. For 'Jessica', it is most importantly a point of pleasant contact with an (unspecified) fandom, although it is not entirely clear what she means by her alternative to seeing it as 'commentary'.

We now consider each person separately. We will see that each one quite closely embodies the overall profile of one of our ideal types.

'Hannah'

'Hannah' participates in many of the qualities of our 'World Watchers'. Their distinguishing marks among 'other activities' were 'debating its merits and faults with other viewers'; 'writing about it online'; 'reading (or re-reading) Martin's books'; and 'enjoying other people's fan productions' – but *not* 'producing fan works'. She matches these exactly. 'Hannah' also closely follows their tendencies with regard to roles for fantasy – her choices again emphasising her philosophical interests: 'a way of thinking, from a distance, about the problems of our world'; 'explore different attitudes and ideas'; 'a source of hopes or ambitions for changing our world', and again, although less markedly, in her naming of 'kinds of story' ('dystopia'; 'medieval political drama'; and 'moral fable'). Although naming herself as a 'book-first kind of a guy', she has no problems with the changes between the books and the TV show – they are different iterations of the same thing. She has a powerful sense of the story's near-uniqueness: 'I love many other works of art, but *Game of Thrones* is so lifelike that it can best be compared to the real world'. This shows again in her answer to our 'Winter is coming …' question:

> Obviously, the white walkers, but also, it makes me think of impending danger, but not necessarily an unpreventable one, or the words would serve no purpose. They serve to warn the Starks, and all of Westeros, that things are only going to get worse, so you need to get stronger, mature, etc, to face this coming danger. It makes me think of these perils, but also of the value of hard work, perseverance, and teamwork in facing these threats.

All these points suggest, that to 'Hannah', thinking about the story-world is closely woven into thinking about our contemporary world.

'Hannah' preferred watching the TV show for the first time on her own, several episodes at a time, but she was happy then to rewatch it with others ('to relive the magic as well as laugh at their surprise'). That does not diminish her awareness of the impact of the rape scene:

> I thought Sophie Turner's thoughts on Sansa Stark's rape scene recently published in the *Huffington Post* summed up this issue perfectly. If we can have all other sorts of terrible things in this Show, it's important to leave nothing out, especially in an issue that's unfortunately so prevalent in modern society. The scene, and some people's reactions to it, have empowered rape survivors and inspired people to keep fighting against this injustice, which has made it all worth it.

Her relations with Sansa are very complicated:

> Sansa Stark!!! Her character growth has been so real, and I've really empathized with her difficult situations, and the fact that she only comes out stronger. She empowers me to keep going, no matter how hard it may seem, and to always do what's right, because that's what Sansa strives to do. She's so powerful as a feminist icon, and I would love to crawl through the pages or the screen and hug her and tell her everything's going to be all right. In younger Sansa, I also see the wide-eyed idealism of my sister, who's away at college,

and sometimes I like seeing a character similar to her (even if Sansa's life is utter tragedy). It helps that Sophie Turner is a great actress, and truly brings the role to life. Due to her portrayal of her character, her awesome and inspiring philanthropy work, and how fun she seems to hang out with, Sophie Turner has become my favorite actress like Sansa has become my favorite fictional character. Sansa means the world to me, and I just want her to be happy, to hang out with her (it only needs to be once in a while, don't judge me), and while I loved what I saw from her in season 6, I'm looking for her to finally step up and just blow everyone else away with her political agency and capability in season 7, and survive to season 8 and beyond, ruling as the Lady of Winterfell and/or Queen in the North (or even the realm??) and reassure us by knowing that a competent and awesome woman will be protecting the realm well after the end of the series. I'm also hoping she'll retain aspects of her own humanity rather than merely vicious, non-trusting traits instilled on her by Joffrey and Ramsay and everyone else, and stay friends with Jon, and pick him over Littlefinger, and finally have a happy, healthy domestic life again, and reunite with Arya and Bran and Tyrion and befriend Dany and all the other characters I love. I know I'm asking for waaaaaay too much from GRRM, but I think Sansa has good odds of surviving the series, but knowing GRRM and how terrible I am at predictions, I'll probably be bawling as she dies a slow, agonizing death, friendless and alone.

Note the variety of levels on which she appreciates Sansa. She is someone to admire and look up to; a feminist icon; a future Queen in the North; empowering; always doing the right thing (a position that Sophie Turner's 'awesome and inspiring philanthropy work' echoes); coming out stronger all the time. But she is also someone to pity because her life is 'utter tragedy', who has yet to completely realise her potential, and who will surely step up soon and overcome 'vicious, non-trusting traits'. She is someone who can be empathised with and worried about – Sansa is both a 'wide-eyed idealist' like her own sister, and a character in a story who might still end up 'friendless and alone'.

'Hannah' moves through an anticipation of several versions of Sansa's fate – she wants to tell Sansa that everything will be alright, she calculates that she has 'good odds' of survival, but worries about being left 'bawling as Sansa dies a slow, agonising death'. Her connection to Sansa moves back and forwards in time, even imagining Sansa's role in protecting the realm 'well after the end of the series', as though the world persists beyond its representation. But this world is governed by its own rules and although she can *hope*, she does not *expect*. The sense of Sansa as both within and outside of the representation is also heightened by the way 'Hannah' acknowledges the story's pages and screen, albeit as something she would love to 'crawl through', to 'hang out' with her. Sansa seems to be melded with Sophie Turner here because of 'how fun she seems to hang out with'.

While Sophie Turner is acknowledged as a performer – a 'great actress' – Sansa's character growth is 'so real'. But whatever happens or might happen to Sansa, she feels no need to *blame* the world, or its creators.

'Jessica'

'Jessica', on the other hand, shares many of the characteristics of our 'Classic Fans'. Like them, hers is a richly active engagement with the TV show: 'debating its merits and faults with others; 'writing about it online'; 'buying/ collecting merchandise'; 're-reading Martin's books'; 'producing fan fiction, fan videos, fan art, or etc'; 'enjoying other people's fan productions'; and 'game-playing, role-playing, or cosplay'. Her 'roles of fantasy' choices have a small overlap with 'Hannah's': such stories are 'a way of enriching the imagination'; 'a way of thinking from a distance about the problems of our world'; and 'a means of escape'. But her 'kinds of story' choices again show a pattern typical of the Classic Fans: 'cruel TV'; 'medieval political drama'; and 'world-building fantasy'.

'Jessica's' watching options in Australia were quite constrained: 'I prefer to watch alone or with a small group, on a television with the DVDs. But as *GoT* is actually airing, the only way I can watch it is on my phone/ laptop streaming it from Foxtel, which is the only legal way to watch in my country.' Her favourite character is Cersei, whom she loves precisely for being so bad:

> When you delve deeper into her character, she has so much to offer. She's a terrible person, yes, but so fascinating. She's so complex & I find her descent into being gradually more & more horrible so interesting. I have a few nitpicks about how the Show writes her, but I still love her nonetheless!

But anything which gets in the way of the wished-for careers of her favourite characters is simply unacceptable. Commenting on her feelings about controversies she writes:

> I could write an essay on this but in short: Sansa's rape, & Cersei's 'unintentional' rape. Both Sansa & Cersei are my fave characters so this was particularly frustrating for me. The sexual assault that occurred added absolutely nothing to either character & they tried to pull it off as a cheap badass arc for Sansa. Guess what, D&D, feminine characters don't need to be raped to become empowered.

Here, the expressions 'adding to character' and 'empowerment' are doing a lot of work, as is the notion of an 'arc'. The ideas recur in her direct remarks on Sansa's rape (under Most Uncomfortable):

> I'm going to throw in the same scene again: Sansa's rape. Sophie was just 18! It never happens to Sansa in the books, and it was just so frustrating and

heart-breaking to watch. It was like seeing D&D ruin her character arc right before my eyes, but having to see a strong female character on her road to empowerment being torn down like that for no reason was terrible.

There are a number of similarities between the accounts given by 'Jessica' and 'Hannah' – for example, both see Sansa as empowering and both mention the actress who plays her, Sophie Turner. 'Jessica's' comment here is made as though the young Sophie is herself actually raped. That concern sits alongside an appeal to the notion of a 'character arc', which simply has to be a 'road to empowerment'. 'Hannah's' account is both more personal and affective, and more philosophical. While she relates to Sansa and Sophie on a number of levels, she is also able to disconnect them, citing, for example, the actress's own discussion of the rape scene. Although she has strong hopes for Sansa's future and clear views about the way she hopes that Sansa will develop, she is able to anticipate a range of possible outcomes for the character. 'Jessica' has a much more rigid view of the character and the TV show; deviations from the book are suspect, sexual assault can only be represented if they 'add to character', representations of women's empowerment require the deployment of a very particular kind of character arc. For 'Jessica', therein lies the only hope. This surely connects with her slightly tentative disconnected answer to our 'Winter is coming ...' question: 'Well in the metaphorical sense I guess "hard times". Could be referring to things like the Great Depression, depression itself, Global Warming, or something else entirely? Just a real sense of foreboding doom.' If there is anything beyond doom, it can only be located in her favourite female characters' arcs, be those innocent (Sansa) or knowing/wicked (Cersei).

Understanding the Sansa controversy

To emphasise again: our top two remembered moments *could* have been responded to in identical ways. Both involved deviations from Martin's authorial version. In both cases, this deviation introduced an element of extreme violence against a woman. Arguably, being murdered – and having your unborn foetus targeted in the process – is a worse fate than being raped by your husband. Both could feasibly be argued to be 'unnecessary' to the narrative. But something substantial marked them apart, allowing the first to become mainly assessed as 'shock': who guessed, who was ready for it, how did it make them feel? Meanwhile, the second was assessed against a corpus of ethical imperatives: is it permissible to treat this character in this way? How could they wreck a character arc? How dare they show a rape in this manner, through the eyes of a male onlooker?

Of course, there is a marked difference in the placement and longevity of the characters involved, Sansa and Talisa (although Catelyn – another female victim, who is indeed allowed to show the gamut of emotional reactions before she dies – has been with us since season 1). There is little doubt that Sansa's unusual character and relations with her devotees is a factor. In Chapter 4 we saw a general portrait of the qualities accorded her by those who favour her, as compassionate, intuitive, vulnerable, empathic and relatable. But there is a further dimension: Sansa's status as a character. To her choosers, she either does not really belong within Westeros, or she requires special consideration and protection. Either way, the (mainly) women who adopt her see her as special, even by comparison to the other favourite female characters who defy convention, such as the defiant tomboyish Arya or the empowered and inspirational leader Daenerys:

> Sansa Stark … was my favorite character in the book, largely because I just enjoy being inside her head, and that has transferred to my feelings about her in the series. I like that she is a traditionally feminine character, in contrast to some of the more stereotypically 'badass' female characters in the series. I also think she is strong and undervalued, and that her character is one of the few that feels the most like a 'real' person to me (no fantastical powers). (#1487)

> Sansa. I feel I can connect with her on a more personal level than I can with other characters. In all honesty if her character is ever killed off I will stop watching, as most of my entire interest in the Show is invested in her now. (#401)

While others do not express their connection to her quite so overtly, there are hints of her perceived difference from other characters in the way, for instance, some say she did not 'deserve' what happened to her:

> Sansa is one of the most misunderstood characters in *Game of Thrones*, and doesn't deserve all the horrible things that have happened to her. Sophie Turner's performance is a big part of this. In the first Season, Sansa was a teenage girl who wanted to be queen, without understanding what it entailed. Some of her actions led to Ned's death, but she isn't solely responsible for her father's execution. The moment I realised Sansa was great was when Joffrey showed her Ned's head on a pike outside the castle. Sansa was trapped in King's Landing, and engaged to a psychopath. The fear she felt when she got her period was heart-breaking, and despite a Season 5 misstep, it's been wonderful to see Sansa grow into a woman. (#7110)

Other rules ought to apply to her. *GoT* has specialised, generally, in ensuring that characters *do not* get what they 'deserve' – or at least, not at the time we might hope: that is part of its generic promise! But Sansa stands apart because she is 'like me' (e.g., #333, #3040, #6747)), 'relatable' (e.g., #437, #2253, #2808); someone who stands for women and their experiences and whose responses to this cannot be enjoyed in the way that the larger-than-life female characters Arya, Dany or Cersei can. There is also a sense here that the kind of heroism that other *GoT* characters show – which is displayed by making choices and choosing paths with little chance of reward or even survival – is not available to Sansa; she does not, at least in the earlier seasons, understand the world she lives in and her story simply does not allow the space to make the kind of 'decision with consequences' that are taken by others. And without this, HBO's 'aesthetic of excess', which in other instances allows viewers to appreciate sexually explicit storylines as potentially complex and meaningful, registers as unacceptable.

In their research into responses to screened sexual violence for the British Board of Film Classification (BBFC), Barker *et al.* (2007) identified a similar phenomenon in relation to one of the five films that they were asked to explore: *House on the Edge of the Park* (dir. Ruggero Deodato, 1980). One character, Cindy, arrives by chance at the house where two noxious working-class men are holding its owners captive – although unknown to them, their invitation was a ploy to set up the scene for revenge for an earlier rape and murder. Cindy is subjected to sexual assault, almost with the connivance of the house's bourgeois owners since it enables them to seize control again. Cindy is 'sacrificed' to the needs of their scheme. Barker *et al.* write (first, quoting one focus group member):

> '… all bets are off when Cindy gets involved, cause it's like fine, if you and your friends want to set up this complicated plot, whatever, you're adults and you can make your own decisions, but you've involved somebody who's got nothing to do with this … so as far as I'm concerned you deserve everything you get right now …' The arrival of Cindy and the 'use' of her by the rich people means they now have lost all rights within the movie for her. (Barker *et al.*, 2007: 180)

Cindy's status is exceptional – she does not 'belong' within the cynical class-based conflicts that dominate the film. Sansa's position within *GoT*'s world is somewhat equivalent. She does not understand Westeros's rules, and survives off a kind of vulnerable femininity that speaks to many of her (especially young, female) viewers.

But this is surely not the complete answer, for which we need to look much more widely into a very large historical phenomenon: the rise of 'rape' as a core metaphor for thinking about the problems, challenges and threats that women face in society, its particular salience for thinking about issues of representing women in popular genres, and the place of both of these in popular and scholarly understandings of controversial forms of media.

Bifurcating understandings

Behind our examination of reactions to our two moments lie two sharply opposed contexts.

Behind reactions to the Red Wedding lie a series of shifts in the ways that people think and talk about the very idea of 'violence'. Although there were always countervailing voices, from the 1960s until the turn of the millennium there were strong currents of argument that 'violence' was something primal. Whether driven directly by inherited tendencies, mediated through maleness, or simply hard-wired into the more primitive areas of the brain, it meant that the word could easily seem to signify a singular phenomenon. As a result, it made sense for communications researchers to *count* the frequency of all moments of conflict and confrontation and simply assume that these would have a unidirectional cumulative pre-cognitive impact on audiences' brains (as in the work of George Gerbner and his associates). But that dominance has been increasingly eroded in recent decades. In the political field, Johan Galtung – who as early as 1969 had argued (against the stream) for the use of a notion of 'structural violence' to capture oppressive states – proposed in 1990 the addition of 'cultural violence', to capture the role of dehumanising ideologies in justifying brutality and murder. From the standpoint of law, the concept was found to be extremely 'slippery', even an 'essentially contested concept' (de Haan, 2008). In other spheres, the role of culture in warranting, for example, domestic violence was studied (see, for instance, Yoshioka *et al.*, 2008). Anthropologists have drawn on understandings of conflict (and its avoidance) in traditional societies to look at our own histories (see, for instance, Scheper-Hughes and Bourgois, 2003). Overarching these was a growing certainty that 'violence' was not a singular, primal force, but something best understood as *culturally shaped, strategic, localised* and needing interdisciplinary study (see, for instance, Turpin and Kurtz, 1996; Bufacchi, 2010; and Bessel, 2016).

Slowly, alongside these wider rethinkings, came more thoughtful attention to the role of the media, and to the responses of audiences. A complex body of work emerged on what has been called the 'seemingly paradoxical enjoyment' of negative or ambivalent emotions (see, for instance, Gaut, 1993; Carroll, 1995; and Bantinaki, 2012). Over the past twenty-five years, within the context of serious study of the horror genre in particular (see, for instance, Carroll, 1990), there has been significant attention to the audiences for horror, violence and schlocky cultural forms – shifting away from the predominantly moralistic tone of work since the late 1960s ('violence' as bad for viewers, cumulatively affecting their sense of the world). In 1997 Andrew Tudor was among the earliest to broach this new mode of thinking, reviewing the main approaches and arguing for a shift to a view of 'a heterogeneous audience capable of taking diverse pleasures from their favoured genre' (1997: 43). In the same year, Mark Kermode wrote of his very particular ways of watching and responding to films as a teenage horror aficionado, and of his delight at sensing similar responses in other corners of the cinema, and Annette Hill published her study of male and female responses to watching extreme cinema. A seismic shift was underway. Remnants of old approaches of course lingered on (as in Weaver and Tamborini's (2001) collection of (mainly) psychological approaches).

From seeing the 'pleasures of horror' as typically male adolescent 'sensation-seeking', the field broadened to include women as horror fans (e.g., Cherry, 1999, 2002). Serious attention began to be given to the fields of 'cult' (e.g., Mathijs, 2007), 'exploitation' (Schaeffer, 1999), 'schlock' (e.g., Holbrook, 1999), and particular subgenres such as 'Asian extreme' cinema (e.g., Dew, 2007; and Pett, 2013). Donovan (2010) has explored the 'thirst for violence' associated with pleasure in action films. All these were moves away from universalist psychological accounts, towards a view of audiences as particularised within historical, cultural and generic contexts.

Meanwhile, commissioned research by British sociological researchers (see Morrison *et al*., 1999; Schlesinger, 1992; Schlesinger *et al*., 1998) laid the basis for the UK BBFC to worry less about presentations of 'violence' in films, but at the same time *more* about 'sexual violence'. Now *that* became a special case, with its own problematics, a case of 'where do you draw the line?'. A new 'figure' was invented to bear the weight of transferred fears: 'young men with little life experience' (on this, see Barker, 2016), seen as potentially 'vulnerable' to disturbance and arousal by any kind of scene of sexual violence. Driving and activating this was a quite distinct set of debates.

These debates do not have a single beginning, but they certainly crystallised in 1975 with the publication of Susan Brownmiller's *Against Our Will*, which mounted a powerful argument that rape was a key tool of male oppression of *all* women. Closely alongside this came a focus on what were termed 'rape myths' (see, e.g., Burt, 1980): the excuses and self-justifications offered by male aggressors for their crimes (on the shifting history of these, see Burke, 2007).

This developing focus on rape was part of a broader shift from early feminist concerns about the production contexts of representations of violence against women to a much narrower focus on the significance of images of sexual violence and their impact on audiences. This 'texts and effects' approach is evident from the 1980s onwards in the most visible and influential of feminist writing and activism which originated in a particular brand of radical feminism in the United States (for a discussion, see Bronstein, 2011). It has been bolstered by academic work on 'sexual objectification', derived from a social psychological perspective, and on the 'male gaze', taken from a psychoanalytically inflected form of film studies. Despite their origins in calling for representations of women which centred on female experiences and agency, both theories now tend towards a view of men as active and aggressive and women as passive and 'put upon', to the extent that succeeding debates about 'sexualisation' offer a narrow understanding of sexual expression and representation (for a discussion, see Paasonen *et al.*, 2020), and a tendency to focus moral concern around an imagined figure of a vulnerable, white, middle-class, assumed-to-be-heterosexual girl (Egan, 2013). The more recent #MeToo movement has been more inclusive and more political, although it has still foregrounded the experiences of white western women; and in particular media celebrities (Zarkov and Davis, 2018; Gill and Orgad, 2018).

Tanya Horeck's notion of 'public rape' (2004) is useful here because of the way that it shows how controversies around rape have become central to the way the politics of gender and sexuality are understood. Representations of rape have taken on a particularly significant role in emblematising issues of power and inequality, to be measured against a properly feminist understanding of women's absence of choice in face of men's violence. Debates about rape (rather than, for example, work conditions, reproductive rights, poverty or literacy – or indeed representations of other kinds of suffering and inequality) have come to 'stand for' feminist politics and thinking, thus a dramatised rape carries forward wider meanings and connections to the broader social reality of victimised women. The growing acceptance that rape, representations of rape and debates about rape must be responsible towards actual victims can be gauged by the current visibility of the term 'rape culture', which suggests that rape permeates contemporary life, protecting men who commit violence and blaming the women they attack, instilling fear in women and working to limit their behaviour. Individual scenes of rape, like those in *GoT*, are then uniquely 'public' in ways that other representations may not be. And in the digital age, as Horeck (2014: 1106) notes, 'public rape' has taken on even greater urgency, with rape culture the subject of 'vociferous discussion and debate', conducted with 'an unprecedented speed and immediacy'.

Debra Ferreday (2015), focusing on the scene where Cersei is raped by Jaime, has shown how responses to representations of rape in *GoT* take place in this context of wider debates about rape culture. In fan communities, for example, dominant discourses about rape were both reproduced and challenged, often through discussions based on competing notions of reality and authenticity. This played out in various ways; whether the scene represented 'what really happened' in the book, whether it showed 'real rape' (2015: 31) (and what counts as real rape), how it might be seen to represent the reality of women's experience in the Dark Ages, how it did not matter because of the series' status as 'just fantasy' (2015: 32), or how it might speak to 'a reality of lived experience' (2015: 31) for many women, presenting an opportunity for 'silenced voices and bodies to speak and be heard' (2015: 34).

As we have noted, some of our participants framed their responses in relation to debates about 'rape culture'; for example, arguing that most of the show's rape scenes 'are made to titillate and shock rather than explore the victims' trauma like the books do' (#4011), or are used as 'a plot point to garner sympathy for female characters' (#9709). That the series had been embraced as one portraying women in a positive way, strengthened the sense of betrayal that some participants felt; ' I love it how D&D portray *GoT* as something where women are empowered while they always end up being raped, abused, sexualized or something else. Is it so difficult to just make them empowered by default?' (#450).

The bleeding of reaction to the scene of Sansa's rape into a broader critique is evident in the following long response which enumerates a wide range of objections, including lack of faithful adaptation, violence to character development, gratuitousness, over-reliance on rape as an element in representations of women, sexualisation and misogyny:

> It wasn't in the books. It was particularly violent and horrifying for Sansa's virginity being such a major topic of discussion throughout the show, and the fact that this is how she loses her virginity is repugnant. She had already been so broken down that in terms of plot and growing the character, the rape wasn't even necessary as a tragic motivator. Regardless, I'm sick of rape being the only tragedy that could ever befall a woman and the only thing that could make her develop or become more interesting as a character. It's misogynist and a thinly veiled excuse for indulging in the male writer's rape fetish, it's lazy and unsympathetic, and ultimately it's unrealistic and shows a lack of comprehension or empathy for the real life impact of rape. Trauma is an immobilizer, and sexual assault is all the more hideous for how it seeks to devalue and dehumanize the victims, and that crisis of self-esteem will likely always linger. In the end, though, writers choosing to employ rape in a narrative never do so as a thoroughly considered and sensitive action. It is merely the automatic response to the question 'what do we do with this female character' and plays into the voyeuristic desires of the writers and male audience. Rarely is rape depicted in visual media (and especially GoT) and not sexualized – rape scenes are often filmed with same angles and lighting as those used in consensual sex scenes elsewhere in the show, to me implying that the director/writers/ whoever else don't genuinely differentiate rape and sex as experiences. And that's terrifying. (#6296)

The way this account moves from the particular – the adaptation of books to TV show, the significance of virginity in Sansa's story, her history of being broken down, the lack of motivating factors for the scene – to broader issues about rape and representation – as a mark of development or interest or tragic fate particularly associated with female characters, as lazy and stupid, 'automatic' and unconsidered, and as evidence of the wider way that male writers and audiences operate in general – is striking. What it exemplifies well is the way that responses to the scene open up into a discussion of rape culture, even though the scene itself can hardly be considered as an example of the glamorisation of rape, or of the lack of differentiation between representations of rape and consensual sex.

Closing remarks

We reiterate what we said at this chapter's outset: that the task of audience research should not be to take sides in any controversy, but to unpack the nature of those 'sides'. What is the nature of the claims being made, what kinds of assumed commitments or normative criteria are involved, and what light can these throw on the 'terrain of debate'? What general positions are taken for granted by participants, even as they argue? Or, are there fundamental disagreements – not so much over the raw facts of the case, but over the basic frames of reference and 'languages' that need deploying. If nothing else, we believe that we have shown how, in significant ways, debates over the Red Wedding and Sansa's rape carry within them and are permeated by distinct long-standing debates, incompatible discourses which belong in different domains.

This does not mean that we, as authors, do not have our own personal convictions and conclusions on these topics, but we have tried as far as we are able to stand aside from these, in developing our analysis. We firmly believe that any worthwhile research must have a 'moment' when, whatever the researchers may themselves believe, the materials and methods must speak for themselves and be evaluated for their inherent strengths and weaknesses. Otherwise, it is not research, only opinion-swapping. Only through this can progress ever be made in debates of the kinds that we have broached in this chapter.

Notes

1 We note in passing that this was a response from an older female participant.
2 See https://twitter.com/redweddingtears?lang=en.
3 The video can be found here: www.youtube.com/watch?v=wiuahPCq1bU.

8

Making predictions for an unpredictable world

In drawing to a conclusion, we return to some of the arguments with which we began our research. As we noted in Chapter 1, scholars across various disciplines are increasingly interested in popular culture and it s connections to political activism, thought and scholarship. Such accounts deploy elements of popular culture (particularly shows or films, e.g., *Star Trek*, *Battlestar Galactica* and *Star Wars*) as sites of meaning creation (Buzan, 2010; Wedeen, 2002). Some scholars have engaged in studies to test how such texts might have 'effects' on political behaviour and/or attitudes – as in, for example, Shaheen's (2009) study of Hollywood's vilification of Arabs or, in relation to *GoT*, accounts of gender and/or feminism (Ferreday, 2015; Clapton and Shepherd, 2017). In the arena of political science, popular culture is understood to offer a 'social grammar' of the contemporary moment (Kiersey and Neumann, 2015: 75), its ability to be 'at least as influential – or, under some conditions, even more influential – in shaping people's world-views as more "respectable" sources' (Furman and Musgrave, 2017: 503) borne out by reference to such visible indicators as *GoT*'s generation of new baby names and contribution to some politicians' rhetorical vocabularies and strategies (Jaworski, 2017).

The TV show's narrative is undoubtedly centred on political manoeuvrings, but this book has demonstrated that even as there are recognisable patterns to responses, *GoT* offers no singular vision of its politics, no essential message. Readers will hopefully remember that we spent some time exploring the nascent literature on audiences of *GoT* and in particular reflecting on Anthony Gierzynksi's work, which saw in the TV show a tendency to persuade viewers that the world is unjust.

The paucity of such approaches that can see only two alternatives – that viewers are entertained or that they receive messages transmitted by popular culture – is, we hope, illustrated in our research. In 2020, the leading fan scholar Henry Jenkins and two colleagues published an important collection of essays entitled *Popular Culture and the Civic Imagination*. Rejecting negative dismissals of popular culture generally, the book instead celebrates a wide range of instances where popular narratives, songs and events have played positive roles in providing stimuli and imagery for radical initiatives. From H. P. Lovecraft's later narratives to the film *Black Panther*, different authors explore the ways that a 'civic imagination' may be sustained and called into action. The book is important not least for its steadfast insistence on the productive role of imagination and fantasy. Amid an impressive array, one essay in particular stands out in its proximity to our study: Lauren Levitt's exploration of the young adult dystopian series *The Hunger Games*. Levitt finds herself caught on the horns of a small dilemma: here is a book and film series appearing to promote revolutionary overthrow of a (US-imagined) government – yet that series is the product of the very business-dominated system that underpins current governmentality in the United States and elsewhere. What can this tell us about the possibilities of utopian and dystopian imaginings? She looks briefly at the emergence of Imagine Better, a grassroots activist campaign, in association with Oxfam, drawing on the symbolism of *The Hunger Games* to address issues of food and farming. (An attempt by film distributors Lionsgate to block their use of the films' images was challenged and quickly withdrawn.) Imagine Better also took part in campaigns and demonstrations for better pay for low-paid (agricultural) workers.

Levitt concludes by reiterating the core argument of the overall book, that – even though they are the products of a money-hungry business orientation – 'engagement with popular culture can lead to civic engagement through the civic imagination' (2020: 50). This is surely very important, but it does leave unexplored the vital question of *how*? Is it, for instance, a condition of this happening effectively that *The Hunger Games*' dystopia is rounded off with a *successful* revolution – that is, the dystopia comes to an end? Is the story strengthened or weakened for these purposes by Katniss Everdeen's withdrawal from public life at the very end of the final film? Are there any identifiable ways that those who take up the narrative's symbolism and ambitions make distinctive understandings of it – for instance, towards actress Jennifer Lawrence's association with the part? We do not mean these queries as criticisms – the book, and this essay, are wonderfully provocative – but we do think that our study of *GoT*'s audiences can go some way towards positing and answering these kinds of question.

As we have seen in our explorations of favourite characters, lands and peoples, *GoT* has offered its audiences rich resources for thinking about the world of Westeros which they have, to varying degrees, taken up, debated, rejected, revelled in and accepted. Some of these ways of engaging have related to real-world politics, questions of environmental change, the position of women inside and outside the narrative, and the nature of power. Others have centred on how television works; what it means to be a fan; to be disappointed in the journey from book to film; and others have shown the importance of particular characters as emotional types, as rejections of generic types. And still there is more that we could have explored and written about.

The pleasures of unpredictability

In this final chapter, we look at just one aspect that might mark *GoT* as quality TV: its unpredictability. In part, this has been prompted by the marketing and transmedia activities in the lead up to the TV show's finale, which we discuss in our Postscript and by Gierzynksi's prognosticating article in the *Chicago Tribune*, in which he stated:

> I'm hoping 'Game of Thrones' has an unhappy ending because, sadly, unhappy endings mimic reality. I recognize the need to occasionally escape from the ugliness of the real world into fictional ones with happy endings. But in a media environment dominated by entertainment, it's also important to be periodically shocked into remembering that things don't always work out so nicely. (2019, n.p.)

Gierzynksi's article was one among many as, in the run up to the final season, the pleasures of speculating on the series' finale became incredibly visible – surely contributing to the retention of audiences and validation of their investments in the series (Kohnen, 2017: 341) as much as offering plausible narrative directions. In what follows, we explore briefly some of the ways that our research points beyond the dismal choice between happy or unhappy ending, distraction or mimicry. It is important to us to move beyond whether such 'imaginings' need first and foremost to be *positive* (utopian) or whether *negative* (dystopian) imaginings can do as well. The comment below is, we think, striking in its openness and commitment to seeing the series as capable of being important beyond being a beloved example of a favourite genre:

> Fantasy is my preferred genre so naturally I love *Game of Thrones*. As social commentary, this remains to be seen because we don't know the ending yet. We have an idea of what the flavor of the ultimate message might be from numerous interviews with Mr. Martin. So I suspect the social commentary in the end will also be extremely important to me. But since I don't know the ultimate message yet I can't say how important it will be to me. I hope it will turn out to be also extremely important to me. That would be awesome. (#6374)

We did not include a question specifically seeking predictions, and we are not interested in asking whether respondents made correct guesses at who would end up on the Iron Throne (if indeed that was going to survive). Rather, our interests here centre on how our seven ideal types envisage different conceptions of 'unpredictability' and 'futures'. Unpredictability is one of the criteria by which TV drama is judged as 'quality'.

The idea that we are currently experiencing a 'golden age of television' is not new. Many academics, critics and journalists have made this observation since Robert Thompson attempted to outline the generic conventions and evaluative elements of quality TV as 'best defined by what it is not: it is not *regular* TV' (1996: 13). The idea of 'quality' has become central to TV-industry culture as a way of thinking about and practising television. Producers and audiences have come to expect 'high production values' (Cardwell, 2007: 26), particularly 'aesthetically ambitious' (Bignell, 2007: 162) with 'external, occasionally exotic locations' (Nelson, 2007: 11) and 'alternative and potentially subversive representations' (Feasey, 2008: 4–5), offering character development through slowly unfolding stories which make episodes 'seem less like a series of shows, and more like chapters in a novel' (Bianculli, 2007: 36) and with seasons that 'build steadily towards a climax through multiple examinations of a particular theme from myriad perspectives' (Santo, 2008: 28). These *signifiers* of quality are inherent *within* quality programming offering rich, intertextual, serious, nuanced and significant storytelling. A concomitant literature examining quality television moves beyond describing what it is, to what it is *for* and what we expect of it – particularly as audiences. And those expectations, as Jenkins, Ford and Green suggest, are not simply about some singular practice of watching. Instead, 'behaviors that were once considered "cult" or marginal are becoming how more people engage with television texts' (2013: 142).

One of the ways in which engagement is understood is through complex, innovative and rewarding interactions between a narrative and its viewers. As David Chase, originator of *The Sopranos* described it: 'All of us have the freedom to do storylines that unfold slowly, to create characters that are complex and contradictory ... to let the audience figure out what's going on rather than telling them what's going on' (David Chase, in Lavery, 2006: 5). 'Figuring out' is a complex process, as we have seen throughout our discussions here, particularly as *GoT* is such a complex game, with different characters starting from different places; some with advantage over others; where skill plays an ambiguous role; as do the character traits that often denote 'the good guy', such as honour and respectability; even the gods cannot guarantee success in this world. While luck might help a character for a while, it cannot be guaranteed; and magic does not save them either. Nonetheless, some aspects of the TV show are predictable: there will be conflict; there will be hardships and challenges; and there will be death. While it is inescapable that the TV show has been scripted, it invites recognition that the relationships within the game are evolving. As it progresses, and characters die, those who remain, along with their various allegiances and strategies, become increasingly well known. The direction of the TV show has tacked and changed, as one set of allegiances is fractured others become clear and perhaps lead to a reimagining of individual characters as a potential leader. We think that our explorations of the seven orientations demonstrate that processes of engaging with this narrative are more than appetites for knowing what happens next (Barthes, 1975).

Interestingly, Thompson (and others) say very little about 'unpredictability' as a virtue – it seems little more than being 'different', which then itself becomes utterly predictable (Thompson, 1996: 16). By searching the frequency of certain keywords (predict, hope, wish, expect, promise, should, theory) and sorting according to our seven orientations, a few striking features about unpredictability emerge. For Just the Show viewers, there is a general awareness of and pleasure in the show's 'unpredictability'. Some make general comments about the TV show making them think about possibilities, but they are too unspecific to analyse ('they make one wonder, reflect, and predict' (#4418); 'prediction of future events is pretty useless' (#4421)). If there is 'unpredictability', it is almost on an episode by episode basis: 'Who will die this week?' (#4428) Or a 'hope' plucked out of visible grounding: '[Winter] also means new ruler, and gosh I hope it's going to be Daenerys!' (#1), or 'I sincerely hope that Jon Snow and the dragon Queen wind up getting married' (#1621) – such comments show no sign of being rooted in anything other than wish-fulfilment.

Mostly 'unpredictability' can be thought of as being for 'fans', rather than the respondent: 'It is an extremely fan show in terms of unpredictability and characters. I do not find it relevant as a political commentary, though, as its references are not realistic – I'd like to think' (#415). Or, answers can signal the show's *failure* to be anything like a viewer's preferred approach: 'To be honest, in my fantasy I for some reason hope for a more moral society than the one I actually live in. I'm constantly disappointed when *Game of Thrones* represents things that plague me in my daily life (rape culture, white privilege. etc.)' (#1909). Again, 'unpredictability' is welcomed by many of our debaters and they seem to enjoy the idea of 'sharing theories' with friends but occasionally someone jibs at the celebration of this as an end in itself: 'it has also become "the thing" of *Game of Thrones* with Martin and his fans boasting death tolls and how he'll kill a character if it's too popular' (#3218). As we have shown previously, this group has a strand of conscious intellectualism in it, which means that predictions are measured against real world moments in a knowing way, as here: 'I pay close attention to the visual foreshadowing and symbolism in the show and it's very well done' (#1967). Mostly, though, unpredictability lies in 'not knowing what comes next': 'I think *Game of Thrones* is special because it's unpredictable, you never know what's going to happen next. I started loving the show the moment when one of the main characters Ned Stark dies in the first season. What a weird way to start the show' (#7526).

As we explored in more depth in Chapter 7, wild hopes and predictions are to be found in 'Winter...' answers, for example: 'Hope that the Walkers destroy the world' (#756) – or alternatively, 'Genuinely scared and concerned for them. I hope all the White Walkers die' (#4044). Otherwise, there is a strand of pessimism, which makes predictions pointless: 'I expect the lives of the characters to get worse before (if) they get better' (#3129). More extensively we see awareness of the mechanics of keeping audiences engaged:

> For me it is a marketing gimmick. Winter has been coming for so bloody long but it never gets here! For me this is a major issue with the programme – it promises so much but never delivers. Winter never comes, the wall is never breached and the dragon lady has only just crossed the narrow sea ... how long did that take her? (#3314)

At various points, we have expressed surprise at how rarely our Book Followers engage in forms of commentary on the TV show and, here, particularly given this group's adherence to knowing the books, it seems unusual that there is little sense of participating in predictions. There is a strong strand of complaint (coming mostly from those for whom the books are just one part of their involvement) about the differences between the books and the TV show, which appear to nullify people's interest in predictions and the like. This is shown here in a mild version: 'I wish that all books had been completed prior to the start of filming since I always prefer to read the book before seeing the filmed product and then go back and reread' (#911). For our Contented Consumers group we find a willingness to parse unpredictability as pleasurable 'twists'. At one extreme, they almost consciously avoid asking these kinds of question: 'Enjoy it but don't relate it to real world. Probably should though. Actually never thought of it' (#1495). But #2531 gives a much longer and committed answer, listing all the things she loves, closing it with a gasp of simple satisfaction:

> [W]hat makes the show so good and one of my favorites is how the combination of all of those aspects create a world with people that we identify with and just want to see succeed. It's a world I can escape to and somehow wish I lived in. I NEED TO KNOW WHAT HAPPENS NEXT! (#5321)

An extreme example of this fleshes it out, without specifying the *results*:

> I see parallels between the story and our world, but I don't see the story's purpose as a commentary on such. As far as following and enjoying, I legitimately feel that *Game of Thrones* is the single greatest television show ever. Furthermore,

> *A Song of Ice and Fire*, the book series, is perhaps the single greatest story ever told. I say this because of how excited for each new episode and book I become, and how disappointed I am when it's over. It's never enough, and I find myself analyzing micro details about the story to try to figure out the next thing. So many details from stories and dreams have foreshadowed major plot points, which causes me to examine other dreams, stories, and seemingly insignificant details to try to figure out what might happen next. I have never been so engaged in trying to figure out the direction of a story and been so impressed with how it ultimately plays out. There's always more unexpected surprises, despite how much I think I know. (#6845)

The pleasure for this respondent lies in its very openness and excess.

Of course, this is not the only orientation. In this group are also some who are dissatisfied, most notably with the disparities between the books and TV show. One exceptional answer is worth noting:

> Winter, in the context of the words of House Stark, is a threat or boast like any other House of Westeros. The Lannisters have 'Hear Me Roar!' the Baratheons 'Ours Is the Fury!' or the Martells 'Unbowed, Unbent, Unbroken.' The Starks of Winterfell had ruled as Kings of Winter for millennia, conquering all of the North under their banner and demanding the conquered lords swear fealty to them as their King and liege-lord. The words 'Winter is Coming' are a threat, meaning 'If you cross us/declare war on us/slight us, expect our armies to march upon you' as, again, the Starks were Kings of Winter. In the series, I think of Arya slaying House Frey out of revenge and killing all those who slighted House Stark or defiled the realm. I think of Robb and Jon as skilled warriors who lead/led armies in the field, scoring victories and securing their name in the annals of Westerosi history for their skill and valor. I think of Sansa and her transformation from a naïve young girl to an intelligent and calculating young woman who will do anything for her house and see to it that Stark honor and pride is preserved. I think of the North and its loyalty to the Starks, and how despite their ancestors being conquered, they would uphold their oaths and loyalties through thick and thin for centuries, answering summons and banner calls for their liege when the time came to see what their words were worth. (#10090)

This is highly unusual in its detailed forecasting but it also offers a glimpse of the Starks as a vision of alternative politics, they are a 'collective' (as per Ned Stark's exhortation that 'the lone wolf dies but the pack survives') who embody a range of attributes – responsibility, loyalty, vengeance, skill, intelligence – that #10090 clearly admires.

For Fans, as we might have expected, we see much more evidence of 'theories' including reference to theory videos, memes and writings. This group differs from the others in that while there is obviously an acknowledgement of 'unpredictability', this is set against hints of specific expectations formed – #1663 writes (as an older woman) about 'theorising, arguing over what will happen next'. We also see a range of ways of expressing expectations of the ending, from 'I hope it's not a cliché' (#1055) to 'Expect the worst, hope for the best' (#2144). Or even, 'I hope we find out soon, though I'm absolutely terrified to' (#354). But only a very few go beyond generalities ('hope vs dread') to indicate what their hopes and fears are based on and pointing towards. Often, their fears are expressed in very wide terms, about the White Walkers (although with occasional hints of knowing what they are, and what they represent). One answer nicely closes with 'Good luck Westeros' (#9241).

Incidentally this group's answers to our 'personal' question pulled up two things of interest: a sharp split between pro-/anti-feminist views, complicated by some interestingly ambivalent ones. One person writes of being bisexual, therefore having mixed feelings about seeing naked women in the show. Another (#6201) writes: 'I'm pansexual ... so I hope there will be empowerment'. There is a strong sense of wider orientations being operative and on show. And debated: this quote is surely revealing – that fan orientations to the show are infested with wider political attitudes, and this is an issue in itself:

> It ... stands out among other TV shows or movies for how far it pushes the boundaries, at least, of what is acceptable for popular shows in the US. For example, the scene where Ramsey Bolton rapes Sansa Stark after their wedding stirred a lot of controversy, which was kind of fascinating. It's not the first show/movie to have a character raped, but in some ways there was a larger outcry than actual rape victims receive. Why? Also, why were viewers so shocked? Ramsey is close to a purely 'evil' character and nothing in his actions or speech would indicate it was an act beyond him and as some responding to the controversy pointed out, the consent of a woman was not often considered in many 'medieval' societies and even the idea of 'raping one's spouse' is relatively new to be accepted. Also, this wasn't the first rape scene in the Show, so why was the reaction so large for this particular one whereas I barely remember a reaction between Khal Drogo and Daenerys? (#9431)

We have shown throughout this book that Fans demonstrate heightened knowledge of the series, debates around it, as well as the location of both. This is a particularly clear example of working through a political issue both within and without the narrative.

The group that overall tended to express most enjoyment in the TV show – the Players – also show clear pleasure in the story's unpredictability ('love its unpredictability' (#3145); 'I love that I can't predict what's going to happen' (#7013); and 'I'll never get tired of it because it will always manage to surprise me and keep me wanting more' (#1840)). This last answer goes on to talk about the scale and impact of these unexpected elements: 'how one small change at one end of the world is going to alter the entire story'. There seems to be no sign at all in this group of declarations of identity driving reactions. The nearest anyone comes is one who marks himself as Puerto Rican, saying that it has made him especially interested in the characterisation of Dorne – the country/culture most recognisable to him – but it does not lead to a critical standpoint, just interest. Comments on 'winter' all seem very general, as in this complete one (#5608): 'The long night. Long lasting struggle and hopelessness. War among the living and the dead.' Even White Walkers get only occasional mention. The decision between being hopeful or hopeless seems almost arbitrary, as in the contrast between these two answers:

> In addition to concrete winter, bad times, austerity and bad times, but also a promise of better things (spring). I might be naïve, but I hope for some happiness in the end. (#3548)

> Ragnarok, the end of the world. It's a very hopeless concept. People are doomed. (#3697)

Our World Watchers (as we now propose they be called) most clearly overlap with the Fans, in their references to theories and to communities, and – to a smaller extent – to identity-based judgements of the TV show (although an interesting exception is the Muslim respondent (#1669) who simply uses their religion as a basis for choosing what to attend to (Dorne) rather than as a basis of judgements). But they also show signs of a degree of philosophising about the overall narrative and world that is not evident in the other orientations. So, #7282 gives a long answer articulating his personal theory about a recurrent re-magicking of the world, for which he provides examples and justifications; and #7490 *threatens* a long answer but restricts himself to a short summation about the 'rebalancing' of the world through the impact of winter. There are of course also simple acceptances for and delights in the series' unpredictability (its 'unmatched unpredictability' (#1762), and 'constant betrayal of expectations' (#5998)), but occasionally an answer explains in a manner that suggests a way of looking which finds general principles at work:

> I love the book series and show. And I think it's great to show that we can all have different opinions on characters in a morally grey world. There is very little black and white in morality in the real world which gets lost in most fantasy/sci fi such as *Harry Potter, Star Wars, Lord of the Rings*. Those are all about heroes that shine like beacons of honor fighting back the tides of dark evil. *Game of Thrones* is more of different greys all converging in a swirl around one central theme: Power. Some want it, some don't. Some think it should be used to help the poor, to overthrow a kingdom, to re-conquer, to hold back tides of undead, etc. They all have different ideas of what to do

with power and they are each justified and you are able to understand each character. If we could only apply that to reality we could go a long way to solving lots of conflict and problems between people. (#7736)

For some this ability to move between different points of view and character perspectives is a key pleasure: 'The really unknown of the future of the series/books and the wild imagination of George R. R. Martin builds a place when you can make your own theses and predictions. And really enjoy even if they don't happen' (#10210).

Revisiting our seven ideal-type orientations

In the light of the preceding chapters, what can we say now about the nature of our seven orientations? It is essential to remember that these are intended as Weberian ideal types. That is to say, they are not simple empirical generalisations (of which we might ask, what proportions of our respondents fit each one?). But nor are they arbitrary segmentations. Rather, they capture *points of attraction, currently available positions* towards which people can be drawn, even if many move between or combine them. The key difference from Weber is that he described his methodological process for generating them as a combination of two analytic processes (abstraction; and purification) with the subjective insight of the sociologist (constructing an account of a cultural rationale). But we believe that the structured nature of the evidence in our database allows us to identify emergent groupings, deliberately exaggerate their distinctiveness by isolating those who most clearly display the key features, but then also use the resulting groups to go on to compare the ways in which they answer our other questions.

An example can hopefully make this clearer. We were quite startled by the profile which emerged for our Book Followers. We had expected that their declared attraction to Martin's written version would make them particularly critical of the TV show for all its deviations. We also expected them to display a distinctive take on spoilers – since they are clearly already 'spoiled' by their book knowledge. Neither is the case. What we have found instead is a *near-indifference* towards the TV show, evincing some of the lowest levels of enjoyment, and interest in commentary, and debates.

This is not to say that there are not plenty of people who *do* castigate the TV show from the angle of the books. But they are people who do so as part of wider commitments. Such people not only read the books alongside the TV show, they also debate, make fan works, play in various ways. The books for such people are part of a wider critical armoury. But that leaves our Book Followers looking all the more interesting because they veer away. We isolated them within the database because their choice of activity beyond viewing was re-/reading the books – and because we had noted (in Table 3.1, see Chapter 3) a tendency for this to be chosen in isolation. Yet they show few signs of adopting *literary* stances (interest in the different qualities of books versus television) or *hierarchical* attitudes (signalling reading as of greater cultural value than watching). In fact, in most ways, the Book Followers stand very close to the Just the Show group. Reading the books for them seems to be 'something to do', for entertainment; so is watching the TV show. They are two semi-separate, low-gravity activities.

In Chapters 4 and 6 we tried to present some at least of the key characteristics of the seven orientations, we shall not repeat them here. But a few general things are worth emphasising. First, there is a clear general *scaling* of levels of engagement. Just the Show respondents display the lowest levels of interest in many ways – although they are just occasionally challenged for the bottom spot by the Book Followers. Debaters are also close in being low on many dimensions – for them, there are clear boundaries around the levels and kinds of engagement. Contented Consumers are the least political of all, and among the least bothered by controversies around the TV show – but on other dimensions (e.g., enjoyment and commentary) they demonstrate considerably higher levels of engagement. At the other end of the scale, Players, Fans and World Watchers 'compete' for the highest levels of engagement on issues of enjoyment, commentary and debates. However, they pull apart on specific dimensions. Players display the highest levels of enjoyment of the TV show and are much taken with its detailed construction. Classic Fans break ranks over most adopted characters, substantially boosting attention to Sansa (whether criticising the rape scene or not) but emphasising emotionality in other ways as well (they score easily the highest on 'exploring emotions' as a role for contemporary fantasy). World Watchers often give the longest answers to open questions and show high levels of engagement in other ways (e.g., nominations for favourite characters and survivors). And their substantially greater investment in *hope* for something after 'winter' – in both Westeros and our world – is an important finding.

Culture is messy. People live out their lives in complicated ways, adapting and mixing among the possibilities that they encounter. They learn new things; they change their minds. But those possibilities are patterned, and persist, at least for a while. They find distinctive modes to embody them. New cultural forms appear, speaking in distinctive ways to those who embrace them. Raymond Williams (e.g., 2007) famously tried to capture this within his notion of 'structures of feeling' – that is, widely shared feelings and attitudes, in themselves almost indescribable, but which find expression and embodiment in very particular cultural materials (e.g., books, plays, films, television, music or dance). Queried and criticised for its vagueness by some, Williams' concept has still been returned to by many scholars – in particular, in combination with his division of cultural forms into three stages: dominant; residual; and emergent. It is beyond the boundaries of this book to explore all that this might mean in relation to *GoT*, but we want to end by pointing to one strongly indicative element: the issue of *naming*.

A 'Grimdark sensibility'?

In Chapter 3 we noted that we might have missed one important option in our questionnaire's list of 'Kinds of Story': 'Grimdark'. Grimdark emerged in 2008 as a composite term for a subgenre of fantasy writing, but also anime and games, among other things, inspired by words in the game series *Warhammer* ('In the grim darkness of the far future, there is *only* war').[1] The expression broadly refers to a kind of story that either lacks heroes, or whose heroes are seriously flawed, living within worlds of conflict, murderous revenges and pointless wars. As this informal definition nicely captures it:

> What is Grimdark? Take what is good about the world and humans, then grab a bucket of shit and dump it all over both. Toss in a horrific amount of blood, even more dry sarcasm, shove in a cast of morally ambiguous, emotionally tortured heroes that probably hate each other and the world at large, and you are aiming in the right direction. (Best Fantasy Books, n.d.)

Authors typically grouped under the label are George R. R. Martin (seen by some as originating and authenticating the style), Joe Abercrombie, Scott Lynch, Scott Bakker, Brent Weeks and Mark Lawrence. There are revealing disagreements over whom to include. One commentator, Rachel Neumeier, for example, excludes Scott Lynch because of the 'beautiful' elements within Locke Lamora's relationships, which she sees as ruled out by Grimdark (see Neumeier, 2014). Some trace origins quite a way back – to Stephen Donaldson, for instance, or to Michael Moorcock (rooting its origins in a riposte to Tolkien's morally unambiguous world). In the other direction, a zine devoted to Grimdark writing is approaching its twentieth issue, having launched in 2014.[2] This is clearly an emergent organising sublabel.

Ongoing debates examine how and whether to distinguish Grimdark, dark fantasy, and horror. 'Dark fantasy' is an interesting case in point here; this one has variously been used to describe deeply pessimistic horror stories, but was then 'borrowed' by some bookshops to shelf-label Stephanie Meyer-esque teen vampire fiction (on this, see Best Fantasy Fiction, 2014). But there is a persistent sense that authors and commentators are feeling that something of importance, in need of thinking and naming, is emerging – see, for instance, Theresa Frohock's (2015) worried musings (herself an author of a number of fantasy books) about the implications of the term; a fascinating discussion by Basil Price (2016) of its generic characteristics; and the thoughtful blog by Daniel Stride (2019) on the nature of 'grimdarkery'.

Perhaps most importantly for us, a number of discussions of the term revolve around its 'nihilism', and whether that is essentially a *story-trope* or a direct reflection of something about the audience and their broader culture. So, an alternative tendency calling itself 'Hopepunk' (first named in 2017 by fantasy author Alexandra Rowland) specifically sets itself at odds with Grimdark, and insists on maintaining hope in the era of Donald Trump and his ilk (see, for instance, Romano, 2018, whose opening sentence is a virtual manifesto: 'In the era of Trump and apocalyptic change, Hopepunk is a storytelling template for #resistance – and hanging onto your humanity at all costs').

There are signs that Grimdark is becoming a substitute term for 'torture porn'. Rhiannon Thomas, for instance, in a thoughtful feminist blog on the topic suggests that there is a shift in the way we are supposed to relate to characters:

> I think that the Grimdark trend, particularly in television, has inspired a shift in the intentions of these 'torture porn' stories. The writers do seem to revel in showing suffering, but the viewers aren't expected to join them. It's not a case where stories are advertised as 'come watch some ridiculous, grisly murders for two hours!' but where the viewers are invited to empathise with and care about characters before they're put through hell. The Shows revel not just in making the characters suffer, but in making the audience suffer as well, all in the name of 'gritty realism', and being Serious, Good Quality Entertainment. (Thomas, 2018)

The ambivalence in here is both striking and relevant. And it is being given warranty by its adoption and promotion by well-established publishers (see, for instance, Penguin, 2020). It is now a *kind of literature* to be checked out, even to be revelled in.

Thinking of Grimdark as an authorial sensibility that is still looking for a settled name raises a question: how can we best characterise the associated *audience* sensibility? We believe that across our project we can see an emergent shape that can be summed up under two – apparently opposite, but in fact interwoven – terms: 'relish'; and 'anguish'. 'Relish' we think captures all the complicated ways that our audiences respond to the horrible, predictably unpredictable, violent and gross elements of *GoT* (the books and the TV show). It captures the fascination that people display with their own and others' startled realisation that things are going to keep turning out badly. Beginning with the shock beheading of Ned Stark, horrifically watched by Sansa and Arya, the story appeared to guarantee a principle of *doom for the good and noble*. It became just a case of how, when and by whom such doom would be enacted. Speculating on futures, making predictions, forming theories all became tactics for finding order in a world apparently ruled by chaotic brutality. 'Relish' captures the feeling behind reaction videos as viewers watch each other being shocked, or behind the bitter irony of merchandised doorstops inscribed with 'HOLD THE DOOR', 'celebrating' the innocent Hodor's self-sacrificial death. On its own, this relish might be thought of simply as bad taste, uncaring pleasure at the suffering of others. But there had to be enough relish – sheer enjoyment of this awful 'ride' – to keep people engaged and still watching.

However, there is a necessary flipside to relish, which is that people must become sufficiently interested in, if not attached to, individual characters, Houses or causes, to keep hoping that someone, something will survive and succeed. Against all narrative odds, people take sides and fall for particular characters, like or unlike themselves. Or maybe they become intrigued by the most villainous of characters, watch their awfulness with fascination, and wonder if and when they will overstep or trip. The wrench that accompanies seeing a favoured character fall foul of forces that they cannot control, we want to call a kind of 'anguish' – because hopes are broken, possible futures disrupted. The anguish speaks to broken 'arcs' of development and something 'undeserved' hitting them. For some who attach particularly strongly, too much anguish can fracture their relations overall with the narrative world – and they will stop reading or viewing. For others, who have been willing to take on the *principle of unstoppable risk* that seems to underlie the narrative, the crunching of their expectations is more a lesson to be learnt about not attaching too closely – or being willing to live with the consequences. *No* arcs are guaranteed, *nobody* gets what they 'deserve' in *GoT*'s world. But that does not do away with the pain of those moments, the anguish of seeing intriguing characters suffer or come to ghastly ends.

'Relish' and 'anguish': two complementary responses that are simultaneously rationales and emotions. The complex ways that these can be balanced make sense, we believe, of a great deal of the variations that we have found among and across our audiences. Thinking of it as a 'sensibility', or as a 'structure of feeling', must raise the question of the ways in which *GoT* sits within broader cultural frames and developments. That is not a question we can answer in this book.

Notes

1 'The shorthand term "Grimdark" entered online usage as early as May 2008, when it was used as a descriptor in a blog post on the Wizards of the Coast about the newly released expansion set *Shadowmoor*. The blog post, titled 'The Two-Sided Coin', details the vision of the writers behind the expansion set. The author notes that they wanted to create a dark world without getting too "grimdark", as there is still humour and hope in this game's world. In May 2008, the term was used on 4chan's /tg/ (traditional games) board to describe a potential game that would take place in a school of dark magic. The following month, Grimdark was added to 1d4chan, a Wiki for tropes discussed on the /tg/ board. That October, the term was defined on Urban Dictionary and the single serving site Grimdark.com was registered, containing a picture of an angel seated on a pile of skulls.' See https://knowyourmeme.com/memes/grimdark.
2 See www.grimdarkmagazine.com/.

Postscript: 'If you think this has a happy ending, you haven't been paying attention'[1]

When we launched our questionnaire, season 6 of *Game of Thrones* was underway, and seasons 7 and 8 had not yet entered production. The responses we gathered captured *GoT* in mid-flight. Of course, it would be fascinating to have also taken responses to the series finale, but in light of the raging disappointment which occurred in the immediate aftermath of those final six episodes it seems likely that the only information that we might have gleaned would be centred on whether the ending was satisfactory, and the revisioning of earlier seasons in light of such evaluation.

Speculation about *GoT*'s final outcomes had been fuelled well before the immediate run up to season 8; back in 2015 Martin had himself signalled the ending in an interview which suggested 'that while Westeros may be dark and full of terrors, there's a light at the end of the tunnel. He's not promising a blissfully happy ending for his epic yarn, but it won't be a heart-breaking bloodbath either' (Robinson, 2015). Anticipation for the final two seasons was high – when HBO live streamed a huge block of ice being melted with torches to reveal the season 7 premiere date, tens of thousands watched for almost an hour. Even if the promo was roundly mocked on social media, it demonstrated both HBO's intentions to tease audiences with information, and audiences' willingness to participate. Digital media enabled the spread of content across platforms and fans and other audiences undertook forms of participatory labour, discussing and producing different kinds of media relating to the 'industrial' object. Across the very many podcasts, YouTube channels and mainstream media there was a flurry of excited commentary about how the series would end. There is no doubt that season 8 generated the most fascinating conversations and flights of fancy about who would die and who win the game of thrones.

A good ending?

In an interview for *Entertainment Weekly* in the week before season 8 aired, David Benioff and D. B. Weiss (often referred to collectively as

'D&D') seemed aware of the challenges in bringing the TV show to its conclusion:

> From the beginning, we've talked about how the Show would end. A good story isn't a good story if you have a bad ending. Of course we worry. It's also part of the fun of any Show that people love arguing about it. (Benioff, quoted in Hibberd, 2019)

> On the one hand, when you've been working on something for 10 years, knowing you're writing the last episodes is harder because there's a lot more weight and pressure on those scenes. 'Is a line right?' seems more important than in seasons past. On the other hand, the motivations behind each scene are something you've been thinking about for five years, so the foundations in your mind are stronger for what you're putting on paper. But you still find yourself spending a lot more time to get it right. (Weiss, quoted in Hibberd, 2019)

That first observation chimes well with literary conceptions of endings as 'the stopping place' (James, 2011: 6) and the 'scaffolding' for interpretation of the whole (Rabinowitz, 1997: 62). Benioff and Weiss were certainly aware of the televisual legacies that they needed to live up to, and the pressure they felt to get it right for Martin, the actors, directors and the fans:

> We want people to love it. It matters a *lot* to us. We've spent 11 years doing this. We also know no matter what we do, even if it's the optimal version, that a certain number of people will hate the best of all possible versions … You hope you're doing the best job you can, that this version works better than any other version, but you know somebody is not going to like it. I've been that person with other things, where people are loving something and I'm going, 'Yeah, that's okay. I was hoping for more.' (Weiss, quoted in Hibberd, 2019)

Television scholarship is increasingly paying attention to this idea of a 'good ending'. Debates have particularly raged about 'quality' TV shows such as *Lost*, *The Sopranos*, *The Wire*, *Breaking Bad*, *Mad Men*, *True Blood* and now *GoT*. What makes an ending 'good' is understood as giving satisfactory closure, while leaving too much hanging at the end is deemed 'bad'. Jason Mittell has suggested that a proper finale is prepared for: 'Finales are not thrust upon creators, but emerge out of the planning process of crafting an ongoing serial, and thus the resulting discourses center around authorial presence and the challenges of successfully ending a series' (2011: para 8). He has also shown how narrative complexity leads to a number of quite different kinds of ending to television narratives linked to a specific production context; for example, he identifies 'stoppage' as sudden cancellation of a programme, while 'conclusion' is a cancelled narrative that is able to construct an ending that's satisfying to a degree. Mittell's taxonomy suggests endings are often disruptive of the intended narrative construction, but sometimes a television narrative can achieve a proper ending, a planned 'finale' in which answers are given and rewards dished out. For another scholar, C. Lee Harrington: 'a good serial death requires creative foresight, "knowing when to fold 'em" and industry support for doing so, careful planning, and a Conclusion or Finale that is internally coherent, satisfies fans and stands the test of time' (2012: 586). Harrington's essay moves beyond the production context to examine the '*discourse* of death and dying' seen in the increasing scholarly interest in television endings, post-object, post-cancellation afterlife and season finales. Harrington introduces the *Ars moriendi* (the 600-year-old Christian manuals on the etiquette or 'art of dying') as a useful metaphor for understanding televisual 'textual finality' as a matter of coherence and preparation – the culmination of a good run – with 'acceptance of death not as the *end* of life but as a *part* of life' (2012: 582).

'A lot of fans will be disappointed'

This is not a book about *GoT*'s textual features, so we do not attempt to examine whether the series ended well or badly from a quality or narrative perspective. As cast members did the obligatory rounds of interviews during the six months preceding the season, it was obvious that opinions would be mixed:

> It was really satisfying for us. Who knows if it will be satisfying for the fans? I think a lot of fans will be disappointed and a lot of fans will be over the moon … it will be really interesting to see people's reactions. (Sophie Turner, quoted in Vejvoda, 2018)

> I think not everyone's going to be happy, you know, and you can't please everyone. My favourite TV Shows are *Sopranos*, *Breaking Bad*, and *The Wire*, and they all ended in a way that … it's never going to satisfy you. (Kit Harrington speaking to *MTV News*, Sharf, 2018)

Zeller-Jacques describes the discourse of closure and finality as 'discourses of satisfaction' (2014: 114), but perhaps 'closure' and 'finality' are not the only ways of understanding *GoT*'s end. In what follows we can only touch on some of the complicated elements of discursive constructions of the TV show's demise, and how our research might suggest ways of understanding the feelings expressed.

'There is only one war that matters. The Great War. And it is here.' (Jon Snow)

On 6 December 2018 the first official teaser trailer for the eighth season was aired and a second teaser on 13 January 2019 announced the premiere date. Throughout February 2019 further promotional materials appeared. By the time that the official full trailer was released on 5 March 2019, social media activity was already turned up to top volume, and across the podcasting communities, anticipation and prediction were in full swing. Since the final series had been confirmed in March 2017 as only six episodes, speculation about how it would all end had been a significant element of transmedia engagements – teased by posters of different characters atop the Iron Throne and promotional activities, such as Sky's Seven Kingdoms Tour (which took the official HBO throne around the United Kingdom so fans could be photographed on it), encouraged anyone to imagine themselves as one of the winners.

Season 8 premiered on 14 April 2019 and concluded on 19 May 2019. It brought the culmination of the series' two primary conflicts: the Great War against the Army of the Dead; and the Last War for control of the Iron Throne. In the first three episodes most of the main characters are at Winterfell with their armies, defeating the Night King and his army of White Walkers and wights. The final three episodes show Daenerys Targaryen launching her attack on King's Landing to defeat Cersei Lannister, and attempting to take the Iron Throne for herself. Although George R. R. Martin had revealed to showrunners how he intended the novels to end, much of season 8 was original content written by Benioff and Weiss. It is important to note that going into season 8 all was not entirely *rosy*. David Sims wrote that season 7 had:

> a weird combination of its story feeling both sped up and stalled out, with Benioff and Weiss giving the viewers bombastic set-pieces in between countless scenes with maddeningly circular dialogue. We're finally ready for the end times, but I've been ready ever since Daenerys took her troops across the Narrow Sea. In the end, this was the season of the White Walkers, the Show's most visually striking, but narratively inert villains, marching ever closer to an inevitable conclusion. That's what we've done this year. I can only hope season 8 offers something more human – and more surprising. (Sims, 2017)

From the off, season 8 received mixed reviews from critics across both social media and traditional media – the *New York Times* called the first episode 'somewhat soapy' – but there was some willingness to welcome the series' return warmly:

> 'Winterfell' is a cracker of a first episode back, that manages to successfully reintroduce everyone and remind us why we've missed these characters over the long break between seasons. In keeping with latter era *Thrones*, it's not exactly subtle. The writing is fairly blunt, as all the plot strands hurtle towards their respective climaxes, but atmospheric direction by David Nutter and stellar performances from all, particularly John Bradley, anchor the proceedings and give a sense of gravitas. (O'Connor, 2019)

But by the time episode 6 aired, general agreement was that *GoT* was ending badly – demonstrating lack of care 'for carefully constructed mythology' and that in truncating the final seasons, the showrunners had made the 'worst choice in recent television history', so much so that 'Daenerys, once the Show's ostensible hero, ended up feeling like a plot point to be dispensed with, rather than a great and tragic figure to be truly mourned and reckoned with' (Rosenberg, 2019).

Season 8 is the lowest rated on both the Rotten Tomatoes and IMDb sites. Again, criticism ranges across the abbreviated runtime and the contraction of the multiple storylines, failures to tie up those storylines adequately and the apparent jettisoning of what had seemed to be important mythology, predictions and in-world lore. But there was still enough praise for direction, musical score, cinematography and other elements of production that season 8 received a record thirty-two Emmy Award nominations and won twelve of those, including outstanding drama series.

'Remake *Game of Thrones* season 8 with competent writers' (Danny D.)

After episode four 'The Last of the Starks' aired on 5 May 2019, Danny D. started a petition on change.org calling for a remake. The petition went viral following 'The Bells' episode and garnered approaching 2 million signatures. This phenomenon of mass rejection needs consideration. The bulk of this book has been devoted to separating out different kinds of audience and exploring the varying ways that people have responded to the series and the phenomenon. But it is clear that at certain moments audiences came together to make a lot of collective noise – and the widespread anger over the final series is just such a moment. We managed to download a mass of the comments from the petition during January 2020 when signatures were still being added daily.

A cursory look at comments reveals suspicion and hostility towards the producers, with widespread abuse of D&D. Even in more temperate commentaries there is an insistence on the separation between D&D and the audience, whether fans or not. And even when there is recognition that some of the narrative/action/character progressions of season 8 had their roots in forms of fan service, this can only be D&D's failure to understand what fans *actually* wanted. The failure to live up to their obligations would mean that fans would no longer support them:

> I'm signing because the disappointment is so great even after almost a month has passed. I guess D&D were just done and moving on. It's not just a couple

of sore fans disliking the mess that was season 8, this is a Universal Failure which I have heard of not one person defending. I can tell you one thing, I am going to personally boycott any and all things D&D May put forth in the future. And, sadly, that means their *Star Wars* collaborations. Big fan of *Star Wars*. Not a big fan of theirs. They don't deserve my time and/or money!

For many commentators, *GoT* was bigger than entertainment, perhaps possessing even philosophical powers which fans had felt an obligation to evangelise: '*Game of Thrones* had that power, to make an impact over many generations to come ... but no one will remember it, I will never spread the word and nor will my peers ... I still feel bad for the ones I did'. The biggest let-down was the ways in which the season failed to meet expectations, not just for a 'good ending'. Questions and enigmas were went unanswered and unsolved, and there was 'just so much unused potential!':

> White walkers – still don't know anything about them. The many faced god – what's his deal? The god of light – you guessed it, no idea. Children of the forest??? Like what the hell *Game of Thrones*. You build up my hopes just to give me some crappy opposite day characters and call it shocking TV. You think that's good writing?

Posters were also deeply enraged about issues of quality and artistry: 'From scripts to storytelling everything SUCKS ... And we the Loyal fans deserve a ton times better farewell for our lovely Show *GoT* ... HBO can't be so cruel to us ... I beg u remake season 8'. Across the petition (and reflected in mainstream and participatory media), the key villains were Weiss and Benioff, avaricious and ambitious at the expense of fans. Their failure to respond to criticisms, and their pulling out of Comic Con, merely confirmed their lack of respect, and condemning all future *GoT* productions to failure: 'The writing on the wall is clear: the Benioff & Weiss fiasco with season 8 proved that the audience won't automatically like anything made in the name of *GoT*. The failure undoubtedly affected all future plans on *GoT* productions.' As time went on, there was pushback from those who had worked on the TV show, from the actors – Sophie Turner in particular – and the production team, among others, but their assertions of having worked hard, of dedicating their lives to *GoT* were dismissed by some posters, as were assertions that nominations for awards indicated the season was a success, as this poster railed:

> Fundamentally, this shows a lack of understanding about critical acclaim in 2019. You can work hard at something, but if the end product is jaw-droppingly bad, viewers have every right to lambast them for it – and so they have. Series 8 won't be remembered by anyone as the well thought thru climax of an awesome Show. It won't be thought of as the icing on the cake of brilliance. The grand finale will forever be thought of as a work significantly worse than

grand, in fact, it'll be viewed with contempt – as being a bit weird and as a missed opportunity, a let-down – and on their heads be it – that's their responsibility.

Perhaps this comment most obviously illustrates Harrington's concept of the *ars moriendi*, and its emphasis on the importance of death being reflective of the life lived – that the ending of a series needs to reflect the best of what went before.

'It doesn't matter what we want. Once we get it, then we want something else.' (Baelish)

Two things were particularly noticeable from our examination of petition comments. Both hinged on the frequency with which the word 'deserve' was being used, hinting at evaluative frames. First, we look at the ways that the *fans* deserve better: 'Because we the *Game of Thrones* fanbase deserve better'. Apparently, an entire community of viewers – the fanbase – were entitled to more. But more of what? And why? Many things are involved here, but while we do not have the space to explore them all, the following are, we think, emblematic:

> Thanks for 8 years of gobbling up my money from years of buying into your Show. I defended these guys through season 7 because I still had faith in them through it all despite what others claimed, but I've reached a point where I'm too angry. There's no more defending these guys anymore. To the Cast and Crew, I love you guys so much and I am so sorry that your hard work got defiled like this. You guys deserve so much better. I have respect for y'alls. To D&D, I hope you take a damn good look at what you have done to this Show because I will NEVER watch anything you morons make in your lives ever again. You have lost the trust of millions worldwide, including myself.

There is surely a sense of 'contractual entitlement' here, a combination of financial investment and loyal viewing which ought to have been rewarded. But loyal viewing meant more than simply staying the course, it meant joining enthusiastically in the 'game' of predictions, theories and clue-spotting: the panoply of fan activities. Just as McNamara (2010) found with viewers of *Lost*, the perceived lack of closure, or 'answers', meant that many talked of wasting ten years of their lives watching the TV show. For another petitioner, the dedication to *GoT* has had less longevity: 'I watched episode one of *Game of Thrones* then didn't sleep until I passed out spending all my time in my room finishing it, barely eating or pissing and this is how I'm repaid'. But the physical toll on this viewer means that they were also entitled to more. As our research has shown, certain kinds of viewer did not just relate to *GoT* as a narrative, they engaged in its world-building, participating in its enigmas, dilemmas, characters and power plays. The wrapping up of the series, along with the news that D&D had refused HBO's offer of plenty of time to conclude, points to the ways in which the series was in the end a *production*. There is a palpable sense of being swindled.

There is a construction of *GoT* fandom as 'rightfully' deserving, that their devotion, and labour mean they ought to matter. As Kelly Lawler (2019b) put it, the TV show left behind 'a hole in the cultural conversation where passion and anger used to thrive'. Jenkins, Ford and Green write that the industry is 'obligated to learn from and respond to fan expectations, not the other way around, since fans do not owe companies anything' (2013: 61). Indeed, Lawler's articles in *USA Today* make it clear that what fans want *matters*, because 'this story was never in the control of Benioff and Weiss or HBO or even Martin. It ballooned out into the world and became something bigger'. Such that in her summing up she writes: '"Game of Thrones" is dead. Long live "Game of Thrones" fans' (2019b).

'But what of my Queen?'

In many ways we might understand this simply as an indication of viewers wanting an ending that made sense of their investment, and their disappointment that too much had been omitted (Torgovnick, 1981: 6) or unexplored, that there had not been the necessary unravelling of the knots of the narrative, nor the tying up of all the threads (Miller, 1978: 6) to repay the hours of viewing. Yet it is striking to us that wishing for a neat, satisfying ending runs counter to the ways in which *GoT* had been celebrated precisely for its unpredictability. Throughout this book and our research, we have seen how important *Game of Thrones*' complex inter-weavings of different characters and their fates have been. In offering numerous 'endings' – Ned Stark's beheading, the Red Wedding, Stannis's defeat at Blackwater and then death at Winterfell, the failure of the Wildling attack at Castle Black and the botched rescue at Hardhome, Hodor's self-sacrificial death, not to mention the numerous arrests of Daenerys' ambitions – the series required from viewers a refiguring of what had gone before, a recognition that something significant had ended, that allegiances might need to shift. And, as we saw in our research, many viewers had been willing and able to move between forms of relishing reversals of fortune and accepting the anguish of broken hopes (see Chapter 8).

Yet the petition points to ways in which some narrative arcs and allegiances were not to be tested, that some characters deserved better:

Because Aegon Targaryen deserves better than the Wall.

Because Daenerys deserves to hurt with the realisation of what she has done before being killed.

Because Cersei deserves to die like a raging queen because she is one. Her passing away should not be hiding in the basement – totally out of character.

Note the different valences of 'deserve' – the idea of in-world reward for Aegon/Jon, the requirement that Daenerys experience remorse (a moral as well as 'judicial' reckoning for her actions), and that Cersei's 'raging queen' is entitled to a spectacular death. Running a search in the petition comments for each of the top six favourite characters (plus one other, Cersei, on a hunch), and looking at raw counts of 'mentions', we found that adding the word 'deserve' produced some interesting results. Overall in our database (see Chapter 4), the running order was: Tyrion, Jon, Arya, Jaime, Daenerys and Sansa. In the petition materials, the running order was completely different: Daenerys (2,371 mentions), Jon (1,879), Cersei (1,496), Arya (750), Jaime (687), Tyrion (259) and Sansa (214). The rates of coupling with 'deserve' run almost parallel, with Daenerys attracting 15.7 per cent, down to Arya's 5.3 per cent. It is perhaps unsurprising that Daenerys' fate should attract a lot of attention and flak, while Sansa has almost dropped out of view. But what was Daenerys owed, and why? In order to examine this idea, we revisited our database for mentions of 'deserve'/'deserts' in answers to our 'most memorable' and 'most uncomfortable' questions.

First, it seems that mentioning 'deserts' allows people to jump to a conclusion without needing to specify the steps they are going through. They rarely feel the need to add 'because ...' – the point they are making is, to them, self-evident. Second, there seem to be several versions of the enthymematic premises that enable the move. One is a sort of universal (moral? justice?) principle: 'nobody deserves ...'. A variant on this hints at emotions being felt by the person writing to us: 'I couldn't bear that ...'. Third, there are character-specific versions: 'The character just didn't deserve ...'; 'Oberyn didn't deserve ...'; or 'Joffrey deserved everything he got ...'. These point to overall character natures and developments, while a variant is more situational: 'It was only time before he got what he deserved ...'. What's not so clear is what such 'deserving' *warrants*. If Sansa did not deserve to be raped, is that just a comment on the raw cruelty of the world, or a condemnation of the TV show for including it? This can vary, and there seem to be no immediate discursive clues to distinguish them, because of the closure effect of reference to 'deserts'. Thus, the most striking thing about these mentions of 'deserts' is the way that they *close an explanation, needing nothing more to be said.* The person making the comment sees it as *hardly needing saying* because it is so 'obvious'.

Here perhaps we could look to thinking about the nature of disappointment in the ending and to the ways in which there were expectations of the 'classic' happy ending even as formulaic as that described by Fritz Lang:

> The traditional happy-ending story is a story of problems solved by an invincible hero, who achieved with miraculous ease all that his heart desired. It is the story of good against evil, with no possible doubt as to the outcome. Boy will get girl, the villain will get his just deserts, dreams will come true as though at the touch of a wand. (1948: 26–7)

With so many characters and so many narrative arcs, perhaps *GoT could* have provided all of those outcomes – but only if viewers were agreed on who might be the 'invincible hero', or on which characters should hook up. As we showed in Chapters 3 and 4, favourite characters were chosen as much for their 'vincibility' as their heroic-ness, their dreams understood as naïve in a world where magic is often thwarted by brute strength, and good versus evil is at the mercy of chaos – so much so that the idea of viewers wanting an 'inevitable outcome' seems anachronistic. Detailed analysis of the many different ways in which petitioners complained about season 8 is beyond our project here, but we think that we can make some tentative suggestions. First, this project has shown that audiences make complex evaluations of *GoT* and that these are *dynamic*. Throughout this book we have tried to show how responses to the series are not simply a matter of likes or dislikes, but evidence a range of emotions and appraisals. While the petition complaints below draw on 'self-evident truths', their laments about Daenerys' and Jon's fates demonstrate the complexity and dynamism of those feelings:

> Someone actually wrote the words, 'Dani loses her marbles and flames an entire city of innocents'. It's like they got amnesia about 8 years' worth of character building. It's just so inconceivable, jarring, un-immersive, frustrating and plain wrong. The viewer is just left dumbstruck – I find it hard to believe anyone watching that said 'oh great plot twist, this is a clever way to alienate Jon from Dani'.

This articulation of being 'flung out' of the narrative and being pushed to reassess Dany's character suggests that disappointment moves through both emotions (surprise and frustration) and evaluations (jarring and plain wrong) to the point where that disappointment outruns language. Underpinning this complaint is a sense that what was proper for a strong female character had not been honoured – our discussion in Chapter 5 uncovered how Daenerys Stormborn is, for a significant group of viewers, a distillation of 'feminist empowerment'. Thus, we would suggest that the complaint here is about recognising that Dany had a purpose and political sensibility that was 'relatable' for contemporary audiences, which meant that manipulating her character at the last minute did violence to her status as a magical role model. Arguments of this type were made in numerous articles across mainstream and social media, for example in Abigail Chandler's '*Game of Thrones* has betrayed the women who made it great' for the *Guardian* (2019) or Kelly Lawler's (2019a) piece in *USA Today* which saw the TV show's 'woman problem' as its 'original sin'.

In a seemingly similar kind of complaint another criterion of disappointment emerges:

> Fuck that shit. Dany should've been a good guy at the end. Fuck the 'mad queen' shit. And the series' moral lesson should've been that politics around who gets to sit on the Iron Throne become irrelevant when thousands of the dead come to threaten the living. In my view the Show should've ended with Jon Snow killing the Night King on an epic battle in Kings Landing and the battle from S8:E3 was lost. And that Dany became a good queen pregnant with Jon's kid when Jon sacrificed himself for the greater good.

Here, once again, Daenerys deserved better, and Jon too should have lived up to the 'epic' role that we discussed in Chapter 5. But perhaps more importantly the role of metaphor and fantasy's unique ability to address contemporary problems is very clear – the Iron Throne (or traditional politics in our world) are not important when humanity faces catastrophe – the White Walkers (Trump? Bolsonaro? climate change? now coronavirus?). The repeated use of 'should've' points to this writer's belief in the obviousness of the permeability of the 'wall between the fantasy-world and ours' (Barker, 2017: 38). There should have been a proper ending for this kind of audience, acknowledging the story as a reflection on our world and thus offering contemporary viewers a lesson they could reflect on.

To close this discussion, let us turn back to the expression of fan deserts:

> WE THE LOYAL FANS WANT OUR PAY OFF!!! SEASON 8 IS A COMPLETE FAILURE, HOUSE TARGARYENS MUST RULE WITH LIVING DRAGONS BY THEIR SIDE. Yes, maybe this is the most predictable outcome however this is one of those stories where the predictable path works and is justified.

Desiring a predictable outcome, as this last writer does, presents a personal position as one shared by 'loyal fans' while at the same time conceding that this is at odds with the ways in which many celebrated *GoT* precisely for being so unpredictable. Yet these last three comments suggest to us how a TV show like *GoT* might offer ways to imagine a better world and a process of change. Overall, the petition and its comments point to a sense of something larger having been lost in season 8 – the opportunity for the series to have made a real difference in the world. Living dragons at the side of a ruling Targaryen? Predictable? Justified? Perhaps this hints at the ways *GoT* offered imaginative possibilities of different institutions, models for change and future possibilities – or, at the very least, topics for further debate?

This postscript hopefully makes clear that we need to understand 'disappointment' as more than unhappiness with an ending. It reveals some very concrete things about the ways that particular kinds of viewer are engaged with the TV show's whole narrative and perhaps an outcome of the rise of 'fan theory' – the fascination with TV shows or films that leave viewers guessing, predicting, explaining, elaborating, but then almost inevitably leave followers let down when there is any kind of a 'closure' (see, for instance, Alexis Nedd's (2019) appraisal). This sees a collective upheaval as the domineering voice of a special minority of highly committed fans, over-colouring the series' terminus. We are mindful that exploring the petition takes us away from our own data and into forms of speculative analysis. Our research materials were gathered more deliberately and systematically than the comments on the petition, so we do not claim that these two datasets can be directly mapped onto each other. Nevertheless, we do think that our investigations can begin to shed light on why nearly 2 million viewers were motivated to complain. What made it possible? The wording of the petition is very careful in this regard, as much for what it *does not* say as for what it does. It does not even hint at how the series *should* have ended, instead posing the issue in terms of incapable writers. The demand became in effect: any ending but this one. The petition thus carefully created a safe common ground on which people who might have very different hopes and expectations could for a moment unite – even if they all mean quite different things under the umbrella of a general mood of complaint.

Notes

1 This sentence, spoken by Ramsay Bolton, has been widely identified as a notable example (among a small number of others) where a character 'broke the fourth wall', speaking as much to viewers as to 'Reek' (to whom it is said within the episode).

Appendix 1: The questionnaire

Thank you for visiting our questionnaire. If you do decide to complete it, please understand that you will only be able to submit *if you have answered all the multiple-choice questions. Beyond these, it is entirely up to you whether you answer the open questions, and how much you tell us. We think it will normally take around 20 minutes to complete it – unless you have a great deal you want to say to us! You will of course be completely anonymous unless you choose to tell us who you are.*

We have only been able (for financial reasons) to present the questions in English, but please feel free to answer them in the language you are most comfortable with – we will cope!

1. How important is Game of Thrones to you, both as something to follow and enjoy, and as a commentary on our world?

   <u>To follow and enjoy:</u> Extremely Very Reasonably Hardly Not at all
   <u>As commentary:</u>   Extremely Very Reasonably Hardly Not at all

2. Can you tell us why you have made these choices?
3. How important has it been for you to follow debates and controversies that have gone on around the series?

   Extremely   Reasonably   Moderately   Hardly   Not at all

4. Is there one debate or controversy that has particularly stood out for you? What were your views on it?
5. How do you feel about Spoilers?

   Hate them.   Dislike them.   Don't mind.   Quite like them. Seek them out.

6. Can you tell us about an actual case where you particularly felt this?
7. What's your preferred way to watch *Game of Thrones*? With others, or alone? One episode at a time, or several? The moment it's available, or delayed until you are ready? Live broadcast, streamed, or DVD? And do you like to rewatch episodes?
8. Who has been your favourite character (whether or not they have managed to survive this far!)? Can you tell us why?

9. Is there another character you have most admired for the 'game' they have played (whether or not it paid off in the end!)? Again, can you tell us why?
10. Which of the following come closest to capturing the *kind* of series *Game of Thrones* is, for you? (We will learn the most from your answers if you choose no more than three):
    Blockbuster TV (expensive, high impact, with claims of HBO 'quality')
    'Cruel TV' (hitting the audience hard with its violence and sense of doom)
    Dark soap opera (all those complicated family and friendship emotions and interactions)
    Dynastic drama (all about who gets to rule, for a while ...)
    Dystopia (in the tradition of *Brave New World*, *1984*, *The Hunger Games*, etc.)
    Epic saga (such as the Norse sagas, with larger-than-life characters)
    Female empowerment (high-achieving female characters in a world generally hostile to women)
    Literary adaptation (to be measured against George R. R. Martin's books)
    Medieval political drama (a fantastical version of real political histories)
    Must-see TV (an example of marathon/box set required viewing)
    Moral fable (a 'warning' about power and its consequences)
    Sexploitation (featuring an excess of nudity, sex and sexual violence)
    World-building fantasy (creating its own multimedia history and geography)
11. *Game of Thrones* is obviously based on an (unfinished) book series. Is that important to you in any way?
12. Are there other films, books, TV series or games that you would compare with *Game of Thrones*? Can you tell us how?
13. *Game of Thrones* presents us with many different lands and kinds of people. Has there been one which has particularly intrigued you?
14. Which of the following come closest to your view of the role that fantasy stories can play in contemporary society? (Again, ideally, choose up to three that seem most relevant to you.)
    They are a way of enriching the imagination
    They are a way of experiencing and exploring emotions
    They are a way of thinking, from a distance, about the problems of our world
    They are a means of escape
    They allow us to explore different attitudes and ideas
    They are mainly a kind of grand storytelling
    They are a form of shared entertainment

They can be a source of hopes or ambitions for changing our world
They are a way of creating alternative worlds
No particular role
15. Do you have a most memorable moment from the series, one that you like retelling to other people? Could you retell it to us?
16. Has there been a scene which has made you particularly uncomfortable or angry? Can you tell us about it?
17. Have you taken part in any of the following activities, in connection with watching the series? (Please choose as many as apply to you)
Debating its merits and faults with other viewers
Writing about it online
Buying/collecting merchandise
Visiting filming locations
Reading (or re-reading) George R. R. Martin's books
Producing fan fiction, fan videos, fan art, etc.
Enjoying other people's fan productions
Game-playing, role-playing, or cosplay
None of the above
18. Your age:
Under 16 16–20 21–25 26–30 31–35 36–40 41–45 46–50
51–55 56–60 61–65 66–70 71–75 76–80 Over 80
19. Your sex (female / male / identify differently)
20. Imagine you are transported to the world of *Game of Thrones*, but you are no richer or poorer, stronger or weaker than in our world. How would you describe your place in society in terms of ranks within Westeros?
Smallfolk ———————————————— Pretender to the throne
          1   2   3   4   5   6   7
21. Back in our world, how would you rate your political views (and we do understand that the terms we are using are very arguable)?

| Extreme Left | Moderate | Middle Left of the road | Moderate Right of the road | Extreme Right | Apolitical |

22. Where do you live? [Pull-down list of countries]
23. Is there anything particular about you personally that would help us understand your feelings about *Game of Thrones* (whether as books or as TV series)?
24. And finally: 'Winter is coming' – surely the series' most famous saying. Ah, but what exactly is 'Winter'? What does it make you think of?

In addition to the above, the database automatically assigned a unique ID to each completed response, along with a column generating a randomised set of 12 letters and numbers, enabling randomised sorts of responses.

Appendix 2: 'Mentions'

In this research we have evolved a practice of counting 'mentions', as a first step in our analyses of answers to our qualitative questions. By 'counting mentions' we mean the simple calculation within the whole database, or selected parts of it, of the frequency of particular words or phrases. While we hope that this book proves the value of doing this, we acknowledge that it does carry a variety of risks – some purely operational, some more conceptually loaded. Looking at perhaps the simplest case – mentions of 'Favourite Characters' – we clearly wanted to know which characters attracted the most attention. We had, first of all, to identify common misspellings ('Tyrion' as 'Tirion', for instance [we obviously chose to search simultaneously under the two], or 'Cersei' as 'Sersei' or as 'Sersey' [our solution proved to be to search under 'Cers' with 'Sers', although this could throw up very occasional errors, such as words like 'officers' or 'users']). There could also be alternative presentations of words to cope with. While 'Littlefinger' found a considerable number of references to Petyr Baelish, 'Little finger' – split as two words – gathered many more (we therefore searched under both versions of Baelish's name, plus 'finger').

But there were also other, more complicated risks. For example, one character could sometimes be mentioned in the course of highlighting some quality in another nominated Favourite. For instance, take the following extract: 'I love that she [Arya] is rough but really just wants a family, like with Gendry and the Hound (though she might deny that she cares for The Hound, but their dynamic was great to watch and they really came to rely on each other)' (#10458). This generates a 'mention' for three characters, although only one of them (Arya) is being named as 'favourite'. This points to a potentially widespread problem of picking up irrelevant mentions. However, we could see no reason why some characters might generate more such secondary mentions than others. For this reason, it seemed reasonably safe to simply count and compare all such mentions, and to assume that secondary mentions would pretty much even out. This then enabled us to identify those characters on whom we should focus most attention. Most importantly, of course, since our portraits of reasons for choosing characters are thereafter entirely based on *qualitative* analysis of those who *do* positively choose each, at the second stage the risks are overcome. The quantitative measure is simply a precursor, and a pointer, to qualitative analysis. However, the search-strings did remain important as we looked to see whether, for instance, character choices were associated with other quantitative factors (e.g., age or gender).

The relative simplicity of simply checking different spellings of names became more complicated as we applied the notion of 'mentions' to other questions, such as people's ways of watching the TV show. This involved finding typifying expressions, such as 'alone' or 'on my own' – but before using these as search expressions, checking if any were using these in negative formations (e.g., 'not on my own' or 'never on my own'). This therefore required a process of refining search-strings in order to obtain comparable groupings.

The idea of counting 'mentions' might then sound as if it is just a useful technique, to be used cautiously and provisionally. But it does in fact have roots in a set of developments in the early 1980s, in which researchers began to theorise the concept of 'cultural indicators'. Out of this came an international symposium, which led to a substantial volume of essays (Melischek *et al.*, 1984). This volume brought together the work of scholars from around the world who were working with versions of this concept. The book is valuable, but also highly problematic in as much as it conflates three very different traditions of work.

The first tradition – and the one which comes closest to our own work – derives in particular from the work of Karl Eric Rosengren, whose essay in that volume presents a way of analysing literary critics' outputs over time, by measuring the frequencies of key evaluative expressions in published Swedish reviews of and debates about theatrical productions. He argues that these reveal important shifts over time in the *terms of debate* through which cultural forms were being evaluated. What is key here is that Rosengren searches for mentions of *naturally occurring terms* within already published materials. In this way, his work is quite similar to what we would call 'reception research', which connects with the tradition developed by, in particular, Janet Staiger (see Staiger's 1992 and 2000 books, in particular): the study of films through the lens of the changing receptions as evidenced in reviews and commentaries. Our use of 'mentions' particularly derives from the work of Ernest Mathijs (2003), who explored the evolution of AIDS references in published responses to David Cronenberg's films.

The second tradition is very different. It draws most prominently on the work of George Gerbner and his colleagues at the Annenberg School of Communication. Their work, especially on the concept of 'violence' in television, has long been highly influential. However, this work was based on concepts and assumptions entirely different than Rosengren's. First, the concept 'violence' was not a naturally occurring one, rather, it was an *analysts' construct* based on highly arguable assumptions that disregarded all differences between genres, styles, narrative contexts and so on (an early statement of these problems can be found in Stuart Hall's (1973) outlining of the 'encoding/decoding' approach). The term 'violence' is not used by the viewers themselves, indeed that is turned into a *critique* – that it can become invisible to 'ordinary viewers'. Second, their approach presumed that in counting quantities, they were measuring *rising influence* – that violence was being 'cultivated' by the media. Again, this is seriously questionable. But this way of conceiving the 'influence' of the media has spread, to be used in relation to various other kinds of media presentation: of smoking, alcohol consumption, homosexuality, or suicide, for instance. 'Cultivation theory' has become one of the stock theorisations of popular media (see, for instance, Gerbner and Gross, 1972; Gerbner, 1998). We stand very much elsewhere.

The third tradition is different again. Its focus is particularly on international cultural comparisons or finding ways of measuring how societies change and develop overall (see, for instance, Madden, 2005; Kates *et al.*, 2005). Researchers look for markers which can be replicated across different countries which might allow comparisons. Public opinion surveys offer one option. Rates of educational achievement at various ages might offer another, as a possible measure of the effectiveness of government spending. Here, the primary challenge is ensuring that the different sources really are compatible with each other (since countries collect statistics in very different fashions). (The 2020 Covid-19 pandemic has given many concrete examples of this, for instance, in the search for ways of managing countries' very different approaches to recording infections and deaths.)

But in one important respect, our aims are distinct from all three traditions. In each case above, the aim has been to *turn qualitative into quantitative* data. Our purpose has been different, to *enable better* qualitative research, by using simple quantitative methods to isolate groups which can then be explored qualitatively. This is in fact a key strand of our overall methodology.

Bibliography

'A Wiki of Ice and Fire'. http://awoiaf.westeros.org/index.php/Mother_(the_Seven)#The_Mother_song.

Akass, Kim and Janet McCabe, 2012. 'It's not TV, it's quality TV: refining television at HBO'. Conference presentation at Sorbonne Nouvelle, CEISME-CIM.

Akass, Kim and Janet McCabe, 2018. 'HBO and the aristocracy of contemporary TV culture: affiliations and legitimatising television culture, post-2007', *Mise au Point*, 10. https://journals.openedition.org/map/2472.

Alesi, Danielle, 2017. 'The power of Sansa Stark: a representation of female agency in late medieval England', in Brian A. Pavlac (ed.), *Game of Thrones versus History: Written in Blood*. Hoboken, NJ: Wiley, 161–70.

Alhayek, Katty, 2017. 'Emotional realism, affective labor, and politics in the Arab fandom of *Game of Thrones*', *International Journal of Communication*, 11(3): 740–63.

Altman, Rick, 1999. *Film/Genre*. London: British Film Institute.

Anglberger, Albert and Alexander Hieke, 2012. 'Lord Eddard Stark, Queen Cersei Lannister: moral judgments from different perspectives', in Henry Jacoby (ed.), *Game of Thrones and Philosophy*. Hoboken, NJ: Wiley, 87–98.

Anon, 2017. 'It has fantasy costumes, flying dragons and mythical lands … but does liking *Game of Thrones* REALLY make you a geek?'. *Sun*, 14 July. www.thesun.co.uk/living/4018627/game-of-thrones-make-you-geeky/.

Appel, Markus and Tobia Richter, 2010. 'Transportation and need for affect in narrative persuasion: a mediated moderation model', *Media Psychology*, 13: 101–35.

Arts Agency, 2011. 'Culture based segmentation'. https://www.artscouncil.org.uk/participating-and-attending/culture-based-segmentation.

Attebery, Brian, 1991. 'The politics (if any) of fantasy', *Journal of the Fantastic in the Arts*, 4(1): 7–28.

Attebery, Brian, 1992. *Strategies of Fantasy*. Bloomington: Indiana University Press.

Azcona, María del Mar, 2010. *The Multi-Protagonist Film*. Oxford: Wiley-Blackwell.

Azcona, Maria del Mar, 2018. 'Email to Martin Barker'. 7 November.

Bantinaki, Katerina, 2012. 'The paradox of horror: fear as a positive emotion', *Journal of Aesthetics and Art Criticism*, 70(4): 383–92.

Barker, Martin, 1989. *Comics: Ideology, Power and the Critics*. Manchester: Manchester University Press.

Barker, Martin, 1998. 'Audiences Я Us', in R. Dickinson, Olga Linné and Ramaswami Harindranath (eds), *Approaches to Audiences*. London: Arnold, 184–91.

Barker, Martin, 2005. '*The Lord of the Rings* and "identification": a critical encounter', *European Journal of Communication*, 20(3): 353–78.

Barker, Martin, 2009. 'Fantasy audiences versus fantasy audiences', in Warren Buckland (ed.), *Film Theory and Contemporary Hollywood Movies*. London: Routledge, 286–309.
Barker, Martin, 2011. 'Watching rape, enjoying watching rape: how does a study of audiences cha(lle)nge film studies approaches?', in Tanya Horeck and Tina Kendall (eds), *The New Extremism in Cinema: from France to Europe*. Edinburgh: Edinburgh University Press, 105–16.
Barker, Martin, 2013. 'Embracing rape: understanding the attractions of exploitation movies', in Feona Attwood *et al.* (eds), *Controversial Images*. London: Palgrave Macmillan, 217–38.
Barker, Martin, 2016. '"Knowledge-U-Like": the British Board of Film Classification and its research', *Journal of British Film and Television*, 13(1): 121–40.
Barker, Martin, 2017. 'Thinking and theorising disappointment: a report from the World Hobbit Project', *Fafnir*, 4(3–4): 31–48. http://journal.finfar.org/fafnir-3-42017/.
Barker, Martin, 2018. 'Review article: the rise of the Qualiquants: on methodological advances and ontological issues in audience research', *Participations*, 15(1): 439–52.
Barker, Martin, 2020. 'An empirical report on young people's responses to adult fantasy films', in Noel Brown (ed.), *The Oxford Handbook of Children's Film*. Oxford: Oxford University Press, forthcoming.
Barker, Martin, Kate Egan, Tom Phillips and Sarah Ralph, 2015. *Alien Audiences: Remembering and Evaluating a Classic Movie*. Basingstoke: Palgrave.
Barker, Martin and Ernest Mathijs, 2012. 'Researching world audiences: the experience of a complex methodology', *Participations*, 9(2): 664–89.
Barker, Martin and Julian Petley, eds, 2001. *Ill Effects: The Media-Violence Debate*. London: Routledge.
Barker, Martin *et al.*, 2007. *Audiences and Receptions of Sexual Violence in Contemporary Cinema*. Report to the British Board of Film Classification. https://bbfc.co.uk/sites/default/files/attachments/Audiences%20and%20Receptions%20of%20Sexual%20Violence%20in%20Contemporary%20Cinema_0.pdf.
Barthes, Roland, 1975. *The Pleasure of the Text*, trans. Richard Howard. London: Macmillan.
Bednarek, Adam, 2018. 'One annihilates the other, one cannot exist without the other: death becomes her', *Kwartalnik Neofilologiczny*, LXV: 206–16.
Berg, Madeline, 2017. 'Why the *Game of Thrones* audience keeps getting bigger', *Forbes*, 14 July. www.forbes.com/sites/maddieberg/2017/07/14'why-the-game-of-thrones-audience-keeps-getting-bigger/.
Bessel, Richard, 2016. *Violence: A Modern Obsession*. New York: Simon & Schuster.
Best Fantasy Books, 2014. 'What is dark fantasy?'. www.unsungstories.co.uk/blog/2014/2/12/what-is-dark-fantasy.
Best Fantasy Books, n.d. 'Best Grimdark fantasy books'. http://bestfantasybooks.com/best-grimdark-fantasy-books.
Beveridge, Andrew and Michael Chemers, 2018. 'The game of *Game of Thrones*: networked concordances and fractal dramaturgy', in Paola Brembrilla and Ilaria A. de Pascalis (eds), *Reading Contemporary Serial Television Universes*. London: Routledge, ch. 12.
Beveridge, Andrew and Jie Shan, 2016. 'Network of Thrones', *Math Horizons*, April, 18–22.

Bianculli, David, 2007. 'Quality TV: a US TV critic's perspective', in Janet McCabe and Kim Akass (eds), *Quality TV: Contemporary American Television and Beyond*. London: I. B. Tauris, 35–7.

Bigelson, Jayne *et al.*, 2016. 'Maladaptive daydreaming: evidence for an under-researched mental health disorder', *Consciousness and Cognition*, 42: 254–66.

Bignell, Jonathan, 2007. 'Seeing and knowing: reflexivity and quality', in Janet McCabe and Kim Akass (eds), *Quality TV: Contemporary American Television and Beyond*. London: I. B. Tauris, 158–70.

Bishop, Jonathan, 2013. *Examining the Concepts, Issues and Implications of Internet Trolling*. Hershey, PA: IGI Global.

Blacharska, K., 2015. 'Ambiguity in the depiction of Melisandre in *A Song of Ice and Fire* by George R. R. Martin', in Bartlomie Blaszkiewicz (ed.), *A Song of Ice and Fire and the Medieval Literary Tradition*. Warsaw: Warsaw University Press, 211–30.

Bolan, Peter, Matthew Kearney and Karla Boluk, 2015. 'Putting tourism on the throne. In *11th Annual Tourism and Hospitality Research in Ireland Conference (THRIC)*, Letterkenny Institute of Technology.

Boni, Marta, 2017. *World Building: Transmedia, Fans, Industries*. Amsterdam: Amsterdam University Press.

Borden, Jane, 2017. 'Who is the Jon Snow of climate change?', *Vanity Fair*, 6 July. www.vanityfair.com/hollywood/2017/07/game-of-thrones-climate-change-white-walkers-global-warming.

Bordwell, David, 1991. *Making Meaning*. New Haven, CT: Harvard University Press.

Bourdaa, M. and J. L. Delmar, 2015. 'Case study of French and Spanish fan reception of *Game of Thrones*', *Transformative Works & Cultures*, 19.

Bourdaa, M. and J. L. Delmar, 2016. 'Contemporary participative TV audiences: identity, authorship and advertising practices between fandom', *Participations*, 13(2): 2–13.

Boyle, Karen, 2017. '*Broadchurch* was a fightback against many rape clichés in TV drama', *Conversation*. https://theconversation.com/broadchurch-was-a-fightback-against-many-rape-cliches-in-tv-drama-76343.

Bronstein, Carolyn. 2011. *Battling Pornography: The American Feminist Anti-Pornography Movement, 1976–1986*. New York: Cambridge University Press.

Brottman, Mikita, 1997. *Offensive Films: Toward an Anthropology of Cinema Vomitif*. Westport, CT: Greenwood Press.

Brownmiller, Susan, 1975. *Against Our Will: Men, Women and Rape*. New York: Simon & Schuster.

Bryman, Alan, 2006. 'Integrating quantitative and qualitative research: how is it done?', *Qualitative Research*, 6(1): 97–113.

Buchwald, E., Pamela Fletcher and Martha Roth, 1993. *Transforming a Rape Culture*. Minneapolis, MN: Milkweed Editions.

Bufacchi, Vittorio, 2010. *Rethinking Violence*. London: Routledge.

Burke, Joanna, 2007. *Rape: A History from 1860 to the Present*. London: Virago.

Burt, Martha R., 1980. 'Cultural myths and supports for rape', *Journal of Personality and Social Psychology*, 38(2): 217–30.

Bustle, 2017. 'Season 7 is feminist but only for one kind of woman'. 25 July. www.bustle.com/p/game-of-thrones-season-7-is-feminist-but-only-for-one-kind-of-woman-70659.

Butler, David, 2009. *Fantasy Cinema: Impossible Worlds on Screen*. London: Wallflower Press.

Butsch, Richard, 2000. *The Making of American Audiences: From Stage to Television, 1750–1990*. Cambridge: Cambridge University Press.
Butsch, Richard, 2008. *The Citizen Audience*. London: Routledge.
Butsch, Richard and Sonia Livingstone, eds, 2014. *Meanings of Audiences: Comparative Discourses*. London: Routledge.
Buzan, Barry, 2010. 'America in space: the international relations of *Star Trek* and *Battlestar Galactica*', *Millennium*, 39(1): 175–80.
Campbell, Jan, 2015. *Film and Cinema Spectatorship*. Cambridge: Polity.
Cardwell, Sarah, 2007. 'Is quality television any good? Generic distinctions, evaluations and the troubling matter of critical judgement', in Janet McCabe and Kim Akass (eds), *Quality TV: Contemporary American Television and Beyond*. London: I. B. Tauris, 19–34.
Carroll, Noël, 1990. *The Philosophy of Horror*. New York: Routledge.
Carroll, Noël, 1995. 'Enjoying horror fictions: a reply to Gaut', *British Journal of Aesthetics*, 35(1): 67–73.
Carroll, Shiloh, 2018. *Medievalism in a Song of Ice and Fire and Game of Thrones*. Woodbridge: D. S. Brewer.
Castellano, M., M. Meimaridis and Junior dos Santos, 2017. 'Game of spoilers: adapted works and fan consumption disputes in Brazil', *Intensities*, 9: 74–86.
Castleberry, G., 2015. 'Game(s) of fandom: the hyperlink labyrinths that paratextualize *Game of Thrones* fandom', in Alison Slade, Amber Narro and Dedria Givens-Carroll (eds), *Television, Social Media, and Fan Culture*. New York: Lexington Books, 129–48.
Celik Rappas, Ipek A., 2019. 'From *Titanic* to *Game of Thrones*: promoting Belfast as a global media capital', *Media, Culture and Society*, 4(4): 539–56.
Chandler, Abigail, 2019. '*Game of Thrones* has betrayed the women who made it great', *Guardian*, 8 May. www.theguardian.com/tv-and-radio/2019/may/08/game-of-thrones-has-betrayed-the-women-who-made-it-great.
Chandler, Daniel and Merris Griffiths, 2004. 'Who is the fairest of them all? Gendered readings of *Big Brother* UK', in Ernest Mathijs and Janet Jones (eds), *Big Brother International*. London: Wallflower Press, 40–61.
Cherry, Brigid, 1999. 'The Female Horror Film Audience: Viewing Pleasures and Fan Practices', PhD thesis, University of Stirling.
Cherry, Brigid, 2002. 'Screaming for release: femininity and horror film fandom in the UK', in Steve Chibnall and Julian Petley (eds), *British Horror Cinema*. London: Taylor & Francis, 42–57.
Clapton, William and Laura Shepherd, 2017. 'Lessons from Westeros: gender and power in *Game of Thrones*', *Politics*, 37(1): 5–18.
Cogman, Brian, 2012. *Inside HBO's Game of Thrones*. London: Gollancz.
Cohen, Jonathan, 1999. 'Favourite characters of teenage viewers of Israeli serials', *Journal of Broadcasting and Electronic Media*, 43(3): 327–45.
Cohen, Jonathan, 2001. 'Defining identification: a theoretical look at the identification of audiences with media characters', *Mass Communication and Society*, 4(3): 245–64.
Connelly, Roxanne, Vernon Gayle and Paul S. Lambert, 2016. 'A review of occupation-based social classifications for social survey research', *Methodological Innovations*, 9: 1–14.
Crawford, Kate, 2011. 'Listening, not lurking: the neglected form of participation', in Hajo Greif, Larissa Hjorth, Amparo Lasén and Claire Lobet-Maris (eds), *Cultures of Participation*. New York: Peter Lang, 63–75.

Cronin, Theresa, 2009. 'Media effects and the subjectification of film regulation', *Velvet Light Trap*, 63: 3–21.
Csicsery-Ronay, Istvan, 2015. 'Science fiction and the imperial audience', *Journal of the Fantastic in the Arts*, 26(1): 7–18.
Cuklanz, L. M., 2000. *Rape on Prime Time*. Philadelphia: University of Pennsylvania Press.
Dasgupta, Rohit K., 2017. '*Game of Thrones* in India: of piracy, queer intimacy and viral memes', in Kavita Mudan Finn (ed.), *Fan Phenomena*. Chicago: University of Chicago Press, 153–61.
de Haan, W., 2008. 'Violence as an essentially contested concept', in Sophie Body-Gendrot and Pieter Spierenburg (eds), *Violence in Europe: Historical and Contemporary Perspectives*. New York: Springer, 27–40.
Deacon, David, Michael Pickering, Peter Golding and Graham Murdock, 2007. *Researching Communications*. London: Bloomsbury.
Deignan, Alice, Elena Semino and Shirley-Anne Paul, 2019. 'Metaphors of climate science in three genres: research articles, educational texts, and secondary school student talk', *Applied Linguistics*, 40(2): 379–403.
Deines, Brooke, 2017. 'Arya Stark and the role of the absent mother in *Game of Thrones*', *Winter is Coming*, 18 November. https://winteriscoming.net/2017/11/18/arya-stark-absent-mother-game-thrones/.
Depken, Craig A., Tomislav Globan and Ivan Kozic, 2017. 'Television induced tourism: evidence from Croatia', *Urban Economics and Regional Studies*. https://ssrn.com/abstract=3002690 or http://dx.doi.org/10.2139/ssrn.3002690.
Desai, Darshan, 2017. 'How the target audience of *Game of Thrones* has changed'. https://geeks.media/how-the-target-audience-of-game-of-thrones-has-changed.
Dew, Oliver, 2007. '"Asia extreme": Japanese cinema and British hype', *New Cinemas*, 5(1): 53–73.
Dockterman, Eliana, 2015. 'Kit Harington has a point about women objectifying men', *Time*, 31 March. https://time.com/3765148/kit-harington/.
Dolitze, Tatia, 2015. 'EU sanctions policy towards Russia: the sanctioner-sanctionees', *Game of Thrones*. CEPS Working Document, No. 402.
Donovan, William Barna, 2010. *Blood, Guns and Testosterone*. Lanham, MD: Scarecrow Press.
Douthat, Ross, 2015. 'The ones who walk away from Westeros', *New York Times*, 20 May. http://douthat.blogs.nytimes.com/2015/05/20/the-ones-who-walk-away-from-westeros/.
Dry, Jude, 2019. 'Nielsen's first LGBTQ ratings report is here, and gay viewers love *Game of Thrones*', *IndieWire*, 18 April. www.indiewire.com/2019/04/nielsen-ratings-lgbt-game-of-thrones-1202060024/.
du Gay, Paul, 2000. *In Praise of Bureaucracy*. London: Sage.
Duncombe, Stephen, 2007. *Dream: Re-imagining Progressive Politics in an Age of Fantasy*. New York: The New Press.
Eder, Jens, 2006. 'Ways of being close to characters', *Film Studies*, 8(1): 68–80.
Eder, Jens, ed., 2016. *Characters in Fictional Worlds*. Berlin: De Gruyter.
Egan, R. Danielle, 2013. *Becoming Sexual: A Critical Appraisal of the Sexualization of Girls*. Cambridge: Polity.
Eidsvåg, Marta, 2016. 'Mother, maiden, crone: motherhood in Westeros', in Anne Gjelsvik and Rikke Schubart (eds), *Women of Ice and Fire*. London: Bloomsbury, 151–70.

Elkus, Adam, 2015. 'Why *Game of Thrones* is making us stupid', *Medium.com*, 11 June. https://medium.com/zero-derp-thirty/why-game-of-thrones-is-making-us-stupid-68b16267ba00.

Ellefson, Randy, 2017. *Creating Life: The Art of World Building, Book 1*. Gaithersburg, MD: Evermore Press.

Elliott, Paul, 2010. 'The eye, the brain, the screen: what neuroscience can teach film theory', *Excursions*, 1(1): 1–16.

Elwood, Rachel L., 2018. 'Frame of thrones: portrayals of rape in HBO's *Game of Thrones*', *Ohio State Law Journal Furthermore*, 113–37.

Emig, Rainer, 2016. 'Fantasy as politics: George R. R. Martin's *A Song of Ice and Fire*', in Gerold Sedlmayer and Nicole Waller (eds), *Politics in Fantasy Media*. Jefferson, NC: McFarland, 85–96.

Evans, T., 2017. 'Vile, scheming, evil bitches? The monstrous feminine meets hegemonic masculine violence in *A Song of Ice and Fire* and *Game of Thrones*', *Aeternum: The Journal of Contemporary Gothic Studies*, 5(1): 14–27.

Fangs for the Fantasy, 2012. 1 June. www.fangsforthefantasy.com/2012/06/motherhood-in-game-of-thrones.html.

Fathallah, Judith, 2016. 'Statements and silence: fanfic paratexts for *ASOIAF/Game of Thrones*', *Continuum*, 30: 75–88.

Feasey, Rebecca, 2008. *Masculinity and Popular Television*. Edinburgh: Edinburgh University Press.

Felten, Pol, 2015. '"Everyone in the realm has a voice": *Game of Thrones*, Twitter and television fan engagement'. Doctoral thesis, Department of Sociology, Istituto Universitario de Lisboa.

Ferreday, Debra, 2015. '*Game of Thrones*, rape culture and feminist fandom', *Australian Feminist Studies*, 30(83): 21–36.

Finn, Kavita Mudan, 2017a. 'High and mighty queens of Westeros', in Brian A. Pavlac (ed.), *Game of Thrones versus History: Written in Blood*. New York: Wiley, 17–31.

Finn, Kavita Mudan, ed., 2017b. *Fan Phenomena: Game of Thrones*. Bristol: Intellect Books.

Firstpost, 2017. '"Game of Thrones" to inspire philosophy course at British university: author titles it "Politics, Power, War"'. 18 June. www.firstpost.com/world/game-of-thrones-to-inspire-philosophy-course-at-british-university-author-titles-it-politics-power-war-3709235.html.

Florini, Sarah, 2019. 'Enclaving and cultural resonance in black *Game of Thrones* fandom', *Transformative Works and Cultures*, 29, special issue, 'Fans of Color, Fandoms of Color', ed. Abigail De Kosnik and André Carrington.

Fortuna, Carolyn, 2019. '*Game of Thrones* is really a wake-up call to climate change'. https://cleantechnica.com/2019/05/05/game-of-thrones-is-really-a-wake-up-call-to-climate-change/.

Fowkes, Katherine A., 2010. *Fantasy Film*. Oxford: Wiley-Blackwell.

Fowler, Rebekah M., 2015. 'Sansa's songs: the allegory of medieval romance in George R. R. Martin's *A Song of Ice and Fire Series*', in Bartlomie Blaszkiewicz (ed.), *A Song of Ice and Fire and the Medieval Literary Tradition*. Warsaw: Warsaw University Press, 71–94.

Framke, Caroline, 2016. 'Somehow, HBO is still surprised by criticism of sexualized violence on its shows', *Vox*, 30 July. www.vox.com/2016/7/30/12332768/hbo-sexual-violence-tca-2016.

Frankel, Valerie Estelle, ed., 2014a. *Symbols in Game of Thrones*. New York: LitCrit Press.

Frankel, Valerie Estelle, 2014b. *Women in Game of Thrones: Power, Conformity and Resistance*. Jefferson, NC: McFarland.

Franklin, T. G., 2018. *World Building Guide and Workbook*. PaperSteel Press.

Frohock, Theresa, 2015. 'Is it Grimdark or it is horror?'. www.tor.com/2015/11/02/is-it-grimdark-or-is-it-horror.

Frost, Warwick and Jennifer Laing, 2016. 'Travel and transformation in the fantasy genre: *the Hobbit*, *Game of Thrones*, and *Dr Who*', in Philip Long and Nigel D. Morpeth (eds), *Tourism and the Creative Industries*. London: Routledge, 164–76.

Furby, Jacqueline, 2011. *Fantasy*. London: Routledge.

Furman, Daniel J. and Paul Musgrave, 2017. 'Synthetic experiences: how popular culture matters for images of international relations', *International Studies Quarterly*, 61: 503–16.

Galtung, Johan, 1990. 'Cultural violence', *Journal of Peace Research*, 27(3): 291–305.

Gaut, Berys, 1993. 'The paradox of horror', *British Journal of Aesthetics*, 34(4): 333–45.

Genz, Stéphanie, 2016. '"I'm not going to fight them, I'm going to fuck them": sexist liberalism and gender (a)politics in *Game of Thrones*', in Anne Gjelsvik and Rikke Schubart (eds), *Women of Ice and Fire*. London: Bloomsbury, 243–62.

Gerbner, George. 1998. 'Cultivation analysis: an overview', *Mass Communication and Society*, 1(3–4): 175–94.

Gerbner, G. and L. Gross, 1972. 'Living with television: the violence profile', *Journal of Communication*, 26(2): 173–99.

Gierzynski, Anthony, 2018. *The Political Effects of Entertainment Media*. Lanham, MD: Lexington Books.

Gierzynski, Anthony, 2019. 'Don't give us a happy ending, "Game of Thrones"', *Chicago Tribune*. www.chicagotribune.com/opinion/commentary/ct-perspec-game-of-thrones-unhappy-ending-20190411-story.html.

Gierzynski, Anthony and Kathryn Eddy, 2013. *Harry Potter and the Millennials*. Baltimore, MD: Johns Hopkins University Press.

Gill, Rosalind and Shani Orgad, 2018. 'The shifting terrain of sex and power: from the "sexualization of culture" to #MeToo', *Sexualities*, 21(8): 1313–24.

Gillett, Stephen L. and Ben Bova, 2015. *World-Building*. ReAnimus Press.

Gjelsvik, Anne, 2016. 'Unspeakable acts of (sexual) terror as/in quality television', in Anne Gjelsvik and Rikke Schubart (eds), *Women of Ice and Fire*. London: Bloomsbury, 57–78.

Gjelsvik, Anne and Rikke Schubart, eds, 2016. *Women of Ice and Fire*. London: Bloomsbury.

Goodwin, Jeff, James M. Jasper and Francesca Polletta, eds, 2001. *Passionate Politics: Emotions and Social Movements*. Chicago: University of Chicago Press.

Green, Melanie C., Timothy C. Brock and Geoff F. Kaufman, 2008. 'Understanding media enjoyment: the role of transportation into narrative worlds', *Communication Theory*, 14(4): 311–27.

Gresham, Karin, 2015. 'Cursed womb, bulging thighs and bald scalp: George R. R. Martin's grotesque queen', in Jes Battis and Susan Johnston (eds), *Mastering the Game of Thrones*. Jefferson, NC: McFarland, 151–69.

Grodal, Torben, 2009. *Embodied Visions: Evolution, Emotion, Culture, Film*. Oxford: Oxford University Press.

Hagen, Ingunn, 1999. 'Slaves of the ratings tyranny? Media images of the audience', in Pertti Alasuutari (ed.), *Rethinking the Media Audience*. London: Sage, 130–50.
Halberstam, Jack, 2017. 'Post-election commentary: winter is coming!', *Educational Studies*, 53(1): 95–7.
Hall, Stuart, 1973. 'Encoding and decoding in the television discourse', Paper for the Council of Europe. https://scholar.google.co.uk/scholar?hl=en&as_sdt=0%2C5&q=Encoding+and+decoding+in+the+television+discourse&btnG=.
Hannell, Briony, 2016. 'Controversy, Sexual Violence and the Critical Reception of Game of Thrones' "Unbowed, Unbent, Unbroken"', PhD dissertation, University of East Anglia.
Hannell, Briony, 2017. 'Restoring the balance: feminist meta-texts and the productivity of Tumblr's *Game of Thrones* fans', in Kavita Mudan Finn (ed.), *Fan Phenomena: Game of Thrones*. Bristol: Intellect Books, 70–81.
Hardt, Michael and Antonio Negri, 2001. *Empire*. New Haven, CT: Harvard University Press.
Harrington, C. Lee, 2012. 'The *ars moriendi* of US serial television: towards a good textual death', *International Journal of Cultural Studies*, 16(6): 579–95.
Harrison, Mia, 2018. 'Power and punishment in *Game of Thrones*', in Joe Leeson-Schatz and Amber George (eds), *The Image of Disability: Essays on Media Representations*. Jefferson, NC: McFarland, 28–43.
Harvey, Dan and Drew Nelles, 2014. 'Cripples, bastards, and broken things: disability in *Game of Thrones*', *Hazlitt*, 10 June. www.randomhouse.ca/hazlitt/feature/cripples-bastards-and-broken-things-disability-game-of-thrones.
Hassler-Forest, Dan, 2014. '*Game of Thrones*: quality television and the cultural logic of gentrification', *TV/Series*, 6.
Hassler-Forest, Dan, 2016a. 'Skimmers, dippers, and divers: Campfire's Steve Coulson on transmedia marketing and audience participation', *Participations*, 13(1): 682–92.
Hassler-Forest, Dan, 2016b. *Science Fiction, Fantasy and Politics*. New York: Rowman & Littlefield.
Hasson, Uri *et al.*, 2008. 'Vase or face? A neural correlate of shape-selecting grouping processes in the human brain', *Journal of Cognitive Neuroscience*, 13(6): 744–53.
Heller-Nicholas, A., 2009. 'Last trope on the left: rape, film and the melodramatic imagination', *Limina*, 15: 1–13.
Henning, Bernt and Peter Vorderer, 2001. 'Psychological escapism: predicting the amount of television viewing by need for cognition', *Journal of Communication*, 51(1): 100–20.
Hibberd, James, 2019. '*Game of Thrones* season 8 showrunners interview: "This is where the story ends"', *Entertainment Weekly*, 9 April. https://ew.com/tv/2019/04/09/game-of-thrones-season-8-showrunners-interview/.
Higgins, L. A. and B. R. Silver, 1991. *Rape and Representation*. New York: Columbia University Press.
Hill, Annette, 1997. *Shocking Entertainment*. Luton: University of Luton Press.
Hill, L., 2015. '"Game of Thrones" recap: another brutal wedding, another vicious rape', *Salon*. www.salon.com/2015/05/18/game_of_thrones_recap_the_honor_of_your_presence_is_requested_at_another_brutal_wedding/.
Historical Materialism, 2002, 10(4), special issue, ed. China Miéville.
Hodgson, N., 2017. 'How *Game of Thrones* reflects historical anxieties about women, motherhood and power', *Conversation*, 21 July. https://theconversation.com/how-game-of-thrones-reflects-historical-anxieties-about-women-motherhood-and-power-81043.

Holbrook, Morris B., 1999. 'Popular appeal versus expert judgments of motion pictures', *Journal of Consumer Research*, 26(2): 144–55.
Holloway, I. and L. Todres, 2003. 'The status of method: flexibility, consistency and coherence', *Qualitative Research*, 3: 345–57.
Hootsuite, 2018. 'How 20 brands are celebrating *Game of Thrones* on social media'. https://blog.hootsuite.com/brands-celebrate-game-thrones-social-media/.
Horeck, Tanya, 2004. *Public Rape: Representing Violation in Fiction and Film*. London: Routledge.
Horeck, Tanya, 2014. '#AskThicke: "Blurred Lines," rape culture, and the feminist hashtag takeover', *Feminist Media Studies*, 14(6): 1105–7.
Horeck, Tanya and Tina Kendall, eds, 2011. *The New Extremism in Cinema: From France to Europe*. Edinburgh: Edinburgh University Press.
Hovey, Jaime, 2015. 'Tyrion's gallantry', *Critical Quarterly*, 57(1): 86–98.
Howe, A., 2015. 'The hand of the artist: fan art in the Martinverse', in Jes Battis and Susan Johnston (eds), *Mastering the Game of Thrones*. Jefferson, NC: McFarland, 243–61.
Hudson, L., 2015. 'Rape scenes aren't just awful. They're lazy writing', *Wired*. www.wired.com/2015/06/rape-scenes/.
Hughes, S., 2011. '*Game of Thrones*: season one, episode nine', *Guardian*, 13 June. www.theguardian.com/tv-and-radio/tvandradioblog/2011/jun/13/game-of-thrones-season-one-episode-nine.
Irimiás, Anna, Ariel Mitev and Gábor Michalkó, 2017. 'Thematic guided tours to co-create film tourism experiences: the case of the *Game of Thrones*', *Revista Turismo & Desenvolvimento*, 27/28: 451–3.
Irwin, William and Henry Jacoby, eds, 2012. *Game of Thrones and Philosophy: Logic Cuts Deeper than Swords*. Hoboken, NJ: John Wiley & Sons.
Itzkoff, D., 2014. 'For "Game of Thrones," rising unease over rape's recurring role', *New York Times*. www.nytimes.com/2014/05/03/arts/television/for-game-of-thrones-rising-unease-over-rapes-recurring-role.html?_r=1.
James, Henry, 2011 [1909]. *The Art of the Novel: Critical Prefaces*. Chicago: University of Chicago Press.
Jancovich, Mark and James Lyons, eds, 2003. *Quality Popular Television*. London: British Film Institute.
Jaworski, Michelle, 2017. '6 ways "Game of Thrones" has changed the real world', *Daily Dot*, 19 September. www.dailydot.com/parsec/game-of-thrones-references-names/.
Jenkins, Henry, 2008. *Convergence Culture*. New York: New York University Press.
Jenkins, Henry, Sam Ford and Joshua Green, 2013. *Spreadable Media*. New York: New York University Press.
Jepson, Rich, 2017. *Brain of Thrones: A Game of Thrones Quiz Book*. Independent Publication.
Johnston, Susan, 2011. '*Harry Potter*, eucatastrophe, and Christian hope', *Logos*, 14(1): 66–90.
Johnston, Susan, 2012. 'Grief poignant as joy: dyscatastrophe and eucatastrophe in A Song of Ice and Fire', *Mythlore*, 31(1): 135–55.
Jones, Rebecca, 2012. 'A game of genders: comparing depictions of empowered women between a *Game of Thrones* novel and television series', *Journal of Student Research*, 1(3): 14–21.
Jowett, L., 2010. 'Rape, power, realism and the fantastic on television', in S. Gunne and Z. B. Thompson (eds), *Feminism, Literature and Rape Narratives*. London: Routledge, 217–32.

Kar, Debarun, *et al.*, 2015. '"A Game of Thrones": when human behavior models compete in repeated Stackelberg security games', *Proceedings of the 14th International Conference on Autonomous Agents and Multiagent Systems.*

Kates, Robert W., Thomas M. Parris and Anthony A. Leiserowitz, 2005. 'What is sustainable development? Goals, indicators, values, and practices', *Environment*, 47(3): 8–21.

Katz, Elihu and David Foulkes, 1962. 'On the use of the mass media as "escape": clarification of a concept', *Public Opinion Quarterly*, 26(3): 377–88.

Kaya, Ş., 2019. 'Gender and violence: rape as a spectacle on prime-time television', *Social Science Information*, 58(4): 681–700.

Kennedy, Julia and Clarissa Smith, 2012. 'His soul shatters at about 0.23: Spankwire, self-scaring and hyperbolic shock', in Feona Attwood *et al.* (eds), *Controversial Images*. Basingstoke: Palgrave Macmillan, 239–53.

Kermode, Mark, 1997. 'I was a teenage horror fan: or, How I learned to stop worrying and love Linda Blair', in Martin Barker and Julian Petley (eds), *Ill Effects*. London: Routledge, 57–66.

Kiersey, Nicholas and Iver Neumann, 2015. 'Worlds of our making in science fiction and international relations', in F. Caso and C. Hamilton (eds), *Popular Culture and World Politics*. Bristol: E-International Publication, 74–82.

Klastrup, Lisbeth and Susana Tosca, 2014. '*Game of Thrones*: transmedial worlds, fandom, and social gaming', in Marie-Laure Ryan and Jan-Noël Thon (eds), *Storyworlds across Media*. Lincoln, NE: University of Nebraska Press, 295–314.

Kohnen, M. E., 2017. 'Fannish affect, "quality", fandom, and transmedia storytelling campaigns', in Melissa A. Click and Susanne Scott (eds), *The Routledge Companion to Media Fandom*. London: Routledge, 337–46.

Kornhaber, S., C. Orr and A. Sullivan, 2015. 'Why Sansa's wedding night was a mistake for "Game of Thrones"', *Atlantic*, 18 May. www.theatlantic.com/entertainment/archive/2015/05/game-of-thrones-roundtable-season-5-episode-six-unbowed-unbent-unbroken/393503/.

Kozinsky, Beth, 2015. '"A thousand bloodstained hands": the malleability of flesh and identity', in Jes Battis and Susan Johnston (eds), *Mastering the Game of Thrones*. Jefferson, NC: McFarland, 170–80.

Kriss, Sam, 2015. '*Game of Thrones* and the end of Marxist theory', *Jacobin*, 4 October. www.jacobinmag.com/2015/04/game-of-thrones-season-five-marxism/.

Kustritz, Anne, 2016. '"They all lived happily ever after. Obviously": realism and utopia in *Game of Thrones*-based alternate universe fairy tale fan fiction', *Humanities*, 5(2): 43.

Lacob, Jace, 2012. 'Kit Harington on *Game of Thrones*, fame, and playing emo hero Jon Snow', *Daily Beast*, 9 April. www.thedailybeast.com/kit-harington-on-game-of-thrones-fame-and-playing-emo-hero-jon-snow.

Lakoff, George and Mark Johnson, 1980. *Metaphors We Live By*. Chicago: University of Chicago Press.

Lang, Fritz, 1948. 'Happily ever after', in Roger Manvell (ed.), *Penguin Film Review* 5. Harmondsworth: Penguin, 22–9.

Lannister, Jammy. 2016. *Game of Scones: All Men Must Dine*. London: Trapeze.

Larrington, Carolyne, 2015. *Winter is Coming: The Medieval World of Game of Thrones*. London: I. B. Tauris.

Larrington, Carolyne, 2019. *All Men Must Die: Lethal Love and Fatal Attraction in Game of Thrones*. London: I. B. Tauris.

Larsson, Mariah, 2016. 'Adapting sex: cultural conceptions of sexuality in words and images', in Anne Gjelsvik and Rikke Schubart (eds), *Women of Ice and Fire*. London: Bloomsbury, 17–38.
Latitude, 2014. 'My *Game of Thrones*: an audience self-portrait'. https://latd.com/blog/study-latitude-gets-close-personal-game-thrones-fans/.
Lavery, David, 2006. *Reading the Sopranos: Hit TV from HBO*. London: Bloomsbury.
Lawler, Kelly, 2019a. 'Sadly, "Game of Thrones" never fixed its problem with women, even in the series finale', *USA Today*, 16 May. https://eu.usatoday.com/story/life/tv/2019/05/16/game-of-thrones-hbo-never-learned-how-write-women-characters-dany-cersei-sansa-mad-queen/3666640002/.
Lawler, Kelly, 2019b. 'The "Game of Thrones" finale tarnished its legacy, but the anger and joy of fans lives on', *USA Today*, 21 May. https://eu.usatoday.com/story/life/tv/2019/05/21/game-of-thrones-tarnished-legacy-fan-anger-series-finale-iron-throne/3692682002/.
Lawler, Kelly, 2019c. 'A disaster ending that fans didn't deserve', *USA Today*, 15 December. https://eu.usatoday.com/story/life/tv/2019/05/19/game-of-thrones-recap-series-finale-season-8-episode-6-the-iron-throne-jon-dany-arya-sansa-bran/3704539002/.
Le Guin, Ursula, 1979. *The Language of the Night*, ed. Susan Wood. New York: Perigee Books.
Leigh, David J., 2008. *Apocalyptic Patterns in Twentieth-Century Fiction*. Notre Dame, IN: University of Notre Dame Press.
Leverette, M., B. L. Ott and C. L. Buckley, eds, 2008. *It's Not TV: Watching HBO in the Post-television Era*. London: Routledge.
Levitas, Ruth, 2013. *Utopia as Method: The Imaginary Reconstitution of Society*. Basingstoke: Palgrave Macmillan.
Levitt, Lauren, 2020. '*The Hunger Games* and the civic imagination', in Henry Jenkins *et al.* (eds), *Popular Culture and the Civic Imagination*. New York: New York University Press, 43–50.
Lewis, Justin, 1997. 'What counts in cultural studies', *Media, Culture and Society*, 19(1): 83–97.
Locke, Hilary Jane, 2018. 'Beyond "tits and dragons": medievalism, medieval history, and perceptions in *Game of Thrones*', in Marina Gerzic and Aidan Norrie (eds), *From Medievalism to Early-Modernism: Adapting the English Past*. New York: Routledge, 171–87.
Lovelock, James, 2016. *Gaia: A New Look at Life on Earth*. Oxford: Oxford University Press.
Lozano Delmar, Javier and Mélanie Bourdaa, 2015. 'Case study of French and Spanish fan reception of *Game of Thrones*', *Transformative Works and Cultures* 19, special issue, 'European Fans and European Fan Objects: Localization and Translation', ed. Anne Kustritz.
Lushkov, Ayelet Haimson, 2017. '*You Win or You Die*': *The Ancient World of Game of Thrones*. London: I. B. Tauris.
Lyons, Margaret, 2012. 'Is *Game of Thrones* for nerds?', *Vulture* (New York), 29 March. www.vulture.com/2012/03/game-of-thrones-nerds-dungeons-dragons.html.
Maccoby, E. E. and W. C. Wilson, 1957. 'Identification and observational learning from films', *Journal of Abnormal and Social Psychology*, 55(1): 76–87.
Madden, Christopher, 2005. 'Indicators for arts and cultural policy: a global perspective', *Cultural Trends*, 14(3): 217–47.

Maibach, Edward, Anthony Leiserowitz, Connie Roser-Renouf, 2009. 'Global warming's six Americas: a segmentation analysis', Yale Project on Climate Change. https://trid.trb.org/view/889822.

Marcotte, A., 2014. 'The director of Sunday's *Game of Thrones* doesn't think that was rape', *Slate*. www.slate.com/blogs/xx_factor/2014/04/21/game_of_thrones_rape_director_alex_graves_says_the_sex_becomes_consensual.html.

Mardorossian, C. M., 2004. 'Toward a new feminist theory of rape', *Gender Studies*, 3: 243–75.

Mares, Nicole M., 2017. 'Writing the rules of their own game: medieval female agency and *Game of Thrones*', in Brian A. Pavlac (ed.), *Game of Thrones versus History*. New York: Wiley, 147–60.

Markelz, Michelle, 2017. 'How Iceland rode a social wave to tourism success', American Marketing Association. www.ama.org/publications/MarketingNews/Pages/how-iceland-rode-a-social-wave-to-tourism-success.aspx.

Marnell, B., 2015. 'Game of Thrones 5.06 "Unbowed, Unbent, Unbroken" review', *Crave Online*. www.craveonline.com/site/857513-game-thrones-5-06-unbowed-unbent-unbroken-review.

Mason, Paul, 2015. 'Can Marxist theory predict the end of *Game of Thrones*?', *Guardian*, 6 April. www.theguardian.com/tv-and-radio/2015/apr/06/marxist-theory-game-of-thrones-lannisters-bankers-sex-power-feudal-westeros-revolution.

Mathews, Jana, 2018. 'Cinematic thanatourism and the purloined past: the "*Game of Thrones* effect" and the effect of *Game of Thrones* on history', in Kathryn M. McDaniel (ed.), *Virtual Dark Tourism*. Basingstoke: Palgrave, 89–112.

Mathijs, Ernest, 2003. 'AIDS references in the critical reception of David Cronenberg: "It may not be such a bad disease after all"', *Cinema Journal*, 42(4): 29–45.

Mathijs, Ernest, ed., 2007. *The Cult Cinema Reader*. Milton Keynes: Open University Press.

Matthews, Jolie Christine, 2018. 'A past that never was: historical poaching in *Game of Thrones* fans' Tumblr practices', *Popular Communication*, 16(3): 225–42.

McCabe, Janet and Kim Akass, 2007. 'Sex, swearing and respectability: courting controversy, HBO's original programming and producing quality TV', in Janet McCabe and Kim Akass (eds), *Quality TV: Contemporary American Television and Beyond*. London: I. B. Taurus, 62–76.

McCabe, Janet and Kim Akass, 2008a. 'What has HBO ever done for women?', in G. R. Edgerton and J. P. Jones (eds), *The Essential HBO Reader*. Lexington, KY: University Press of Kentucky, 303–14.

McCabe, Janet and Kim Akass, 2008b. 'It's not TV, it's HBO's original programming: producing quality TV', in Mark Leverette, Brian L. Ott and Cara Louise Buckley (eds.), *It's Not TV: Watching HBO in the Post-television Era*. London: Routledge, 95–106.

McCabe, Janet and Kim Akass, eds, 2007. *Quality TV: Contemporary American Television and Beyond*. London: I. B. Tauris.

McKay, Hattie, 2018. 'The feminists are coming: a critical analysis of Melisandre and feminism in *Game of Thrones*', *Relics, Remnants, and Religion: An Undergraduate Journal*, 3(1): article 7.

McNally, V., 2015. 'An expert explains why "Game Of Thrones" can't "just throw" their rape story line in one episode', *MTV News*. www.mtv.com/news/2163324/game-of-thrones-rape-portrayal.

McNamara, M., 2010. 'Of love "lost"', *Los Angeles Times*, 24 May. www.latimes.com/entertainment/tv/la-et-lost-review-20100524-story.html.

McNeill, Kate, 2017. 'Torrenting *Game of Thrones*: so wrong, and yet so right', *Convergence*, 23(5): 545–62.

McNutt, Myles, 2018. *Game of Thrones: A Viewer's Guide*. San Francisco: Chronicle Books.

MediaCom, 2015. 'Client: Sky campaign: *Game of Thrones* best newspaper campaign'. www.newsworks.org.uk/write/MediaUploads/1%20Research/Case%20Studies/2015/Awards/Sky_-_Game_of_Thrones_case_study.pdf.

Meisterhans, Nadja, 2016. 'The World Health Organization in crisis – lessons to be learned beyond the ebola outbreak', *Chinese Journal of World Governance*, 2:1.

Melischek, Gabriele, Karl Erik Rosengren and James Stappers, eds, 1984. *Cultural Indicators: An International Symposium*. Vienna: Verlag der Osterreichen Akademie der Wissenschaften.

Mendlesohn, Farah, 2008. *Rhetorics of Fantasy*. Middletown, CT: Wesleyan University Press.

Michelle, Carolyn, 2007. 'Modes of reception: a consolidated analytical framework', *Communication Review*, 10(3): 181–222.

Michelle, Carolyn, Charles H. Davis, Ann Hardy and Craig Hight, 2018. 'Response to Martin Barker's "Rise of the Qualiquants"', *Participations*, 15(2): 376–99.

Michelle, Carolyn, Charles H. Davis and Florin Vladica, 2012. 'Understanding variation in audience engagement and response: an application of the composite model to receptions of *Avatar* (2009)', *Communication Review*, 15: 106–43.

Milkoreit, Manjana, 2019. 'Pop-cultural mobilization: deploying *Game of Thrones* to shift US climate change politics', *International Journal of Politics, Culture & Society*, 32(1): 61–82.

Miller, Clark A., 2006. 'Climate change and global political order', in Sheila Jasanoff (ed.), *States of Knowledge: The Co-Production of Science and the Social Order*. New York: Routledge, 46–66.

Miller, J. H., 1978. 'The problematic of ending in narrative', *Nineteenth-Century Fiction*, 33(1): 3–7.

Mills, J., 1995. 'Screening rape', *Index on Censorship*, 24(6): 37–40.

Mittell, Jason, 2011. 'Preparing for the end: metafiction in the final seasons of *The Wire* and *Lost*', presentation at Society for Cinema and Media Studies Conference, New Orleans. https://justtv.wordpress.com/2011/03/13/preparing-for-the-end-metafiction-in-the-final-Seasons-of-the-wire-and-lost/.

Mølstad, Christina E., Daniel Petterson and Eva Forsberg, 2017. 'A game of thrones: organising and legitimising knowledge through PISA research', *European Education Research Journal*, 16(6): 869–84.

Monleón, José, 1990. *A Spectre is Haunting Europe*. Princeton, NJ: Princeton University Press.

Monroe-Cassel, Chelsea and Sarian Lehrer, 2012. *Game of Thrones: A Feast of Ice and Fire*. Harmondsworth: Penguin.

Mooney, Skyler J., Diana E. Peragine, Georgia A. Hathaway and Melissa M. Holmes, 2014. 'A game of thrones: neural plasticity in mammalian social hierarchies', *Social Neuroscience*, 9(2): 108–17.

Morley, David, 1980. *The Nationwide Audience: Structure and Decoding*. London: British Film Institute.

Moroney, Murphy, 2017. 'The ultimate ranking of *Game of Thrones* moms', 16 July. www.popsugar.com/moms/Moms-Game-Thrones-Ranked-Worst-Best-43732717.

Morrison, David, B. MacGregor, M. Svennevig and J. Firmstone, 1999. *Defining Violence: The Search for Understanding*. Bloomington, IN: Indiana University Press.
Morton, Ashley, 2016. '5 mothering moments from GoT moms', 8 May. www.makinggameofthrones.com/production-diary/mothers-day-5-got-characters.
Moylan, Tom, 2000. *Scraps of the Untainted Sky*. New York: Perseus.
Murphy, Shaunna, 2015. 'Can *Game of Thrones* be dangerous for you? A psychologist weighs in', *MTV*, 22 May. www.mtv.com/news/2167396/game-of-thrones-sansa-rape-effect-on-teens/.
Murray, Noel, 2016. 'GoT Belfast? How a television epic about a war-torn land was employed to rebrand Northern Ireland', in Ahmet Bayraktar and Can Uslay (eds), *Global Place Branding Campaigns across Cities, Regions, and Nations*. Business Science Reference.
Naylor, Alex, 2016. '"My skin has turned to porcelain, to ivory, to steel": feminist fan discourses, *Game of Thrones*, and the problem of Sansa', in Elyce R. Helford, Shiloh Carroll, Sarah Gray and Michael R. Howard (eds), *The Woman Fantastic in Contemporary American Media Culture*. Jackson, MS: University Press of Mississippi, 39–60.
Nedd, Alexis, 2019. 'Fan theory culture peaked with "Game of Thrones": what now?', 16 May. https://mashable.com/article/game-of-thrones-fan-theory-culture/?europe=true.
Needham, Jessica K., 2017. 'Visual misogyny: an analysis of female sexual objectification in *Game of Thrones*', *Femspec*, 17(2): 3–19.
Nelson, Mark, 2019. *Creative World-Building and Creature Design*. New York: Dover Books.
Nelson, Robin, 2007. 'Quality TV drama: estimations and influences through time and space', in Janet McCabe and Kim Akass (eds), *Quality TV: Contemporary American Television and Beyond*. London: I. B. Tauris, 38–51.
Neumeier, Rachel, 2014. 'Gritty fantasy versus dark fantasy'. www.rachelneumeier.com/2014/10/20/gritty-fantasy-vs-dark-fantasy.
Nguyen, H., 2015. 'Why Sansa's wedding night was the most traumatizing *Game of Thrones* scene ever', *TV Guide*. www.tvguide.com/news/game-of-thrones-recap-sansa-rape-unbowed-unbent-unbroken/.
Nonnecke, Blair, Dorine Andrews, Jenny Preece and Russell Voutour, 2004. 'Online lurkers tell why', Proceedings of the Tenth Americas Conference on Information Systems, New York. https://aisel.aisnet.org/cgi/viewcontent.cgi?article=1897&context=amcis2004.
O'Connor, Anthony, 2019. '*Game of Thrones*, Season 8 Episode 1: Winterfell', *FilmInk*. www.filmink.com.au/reviews/game-thrones-season-8-episode-1-winterfell/.
Ormrod, James, 2014. *Fantasy and Social Movements*. Basingstoke: Palgrave.
Orr, C., 2015. 'Why does *Game of Thrones* feature so much sexual violence?', *Atlantic*, 17 June. www.theatlantic.com/entertainment/archive/2015/06/game-of-thrones-sexual-violence/396191/.
Otero, H. A., 2015. '*Game of Thrones* Season 5 Episode 6 Review: Unbowed, Unbent, Unbroken', *TV Fanatic*. www.tvfanatic.com/2015/05/game-of-thrones-season-5-episode-6-review-unbowed-unbent-unbroken/.
Paasonen, Susanna, Feona Attwood, Alan McKee, John Mercer and Clarissa Smith, 2020. *Objectification: On the Difference between Sex and Sexism*. London: Routledge.
Pajares Tosca, Susana and Lisbeth Klastrup, 2016. 'The expert female fan recap on YouTube', in Anne Gjelsvik and Rikke Schubart (eds), *Women of Ice and Fire*. London: Bloomsbury, 219–42.

Pantozzi, Jill, 2015. 'We will no longer be promoting *Game of Thrones*', *The Mary Sue*, 18 May. www.themarysue.com/we-will-no-longer-be-promoting-hbos-game-of-thrones/.

Patel, Charul, 2014. 'Expelling a monstrous matriarchy: casting Cersei Lannister as abject in *A Song of Ice and Fire*', *Journal of European Popular Culture*, 5(2): 135–47.

Pavlac, Brian A., 2017. *Game of Thrones versus History: Written in Blood*. Hoboken, NJ: John Wiley & Sons.

Penguin, 2020. 'So you want to read Grimdark: here's where to start'. www.penguinrandomhouse.com/the-read-down/want-read-grimdark-heres-start.

Pérez, Hector J. and Rainer Reisenzein, 2019. 'On Jon Snow's death: plot twist and global fandom in *Game of Thrones*', *Culture & Psychology*, 26(3): 1–17.

Pett, Emma, 2013. '"People who think outside the box": British audiences and Asian extreme films', *Cine-Excess* eJournal. www.cine-excess.co.uk/issue-1-subverting-the-senses.html.

Phipps, A., 2009. 'Rape and respectability: ideas about sexual violence and social class', *Sociology*, 43(4): 667–83.

Preece, Jenny, Blair Nonnecke and Dorine Andrews, 2004. 'The top five reasons for lurking: improving community experiences for everyone', *Computers in Human Behavior*, 20: 201–23.

Price, Basil, 2016. 'Beware of heroes: a guide to Grimdark'. https://medium.com/dice-addicts-weekly/beware-of-heroes-a-guide-to-grimdark-f9cea0a1df46.

Probyn, Elspeth, 2000. *Carnal Appetites: FoodSexIdentities*. London: Routledge.

Projansky, Sarah, 2001. *Watching Rape: Film and Television in Postfeminist Culture*. New York: New York University Press.

Projansky, Sarah, 2014. *Spectacular Girls: Media Fascination and Celebrity Culture*. New York: New York University Press.

Pulrang, Andrew, 2013. 'Pop culture review: Tyrion Lannister, "Game of Thrones"', *Disability Thinking*, 1 May. http://disability-thinking-blogspot.com.au/2013/05/pop-culture-review-tyrion-lannister-html.

Rabinowitz, Peter J., 1997. *Before Reading: Narrative Conventions and the Politics of Interpretation. The Theory and Interpretation of Narrative Series*. Ohio: Ohio State University Press.

Rafaeli, Shaifaz, Gilad Ravid and Vladimir Soroka, 2004. 'De-lurking in virtual communities: a social communication network approach to measuring the effects of social and cultural capital'. Proceedings of the 37th Hawaii International Conference on System Sciences. https://ieeexplore.ieee.org/abstract/document/1265478/.

Rawson, Andrew, 2015. *The Real Game of Thrones*. Stroud: The History Press.

Rebora, Simone, 2019. 'On fantasy's transmediality: a cognitive approach', *Corporatismi*, 217–32. https://www.ledijournals.com/ojs/index.php/comparatismi/article/view/872.

Reeves, Jacob A., 2017. 'Yaaaas Queen! Daenerys Targaryen as a Contemporary Feminist'. Doctoral dissertation, Appalachian State University.

Reijnders, Stijn, 2015. 'Stories that move: fiction, imagination, tourism', *European Journal of Cultural Studies*, 19(6): 672–89.

Reinhart, Matthew, 2014. *A Pop-up Guide to Westeros*. London: Bantam Press.

Reisener, Matthew, 2019. '*Game of Thrones* meets international relations: a match made in heaven?', *The National Interest*, 13 April. https://nationalinterest.org/feature/game-thrones-meets-international-relations-match-made-heaven-52007.

Ridings, Catherine, David Gefen and Bay Arinze, 2006. 'Psychological barriers: lurker and poster motivation and behaviour in online communities', *Communications of the Association for Information Systems*, 18: 329–54.

Ritzer, George and Zeynep Atalay, 2010. *Readings in Globalization*. Oxford: Wiley-Blackwell.
Robinson, J., 2015. '*Game of Thrones* absolutely did not need to go there with Sansa Stark', *Vanity Fair*. www.vanityfair.com/hollywood/2015/05/game-of-thrones-rape-sansa-stark.
Romaine, Suzanne, 1996. 'War and peace in the global greenhouse: metaphors we live and die by', *Metaphors and Society*, 11(3): 175–94.
Romano, Aja, 2018. 'Hopepunk, the latest storytelling trend, is all about weaponized optimism', *Vox*. www.vox.com/2018/12/27/18137571/what-is-hopepunk-noblebright-grimdark.
Rosenberg, Alyssa, 2011. '*Game of Thrones*: HBO shows the ugly edge of fantasy', *Atlantic*, 11. www.theatlantic.com/entertainment/archive/2011/04/game-of-thrones-hbo-shows-the-ugly-edge-of-fantasy/237033/.
Rosenberg, Alyssa, 2012. 'Men and monsters: rape, myth-making and the rise and fall of nations in *A Song of Ice and Fire*', in James Lowder (ed.), *Beyond the Wall: Exploring George R. R. Martin's* A Song of Ice and Fire. Dallas, TX: BenBella Books, 15–28.
Rosenberg, Alyssa, 2015. '"Game of Thrones" has always been a show about rape', *Washington Post*, 19 May. www.washingtonpost.com/news/act-four/wp/2015/05/19/game-of-thrones-has-always-been-a-show-about-rape/?tid=pm_pop_b.
Rosenberg, Alyssa, 2019. '*Game of Thrones* Season 8, Episode 6 review: "The Iron Throne" melts', *Washington Post*, 19 May. www.washingtonpost.com/opinions/2019/05/20/game-thrones-season-episode-review-iron-throne-melts/?arc404=true.
Rosenfield, K., 2015. '11 former "Game of Thrones" fans who are "done" after last night', *MTV News*. www.mtv.com/news/2163340/game-of-thrones-sansa-outrage/.
Rosengren, Karl Erik. 1984. 'Time and culture: developments in the Swedish literary frame of reference', in Gabriele Melischek, Karl Erik Rosengren and James Stappers (eds), *Cultural Indicators: An International Symposium*. Vienna: Verlag der Osterreichen Akademie der Wissenschaften, 237–58.
Ryan, Marie-Laure and Alice Bells, eds, 2019. *Possible Worlds Theory and Contemporary Narratology*. Lincoln, NE: University of Nebraska Press.
Santo, Avi, 2008. 'Para-television and discourses of distinction: the culture of production at HBO', in Marc Leverette, Brian L. Ott and Cara Louise Buckley (eds), *It's Not TV: Watching HBO in the Post-Television Era*. New York: Routledge, 19–45.
Saraiya, S., 2014. 'Rape of Thrones', *The A.V. Club*. www.avclub.com/article/rape-thrones-203499.
Sarikakis, Katherine, Claudia Krug and Joan Rodriguez-Amat, 2017. 'Defining authorship in user-generated content: copyright struggles in *The Game of Thrones*', *New Media and Society*, 19(4): 542–59.
Schaeffer, Eric, 1999. *'Bold! Daring! Shocking! True': A History of Exploitation Films, 1919–1959*. Durham, NC: Duke University Press.
Schallegger, René, 2012. 'The nightmares of politicians: on the rise of fantasy literature from subcultural to mass-cultural phenomenon', in Lars Schmeink and Astrid Böger (eds), *Collision of Realities: Establishing Research on the Fantastic in Europe*. Berlin: De Gruyter, 29–48.
Scheper-Hughes, Nancy and Philippe Bourgois, 2003. *Violence in War and Peace: An Anthology*. Oxford: Basil Blackwell.
Schiappa, Edward, 2008. *Beyond Representational Correctness*. New York: State University of New York Press.
Schlesinger, Philip, 1992. *Women Viewing Violence*. London: British Film Institute.

Schlesinger, Philip, Richard Haynes and Raymond Boyle, 1998. *Men Viewing Violence*. London: Broadcasting Standards Commission.

Schlutz, Daniela M., 2016. 'Contemporary quality TV: the entertainment experience of complex serial narratives', *Annals of the International Communication Association*: 95–124.

Schmeink, Lars, 2016. 'How Bilbo lost his innocence: media audiences and the evaluation of *The Hobbit* as a "children's film"', *Participations*, 13(2): 430–9.

Schmeink, Lars and Astrid Böger, eds, 2012. *Collisions of Realities: Establishing Research on the Fantastic in Europe*, Berlin: De Gruyter.

Schoenbach, Klaus, 2001. 'Myths of media and audiences', *European Journal of Communication*, 16(3): 361–76.

Schröter, Felix, 2016. 'Sworn swords and noble ladies: female characters in *Game of Thrones* video games', in Anne Gjelsvik and Rikke Schubart (eds), *Women of Ice and Fire*. London: Bloomsbury, 79–103.

Schröter, F., B. Beil, K. Sachs-Hombach and N. J. Thon, 2015. 'The game of *Game of Thrones*. George R. R. Martin's *A Song of Ice and Fire* and its video game adaptations'. *Media Convergence and Transmedial Worlds (Part 3)/Medienkonvergenz und transmediale Welten*, 3, special issue IMAGE, 22: 65–82.

Sedlmayer Gerold and Nicole Waller, eds, 2016. *Politics in Fantasy Media*. Jefferson, NC: McFarland.

Selcke, Dan, 2017. 'What are *Game of Thrones* fans like? Check out the results of this demographic survey'. https://winteriscoming.net/2017/01/16/results-song-of-ice-and-fire-game-of-thrones-demographic-survey/.

Selcke, Dan, 2018a. 'Survey results: how do fans of different races, genders, and political affiliations rate *Game of Thrones*?'. https://winteriscoming.net/2018/08/01/survey-results-fans-different-races-genders-political-affiliations-rate-game-thrones/.

Selcke, Dan, 2018b. 'HBO spotlights *Game of Thrones* merch for Mother's Day', *Winter is Coming*, 9 May. https://winteriscoming.net/2018/05/09/hbo-spotlights-game-thrones-merch-mothers-day/.

Shacklock, Z., 2015. '"A reader lives a thousand lives before he dies': transmedia textuality and the flows of adaptation', in Jes Battis and Susan Johnston (eds), *Mastering the Game of Thrones*. Jefferson, NC: McFarland, 262–79.

Shaheen, Jack, 2009. *Reel Bad Arabs: How Hollywood Vilifies a People*. Northampton: Olive Branch Press.

Shannon Duval, R., 2012. 'The things I do for love: sex, lies, and game theory', in Henry Jacoby (ed.), *Game of Thrones and Philosophy*. Oxford: Blackwell, 250–63.

Sharf, Zack, 2018, '"Game of Thrones": Kit Harington evokes "Sopranos" and "Breaking Bad" endings while teasing divisive series finale', *IndieWire*, 12 September. www.indiewire.com/2018/09/game-of-thrones-kit-harington-series-finale-breaking-bad-sopranos-1202003060/.

Siebert, Horst, 2008. 'The concept of a world economic order', *Kiel Working Papers*. http://citeseerx.ist.psu.edu/viewdoc/download?doi=10.1.1.628.9971&rep=rep1&type=pdf.

Silverman, Eric J. and Robert Arp, eds, 2017. *The Ultimate Game of Thrones and Philosophy: You Think or You Die*. Chicago: University of Chicago Press.

Simpson, William, 2019. *Game of Thrones: The Storyboards*. Los Angeles: Insight Editions.

Sims, David, 2017. 'What did *Game of Thrones* accomplish this year? Three *Atlantic* staffers discuss "The Dragon and the Wolf", the Season 7 finale (with Lenika Cruz and Megan

Garber)', *Atlantic*, 27 August. www.theatlantic.com/entertainment/archive/2017/08/game-of-thrones-season-7-episode-7-the-dragon-and-the-wolf-roundtable/537999/.

Smith, Clarissa, Martin Barker and Feona Attwood, 2015. 'Why do people watch porn? Results from PornResearch.Org', in Lynne Cornella and Shira Tarrant (eds), *New Views on Pornography*. New York: Praeger, 267–85.

Smith, Murray, 1995. *Engaging Characters: Fiction, Emotion and the Cinema*. Oxford: Oxford University Press.

Somer, Eli, et al., 2017. 'Maladaptive daydreaming: proposed diagnostic criteria and their assessment with a structured clinical interview', *Psychology of Consciousness: Theory, Research, and Practice*, 4(2): 176–89.

Spanò, C., 2016. 'Audience engagement with multi-level fictional universes: the case of *Game of Thrones* and its Italian fans', *Participations*, 13(2): 625–55.

Spector, Caroline, 2012. 'Power and feminism in Westeros', in James Lowder (ed.), *Beyond The Wall: Exploring George RR Martin's A Song of Ice and Fire*. Smartpop, 169–88.

Staiger, Janet. 1992. *Interpreting Films*. Princeton, NJ: Princeton University Press.

Staiger, Janet. 2000. *Perverse Spectators*. New York: New York University Press.

Steiner, Tobias, 2015. 'Steering the author discourse: the construction of authorship in quality TV, and the case of *Game of Thrones*', *Series*, 2: 181–92.

Stevenson, Ana, 2017. 'Maidens, mothers, matriarchs: the women of *Game of Thrones*', *Australian Women's History Network*, 16 July. www.auswhn.org.au/blog/women-game-of-thrones/#:~:text=This%20collection%20of%20essays%20examines,%2C%20and%20its%20transmedial%20universe.

Stride, Daniel, 2019. 'Pinning down Grimdark'. https://phuulishfellow.wordpress.com/2019/02/10/pinning-down-grimdark.

Tal-Or, Nurit and Jonathan Cohen, 2010. 'Understanding audience involvement: conceptualizing and manipulating identification and transportation', *Poetics*, 38(4): 402–18.

Tasker, Yvonne and Lindsay Steenberg, 2016. 'Women warriors from chivalry to vengeance', in Anne Gjelsvik and Rikke Schubart (eds) *Women of Ice and Fire*. London: Bloomsbury, 171–92.

Thomas, Rhiannon, 2018. 'Redefining "torture porn"'. www.feministfiction.com/2016/07/08/redefining-torture-porn.

Thompson, Robert J., 1996. *Television's Second Golden Age*. New York: Syracuse University Press.

Tolkien, J. R. R., 2008. 'On fairy stories' [1947], in Verlyn Flieger and Douglas A. Anderson (eds), *Tolkien on Fairy-stories*. New York: Harper Collins, 27–84.

Torgovnick, Marianna, 1981. *Closure in the Novel*. Princeton, NJ: Princeton University Press.

Tourish, Dennis and Owen Hargie, 2012. 'Metaphors of failure and the failures of metaphor: a critical study of root metaphors used by bankers in explaining the banking crisis', *Organization Studies*, 33(8): 1045–69.

Trolio, J., 2015. '*Game of Thrones*' latest rape scene made viewers very angry. And rightfully so', *Vox Culture*. www.mtv.com/news/2163340/game-of-thrones-sansa-outrage/.

Tudor, Andrew, 1997. 'Why horror? The peculiar pleasures of a popular genre', *Cultural Studies*, 11(3): 443–63.

Turpin, Jennifer E. and Lester R. Kurtz, 1996. *The Web of Violence: From Interpersonal to Global*. Chicago: University of Illinois Press.

Tyrer, Ben, 2018. 'The reality of fantasy: VFX as fantasmatic supplement in *Game of Thrones*', in Christopher Holliday and Alexander Sergeant (eds), *Fantasy/Animation*. London: Routledge, 91–106.

Tzanelli, Rodanthi, 2010. *The Cinematic Tourist*. London: Routledge.

Tzanelli, Rodanthi, 2016. 'From *Game of Thrones* to game of sites/sights: reconfiguring a transnational cinematic node in Ireland's e-tourism', in K. Hannam, M. Mostafanezhad and J. Rickly (eds), *Event Mobilities*. London: Routledge.

United Nations, 2004. 'High level panel on threats, challenges and change'. https://peacekeeping.un.org/en/report-of-high-level-panel-threats-challenges-and-change-more-secure-world-our-shared-responsibility.

Urry, John, 1990. *The Tourist Gaze*. London: Sage.

Valente, Joanna C., 2017. '"Game of Thrones" explores complicated and cunning mothers', 24 July. www.kveller.com/game-of-thrones-explores-complicated-and-cunning-mothers/.

van Laer, Tom, 2017. 'Is *Game of Thrones* the perfect metaphor for where we stand as a society?', *Business Standard*, 14 July. www.business-standard.com/article/current-affairs/game-of-thrones-is-the-perfect-metaphor-for-where-we-stand-as-a-society-117071400136_1.html.

Vandermeer, Anne and Jeff Vandermeer, 2008. *The New Weird*. San Francisco: Tachyon Publications.

VanDerWerff, T., 2015. '*Game of Thrones* excels at staging shocking moments, but keeps screwing up their aftermaths', *Vox*. www.vox.com/2015/5/21/8632319/game-of-thrones-repetition.

Vejvoda, Jim, 2018. '*Game of Thrones*: Sophie Turner thinks series finale will divide fans', *IGN*, 29 September. https://uk.ign.com/articles/2018/09/29/game-of-thrones-season-8-sansa-stark-sophie-turner-hbo-series-finale-will-divide-fans-will-be-disappointed.

Vice, 2016. '*Game of Thrones* is suddenly all about powerful women getting their way', 16 May. www.vice.com/en_us/article/wdbqqm/game-of-thrones-is-suddenly-all-about-powerful-women-getting-their-way.

Vincent, A., 2014. 'George RR Martin: "I never discussed the rape scene with *Game of Thrones* producers"', *Telegraph*, 22 April. www.telegraph.co.uk/culture/tvandradio/game-of-thrones/10779097/George-RR-Martin-I-never-discussed-the-rape-scene-with-Game-of-Thrones-producers.html.

Vincent, A., 2015. 'George RR Martin defends *Game of Thrones* rape', *Telegraph*, 19 May. www.telegraph.co.uk/culture/tvandradio/game-of-thrones/11614634/George-RR-Martin-defends-Game-of-Thrones-rape.html.

Vincent, A. and R. Hawkes, 2015. 'Rape on TV: has *Game of Thrones* gone too far?', *Telegraph*, 18 May. www.telegraph.co.uk/culture/tvandradio/game-of-thrones/11612290/rape-game-of-thrones.html.

Virino, Concepción Cascajosa and Vicente Rodríguez Ortega, 2019. 'Daenerys Targaryen will save Spain: *Game of Thrones*, politics, and the public sphere', *Television & New Media*, 20(5): 423–42.

Walsh, Michael, 2017. 'Like it not, *Game of Thrones* is our biggest analogy for climate change', *Nerdist*, 2 August. https://nerdist.com/game-of-thrones-climate-change/.

Walters, James, 2011. *Fantasy Film: A Critical Introduction*. Oxford: Berg.

Walters, John. 2016. 'Sunday's "Game of Thrones" tackled presidential politics', *Newsweek*, 23 May. www.newsweek.com/door-game-thrones-mirrors-2016-american-p-462701.

Watercutter, Angela, 2013. 'Yes women really do like *Game of Thrones* (we have proof)', *Wired*. www.wired.com/2013/06/women-game-of-thrones/.

Watercutter, Angela, 2017. 'This is how *Game of Thrones* ends in total matriarchy', *Wired*, 14 July. www.wired.com/story/game-of-thrones-total-female-domination/.
Watts, Simon and Paul Stenner, 2012. *Doing Q Methodological Research*. London: Sage.
Waysdorf, Abby and Stijn Reijnders, 2017. 'The role of imagination in the film tourist experience: the case of *Game of Thrones*', *Participations*, 14(1): 170–91.
Weaver, James B. and Ron Tamborini, eds, 2001. *Horror Films: Current Research on Audiences Preferences and Reactions*. Mahwah, NJ: Lawrence Erlbaum.
Weber, Max, 1997. *The Methodology of the Social Sciences*, trans. Edward A. Shils and Henry A. Finch. New York: Free Press.
Wedeen, Lisa, 2002. 'Conceptualizing culture: possibilities for political science', *The American Political Science Review*, 96(4): 713–28.
Wells-Lassagne, Shannon, 2013. 'Prurient pleasures: adapting fantasy to HBO', *Journal of Adaptation in Film and Performance*, 6(3): 415–26.
Wells-Lassagne, Shannon, 2014. 'High fidelity: adapting fantasy to the small screen', *TV/Series*, 6.
Williams, Raymond, 2007 [1977]. *Marxism and Literature*. Oxford: Oxford University Press.
Winteriscoming, 2013. '*Game of Thrones* wins award honouring disability awareness'. https://winteriscoming.net/2013/10/22/game-of-thrones-wins-award-honoring-disability-awareness/.
Wolf, Mark J. P., 2012. *Building Imaginary Worlds*. New York: Routledge.
Woods, Faye, 2015. 'Girls talk: authorship and authenticity in the reception of Lena Dunham's *Girls*', *Critical Studies in Television*, 10(2): 37–54.
Yoshioka, Marianne R. and Deborah Y. Choi, 2008. 'Culture and interpersonal violence research: paradigm shift to create a full continuum of domestic violence services', *Journal of Interpersonal Violence*, 20(4): 513–19.
Young, H., 2014. 'Race in online fantasy fandom: whiteness on Westeros.Org', *Continuum*, 28(5): 737–47.
Young, Joseph, 2017. 'Enough about whores: sexual characterization in *ASOIAF*', *Mythlore*, 35(2): 45–61.
Zarkov, Dubravka and Kathy Davis, 2018. 'Ambiguities and dilemmas around #MeToo: #ForHow Long and #WhereTo?', *European Journal of Women's Studies*, 25(1): 3–9.
Zeller-Jacques, Martin, 2014. 'Don't stop believing: textual excess and discourses of satisfaction in the finale of *The Sopranos*', in Michael Stewart (ed.), *Melodrama in Contemporary Film and Television*. Basingstoke: Palgrave Macmillan, 114–29.
Zillmann, Dolf, 1980. 'Anatomy of suspense', in P. H. Tannenbaum (ed.), *The Entertainment Function of Television*. Hillsdale, NJ: Laurence Erlbaum, 137–63.
Zillmann, Dolf, 1994. 'Mechanisms of emotional involvement with drama', *Poetics*, 23(1–2), 33–51.

Index

adaptation 5–6, 128–9, 141
Akass, Kim 5, 73, 126
Alesi, Danielle 5
Alhayek, Katty 10
Altman, Rick 23
Appel, Markus 49
Arp, Robert 3
Arts Agency 34
Atalay, Zeynep 102
Attebury, Brian 7, 72–3
audience typologies 33–46, 152–4
   Book-Followers 39–45, 94, 97–101, 108–11, 113–14, 147–51
   Classic Fans 38–43, 94, 97–101, 108–11, 113–14, 134–5, 147–51
   Contented Consumers 38–43, 94, 97–101, 108–11, 113–14, 147–51
   Debaters 38–42, 94, 97–101, 108–11, 113–14, 147–51
   Fan Watchers (World Watchers) 38–44, 94, 97–101, 108–11, 113–14, 115–16, 131–4, 147–51
   Just the Show 37–42, 97–101, 108–11, 113–14, 134–5, 147–51
   Players 39–43, 97–101, 108–11, 113–14, 134–5, 147–51
Azcona, Maria del Mar 71–2

Barker, Martin 7, 11, 13, 16, 17, 21, 32, 49, 51, 58, 70, 127, 137, 139, 168
Barthes, Roland 147
Bells, Alice 7

Ben Bova 102
Bentinaki, Katerina 138
Berg, Madeline 9
Bessel, Richard 138
Best Fantasy Fiction 154, 155
Beveridge, Andrew 69
Bianculli, David 146
Bigelson, Jayne 51
Bignell, Jonathan 146
Bishop, Jonathan 39
Böger, Astrid 8
Bolan, Peter 6
Boni, Marta 102
Bordwell, David 50
Bourdaa, M. 10
Bourgois, Philippe 138
Bronstein, Carolyn 139
Brottman, Mikita 118
Brownmiller, Susan 139
Bryman, Alan 18
Bufacchi, Vittorio 138
Burke, Joanna 139
Burt, Martha 139
Bustle 5
Butler, David 7
Butsch, Richard 34
Buzan, Barry 143

Campbell, Jan 33
Cardwell, Sarah 146
Carroll, Noël 50, 138
Carroll, Shiloh R. 3
Castellano, M. 10
Celik Rappas, Ipek A. 6
Chandler, Abigail 168
Chandler, Daniel 75
change.org petition 162–9

characters 15, 47–70
    character arcs 55–69
        Arya Stark 59–60, 81–3
        Cersei Lannister 65–6
        Daenerys Targaryen 60–1, 83–5
        Jaime Lannister 67–8, 85–7
        Jon Snow 57–8, 79–81
        Lord Varys 64–5
        Petyr Baelish 63–4
        Sansa Stark 61–3, 118–42
        Tyrion Lannister 55–7
Chemers, Michael 69
Cherry, Brigid 139
Choi, Deborah Y. 138
Clapton, William 143
Cogman, Brian 2
cognitive film studies 50–2
Cohen, Jonathan 49–50
Connelly, Roxanne 31
Crawford, Kate 39
Cronin, Theresa 34
Csecsery–Ronay, Istvan 93
cultivation 138, 175

Dasgupta, Rohit K. 3, 10
Davis, Kathy 140
de Haan, W. 138
Deacon, David 16
Delmar, J.L. 10
Depken, Craig A. 6
Desai, Darshan 10
deserving/deserts 56, 136–7, 164–9
Dew, Oliver 139
Dockterman, Eliana 79
Dolitze, Tatia 4
Donovan, William Barna 139
Douthat, Ross 126
Dry, Jude 9
du Gay, Paul 27
Duncombe, Stephen 7

Eder, Jens 48
Egan, R. Danielle 140
Eidsvåg, Marta Frankel 4
Elkus, Adam 126
Ellefson, Randy 102
Elliott, Paul 51
Elwood, Rachel L. 5
Emig, Rainer 38
empathy 49

endings 145–6, 160–2
Evans, T. 5

fantasy 1–2, 7–9, 13, 14–16, 23, 27–8,
    29, 71, 72–4, 101–15
    escapism 105–6, 116
Fathallah, Judith 6, 10
Feasey, Rebecca 146
Ferreday, Debra 5, 10, 126, 140–1,
    143
Finn, Kavita Mudan 4, 10
Firstpost 3
Florini, Sarah 10
Fortuna, Carolyn 88
Foulkes, David 116
Fowkes, Katherine A. 7
Framke, Caroline 126
Frankel, Valerie Estelle 3, 4, 5, 126–7
Franklin, T. G. 102
Frohock, Theresa 155
Frost, Warwick 6
Furby, Jacqueline 7
Furman, Daniel J. 143

Galtung, Johan 138
Game of Thrones peoples/cultures
    Braavos (Faceless Men) 91, 93
    Dorne 91, 92, 151
    Dothraki 90–1, 93
    Starks (the North) 90–1, 92, 95,
        99–100, 101, 124, 149
    Valyria 91, 92, 93, 116
    Wildlings 90, 91, 92
Gaut, Berys 138
Genz, Stéphanie 5, 127
Gerbner, George 138, 174–5
Gierzynski, Anthony 10–12, 143, 145
Gill, Rosalind 140
Gillett, Stephen L. 102
Gjelsvik, Anne 5, 126
Goodwin, Jeff 7
Green, Melanie C. 49
Gresham, Karin 5
Griffith, Merris 75
grimdark 23, 154–6, 157
Grodal, Torben 51

Hagen, Ingunn 34
Halberstam, Jack 4
Hall, Stuart 34, 175

Hardt, Michael 8
Harrington, C. Lee 160, 164
Harrison, Mia 4
Harvey, Dan 4
Hassler-Forest, Dan 5, 8
Hasson, Uri 51
Henning, Bernt 116
Hibberd, James 59
Hill, Annette 139
Historical Materialism 7
Hobbit, The 14, 17, 20, 21
Holbrook, Morris B. 139
Holliday, Christopher 8
Home Box Office (HBO) 1, 5, 71, 73, 126, 158, 161, 163–5
Hootsuite 2
Horeck, Tanya 140
Hovey, Jamie 4

identification 11–12, 48–9, 50
Irimiás, Anna 6
Irwin, William and 3

Jacoby, Henry 3
James, Henry 159
Jancovich, Mark 5
Jaworski, Michelle 143
Jenkins, Henry 34, 52, 102, 143, 146, 165
Jepson, Rich 2
Johnson, Mark 90
Johnston, Susan 74
Jones, Rebecca 5
Journal of the Fantastic in the Arts 7

Kar, Debarun 4
Kates, Robert W. 175
Katz, Elihu 116
Kennedy, Julia 124
Kermode, Mark 129
Kiersey, Nicholas 143
Klastrup, Lisbeth 10
Kohnen, M.E. 145
Kozinsky, Beth 4
Kriss, Sam 9
Kurtz, Lester R. 138
Kustritz, Anne 3, 10

Lacob, Jace 87
Laing, Jennifer 6
Lakoff, George 90

Lang, Fritz 167
Lannister, Jammy 2
Larrington, Carolyne 3
Larsson, Mariah 5
Latitude 10
Lavery, David 146
Lawler, Kelly 165, 168
Le Guin, Ursula 13
Lehrer, Sarian 2
Leigh, David J. 116
Leverette, M. 5.
Levitt, Lauren 144
Lewis, Justin 16
Livingstone, Sonia 34
Locke, Hilary Jane 3
Lord of the Rings, The 14, 17, 20, 21, 47, 70
Lovelock, James 102
Lushkov, Ayelet Haimson 3
Lyons, James 5
Lyons, Margaret 33

Maccoby, E.E. 49
Madden, Christopher 175
Maibach, Edward 46
Markelz, Michelle 6
Mason, Paul 9
Mathews, Jana 6
Mathijs, Ernest 16, 139, 174
Matthews, Jolie Christine 10
McCabe, Janet 5, 73, 126
McNamara, M. 164
McNeill, Kate 9
McNutt, Myles 3
media psychology 11, 48–50, 116
media tourism 6–7
MediaCom 9
medieval history 2–3, 5, 45, 110
Meisterhans, Nadja 102
Melischek, Gabriele 174
Mendlesohn, Farah 7, 102
mentions 20, 173–5
metaphors 3–4, 88–95
methodology 16–31
 analysis 20–2, 25–32
 ideal-types 22–4, 37–46, 94, 98, 113–15
 portraits 20–1, 131–5
 qualiquantitative 15–18, 35
 research design 16–21
Michelle, Carolyn 16, 24, 32, 34

Miéville, China 7
Milkoreit, Manjana 4, 89
Miller, Clark 102
Miller, J.H. 165
Mills, Jane 126
Mittell, Jason 139
Mølstad, Christina E. 3
Monleón, José 7
Monroe-Cassel, Chelsea 2
Mooney, Skyler J. 3
Morley, David 34
Morrison, David 139
Murphy, Shaunna 33
Murray, Noel 6
Musgrave, Paul 143

Naylor, Alex 10
Nedd, Alexis 169
Negri, Antonio 8
Nelles, Drew 4
Nelson, Mark 102
Nelson, Robin 146
Neuermeier, Rachel 154
Neumann, Iver 143
Nonnecke, Blair 38

O'Connor, Anthony 161
Orgad, Shani 140
Ormrod, James 7
Ortega, Vicente 3

Paasonen, Susanna 140
Pantozzi, Jill 5, 126
Patel, Charul 5
Pavlac, Brian A. 3
Penguin 155
Pérez, Hector J. 10
Pett, Emma 139
philosophy 3
politics 3, 7–9
Preece, Jenny 38
Price, Basil 155
Projansky, Sarah 126
Pulrang, Andrew 4

Q-methodology 24–5, 52
quality TV 51, 73, 145–6, 159

Rabinowitz, Peter J. 159
Rafeoli, Shaifaz 39
Rawson, Andrew 3

Rebora, Simone 51–2
Red Wedding 118–25
Reijnders, Stijn 6
Reinhart, Matthew 2
Reisener, Matthew 88
Reisenzein, Rainer 10
relish/anguish 155–6
representation 4–5, 135, 139–42, 146
Richter, Tobias 49
Ritzer, George 102
Robinson, J. 158
Romano, Aja 155
Rosenberg, Alyssa 5, 126, 161
Rosengren, Karl Erik 174
Ryan, Marie-Laure 7

Santo, Avi 146
Sarikakis, Katharine 10
Schaeffer, Eric 139
Schallegger, René 8
Scheper-Hughes, Nancy 138
Schiappa, Edward 34
Schlesinger, Philip 139
Schlutz, Daniela M. 5
Schmeink, Lars 8, 20
Schoenbach, Klaus 34
Schröter, F. 6, 10
Schubart, Rikke 126
Selcke, Dan 9
Sergeant, Alexander 8
Shacklock, Z. 6, 10
Shaheen, Jack 143
Shan, Jie 69
Sharf, Zack 160
Shepherd, Laura 143
Siebert, Horst 102
Silverman, Eric J. 3
Simpson, William 2
Sims, David 161
Smith, Clarissa 17, 124
Smith, Murray 50–1
Somer, Eli 51
Spanò, C. 10
Staiger, Janet 174
Steenberg, Lindsay 4
Steiner, Tobias 6, 10
Stenner, Paul 24
Stride, Daniel 155

Tal-Or, Nurit 49
Tamborini, Ron 139

Tasker, Yvonne 4
theories of sexual violence 139–42
theories of violence 15, 138–9
Thomas, Rhiannon 155
Thompson, Robert 73, 146, 147
Torgovnick, Marianna 165
Tosca, Susana 10
Transformative Works and Cultures 34
transportation 49, 52, 79
Tudor, Andrew 138
Turpin, Jennifer E. 138
Tyrer, Ben 8
Tzanelli, Rodanthi 6

United Nations 102
unpredictability 145–52

Vaage, Bruun 127
van Laer, Tom 4
Vandermeer, Anne 7
Vandermeer, Jeff 7
Vejvoda, Jim 160
Vice 5
Virino, Concepción 3
Vorderer, Peter 116

Walsh, Michael 4
Walters, John 7
Watercutter, Angela 9, 13
Watts, Simon 24
Waysdorf, Abby 6
Weaver, James B. 139
Weber, Max 27–8, 152
Wedeen, Lisa 143
Wells-Lassagne, Shannon 73–4
Williams, Raymond 153–4
Wilson, W.C. 49
Winteriscoming 4
'Winter is coming' 10, 21, 25, 88–116
Wolf, Mark 102
Woods, Faye 126
world-building 102–3, 110–11, 114

Yoshioka, Marianne R. 138
Young, H. 5
Young, Joseph 10

Zarkov, Dubravka 140
Zeitschrift für Fantastikforschung 7
Zeller-Jacques, Martin 160
Zillman, Dolf 49, 70

EU authorised representative for GPSR:
Easy Access System Europe, Mustamäe tee 50,
10621 Tallinn, Estonia
gpsr.requests@easproject.com

www.ingramcontent.com/pod-product-compliance
Lightning Source LLC
Chambersburg PA
CBHW070356240426
43671CB00013BA/2525